THE

HOW INDIA'S TOP BUSINESS LEADERS

INDIA

ARE REVOLUTIONIZING MANAGEMENT

WAY

PETER CAPPELLI · HARBIR SINGH

JITENDRA SINGH · MICHAEL USEEM

HARVARD BUSINESS PRESS

BOSTON, MASSACHUSETTS

Library of Congress Cataloging-in-Publication Data
The India way : how india's top business leaders are revolutionizing management /
Peter Cappelli . . . [et al.].
    p. cm.
  Includes bibliographical references.
  ISBN 978-1-4221-4759-7 (hardcover : alk. paper)   1. Management—India.
2. Corporate culture—India.   3. Corporate governance—India.   I. Cappelli, Peter.
  HD70.I4I53 2010
  658—dc22

                                                              2009039154

Contents

CHAPTER ONE

Indian Business Rising

The Contemporary Indian Way of Conducting Business

AT 9:20 P.M. on Wednesday, November 26, 2008, ten terrorists launched a shockingly violent attack on India's main business center, targeting a hospital, restaurant, railway station, Jewish center, and two luxury hotels, all in Mumbai. As the world watched in horror on live television, bystanders ducked bullets, and flames devoured a landmark. The three-day rampage— what some have termed India's "26/11"—ended with the death of more than 170 people, including 28 foreigners, the chief of Mumbai's antiterrorist squad, and the chairman of Yes Bank.

We watched these events unfolding with special interest. Our ties to India and the Indian business community ran deep, our concerns were many, and we were, after all, in the midst of writing a book about the Indian business juggernaut. But we had a more immediate concern, too. One of India's most prominent business leaders, Anil D. Ambani, executive chairman of Reliance ADA Enterprises, was scheduled to address a ceremony at the University of Pennsylvania's Wharton School on Monday, December 1, only days after the attack ended. The occasion was the dedication of a lecture hall to his late father, who had founded a company that Anil Ambani and his brother, Mukesh, had now transformed into two of India's largest conglomerates.[1] Would he be able to make the dedication?

In fact, the ceremony had to be deferred, but the delay came not because Anil Ambani's firm had been significantly affected. Rather, the country's prime minister, Manmohan Singh, asked him to remain in India to serve, in the words of our dean's announcement of the postponement, "as a visible beacon of national stability." Anil Ambani heeded the call, and in a well-publicized event, the veteran marathoner jogged with several friends near a scene of the carnage just hours after it had been secured, in what one newspaper termed "a symbolic display of the resilience for which Mumbai is widely admired."[2]

In America, the financial crisis of 2008–2009 had shattered public confidence in corporate leaders ranging from the executives of Lehman Brothers and Fannie Mae to those of Merrill Lynch and General Motors, a confidence already weakened by bonus payments, company jets, and golden parachutes. Financial institutions were reeling, factories were shuttering, unemployment was climbing to levels unseen in most lifetimes. Far from being able to claim a mantle of national leadership, U.S. executives had plummeted in virtually every measure of public esteem.

In India, by contrast, big business leaders had come to be emblematic of national achievement and fortitude. Firms that had been the scene of horrible events were springing back to life in time frames almost unthinkable by post-9/11 standards. The Taj Mahal Hotel, devastated by the attacks, needed only three weeks to reopen for business. And the world had taken notice. When Hillary Clinton visited India a half year after the terrorist attack, the U.S. secretary of state began her stay in Mumbai, the country's business capital, not New Delhi, its political capital. Taking up residence in the by then fully restored

Taj Mahal Hotel, she opted to meet first with Indian business leaders, including Mukesh Ambani, executive chairman of Reliance Industries, and Ratan Tata, head of the $62 billion Tata Group.

"India's booming economy has turned some business executives into rock stars," the *New York Times* correspondent wrote of the meeting, and it was thus "not surprising" that the secretary of state "would stop first in India's commercial capital for a power breakfast with bankers and billionaires."[3]

Mukesh Ambani, whose estimated personal wealth exceeded $19 billion at the time of the meeting, told Hillary Clinton of the need for technological innovation to curb emissions, a creative solution to an emerging tension between developed and developing nations. Ratan Tata, whose companies are ubiquitous throughout the subcontinent, explained to the American emissary how his enterprise was providing nutrients to children across India through the enriched milk it delivers.

This melding of business and national leadership is central to the Indian way of doing business. Many business leaders are deeply involved in societal issues, and they deem it entirely appropriate—even requisite—to voice their views on subjects ranging from climate change to child nutrition. Some of this has to do with the imperatives of development: many Indian firms believe that national growth is essential for their own profitable expansion. Some derives from a long-standing tradition of business largesse, with many companies committed to social goals through philanthropic giving and infrastructure investing near production facilities. Yet the melding goes well beyond private profits and public charity, with national purpose as much a part of the business mind-set as financial results and reputational gain.

This mind-set can be seen in the willingness of the cochairman and former chief executive of Infosys Technologies, Nandan Nilekani, to accept the call to direct India's mammoth national effort to provide a unique digital identification number to all of its 1.1 billion citizens, deemed essential for effective delivery of social services across the country.[4] It is found in the personnel mantra at HCL, the fast-growing international IT service firm: "Employee First, Customer Second."

Principal Practices of the India Way

1. **Holistic engagement with employees.** Indian business
   leaders see their firms as organic enterprises where sustaining employee morale and building company culture
   are treated as critical obligations and foundations of their
   success. People are viewed as assets to be developed,
   not costs to be reduced; as sources of creative ideas
   and pragmatic solutions; and as bringing leadership at
   their own level to the company. Creating ever-stronger
   capabilities in the workforce is a driving objective.

2. **Improvisation and adaptability.** Improvisation is also
   at the heart of the India Way. In a complex, often volatile
   environment with few resources and much red tape,
   business leaders have learned to rely on their wits to
   circumvent the innumerable hurdles they recurrently
   confront. Sometimes peppering English-language
   conversations, the Hindi term *jugaad* captures much
   of the mind-set. Anyone who has seen outdated equipment nursed along a generation past its expected
   lifetime with retrofitted spare parts and jerry-rigged

The mind-set is embedded in Hindustan Unilever's Project Shakti,
which has used the principles of microfinance to create a sales
force in some of the subcontinent's most remote regions. It reveals
itself in community hospitals and grade schools and virtual universities built across the country by name-brand businesses. Most significant, what we have come to term *the India Way* expresses itself
in an economy that even in perilous global times remains a dynamo,
driven by big companies bent on growing at prodigious rates and
competing globally.

solutions has witnessed *jugaad* in action. Adaptability is crucial as well, and it too is frequently referenced in an English-Hindi hybrid, *adjust kar lenge*—"we will adjust or accommodate."

3. **Creative value propositions.** Given the large and intensely competitive domestic market with discerning and value-conscious customers, most of modest means, Indian business leaders have of necessity learned to be highly creative in developing their value propositions. Though steeped in an ancient culture, Indian business leaders are inventing entirely new product and service concepts to satisfy the needs of demanding consumers and to do so with extreme efficiency.

4. **Broad mission and purpose.** Indian business leaders place special emphasis on personal values, a vision of growth, and strategic thinking. Besides servicing the needs of their stockholders—a necessity of CEOs everywhere—Indian business leaders stress broader societal purpose. The leaders of Indian business take pride in enterprise success—but also in family prosperity, regional advancement, and national renaissance.

The India Way

The India Way comprises a mix of organizational capabilities, managerial practices, and distinctive aspects of company cultures that set Indian enterprises apart from firms in other countries. The India Way is characterized by four principal practices: holistic employee engagement, improvisation and adaptability of managers, creative value delivery to customers, and a sense of broad mission and purpose (see "Principal Practices of the India Way").

Bundled together, these principles constitute a distinctly Indian way of conducting business, one that contrasts with combinations found in other countries, especially the United States, where the blend is centered more around delivering shareholder value. Indian business leaders as a group place greater stress on social purpose and transcendent mission, and they do so by devoting special attention to surmounting innumerable barriers with creative solutions and a prepared and eager workforce.

Purpose, pragmatism, and people aptly capture much of the essence of the India Way, but allow us to stress at the outset that we are writing about generalized qualities. To travel any distance in India is to experience firsthand the maddening bureaucratic delays that remain an endemic though diminishing part of everyday Indian life. Nor do Indian firms and their leaders have a monopoly on virtue. Corruption and malfeasance can be found in the Indian business community as surely they can be found in all business communities. Note, for instance, the scandal involving Satyam Computers and its CEO, Ramalinga Raju, who sits in an Indian jail as we write.

Not all Indian business leaders, in short, are saints or sages, just as not all American CEOs are focused laserlike on delivering shareholder value while ignoring larger societal concerns. That said, the attributes of the India Way we describe in these pages appear often enough and especially among the most successful companies that they have come, we believe, to constitute a clear and distinctive model. Drawn from the voices of Indian business leaders, and from our observations of Indian leaders and companies in action, the set of four attributes above captures much of the modern Indian way of conducting business.

Why It Matters

When Westerners think of India, names like Bajaj Auto and Dr. Reddy's Laboratories are hardly the first to come to mind. The Taj Mahal's beauty and Calcutta's squalor are far more defining, with the vale of Kashmir and bustling bazaars of Chandni Chowk in New Delhi not far behind.

Yet increasingly, India is also a world leader in business, with everything from medical procedures to investment banking either migrating from the United States and elsewhere to India or springing up from within. Simultaneously, Reliance, ICICI, Infosys, and hundreds of India's other top companies have been clambering onto the world stage to compete directly against Western multinationals in virtually all sectors. In mastering the art of high-quality *and* efficient production—and in developing unique ways of managing people and assets to achieve it—Indian executives have delivered growth rates that would be the envy of any Western executive. During much of the 2000s, India's gross domestic product (GDP) had been rising by better than 9 percent per year—several times that of the United States and nearly that of China. That 9 percent–plus GDP growth, we should note, represents Indian businesses as a whole (additional indicators of India's fast growth can be found in appendix A). Many of the nation's *premier* companies—the focus of our inquiry— reported that they were growing at twice the rate of the general economy, or more. Chairman Subhash Chandra of Zee Entertainment Enterprises—India's largest media and entertainment company— told us, for instance, that his company had grown from $400 million in annual revenue six years earlier to $2 billion at the time of our interview with him. Managing director G. R. Gopinath of Deccan Aviation said before his acquisition by Kingfisher Airlines in 2007 that he had been adding a new aircraft every month to the fleet, growing from one to forty-five planes in less than four years. Infosys Technologies' chairman Narayana Murthy had presided over a company that employed 10,700 and drew $545 million in revenue in 2002; seven years later, his company employed 104,900 and earned revenue of $4.6 billion.

We have come to believe that undergirding the rapid expansion of the Indian economy—and above all the stunning growth of its largest companies—is an innovative and exportable way of doing business, but we did not approach this project with that conclusion in mind. In fact, we had expected much the opposite: with the triumph of American-style capitalism, at least until it came under a cloud during the financial crisis of 2008–2009, managers around the world had often sought to understand the leadership secrets of U.S. companies like Apple Computer and General Electric. In commencing our study of Indian business leaders, we had anticipated a cross-national convergence on American terms, with Indian companies looking to adopt the management methods of Steve Jobs, Jack Welch, and other leaders of American enterprise.

What we found instead was a mantra of "not invented there." Though well aware of Western methods, Indian business leaders have been blazing much their own path. And though rooted in the traditions and times of the subcontinent, the value of their distinctive path can, we believe, transcend the milieu from which it arose. When Indian companies, for instance, take over publicly traded American firms—such as Tata Motors' acquisition of Ford's Jaguar and Land Rover divisions in 2008—research confirms that the acquired firms increased both their efficiency and their profitability.[5] Rather than appreciating the value of the India Way only upon acquisition, Western firms might be well advised to learn from the Indian experience in advance. Indeed, we believe that understanding the India Way and its drivers has become vital for business managers everywhere.[6]

In completing this study of Indian business leaders, we were repeatedly reminded of the remarkable impact that Japanese business leaders and the Toyota Way have had on the auto-making world and far beyond. The methods of lean production pioneered by Eiji Toyoda and his company—treating all buffers as waste and seeking continuous improvement in all aspects of production—originated in the cultural traditions and austere times of postwar Japan. But the methods have proved powerful drivers far beyond that context, enhancing both quality and productivity in everything from Porsche manufacturing in Germany to hospital processing in the United States.[7] With a model originally built in Japan, Toyota has become the world's largest automaker, and its methods have come to be widely emulated by managers far beyond Japan.

Much the same applies to the India Way. It was born of the circumstances facing Indian business during the past two decades, but like the Toyota Way, it is also a model that can readily transcend its origins, providing a template for Western business leaders to reinvigorate their own, often sluggish growth rates. Think of it pragmatically: if applying the principles of the India Way were to generate even a single extra percentage point in yearly growth—say, increasing the annual growth rate from 3 to 4 percent—over the next five years, the 4 percent–rate companies would see their value doubled, compared to 3 percent–rate firms. Over ten years, they would triple their worth, compared to the slower-growing companies.

Who We Interviewed

India is a vast economy with a wide variety of practices and arrangements across its more than seven hundred thousand companies. To understand the company capabilities and leadership capacities that have constituted a vital factor in the nation's growth, we focused on the country's largest firms—those that have played a leading role in India's rapid development and have come to serve as models of business enterprise for entrepreneurs and managers throughout the nation. Our approach has been to interview those at the top of the pyramid, the leaders of India's largest firms. That is where the critical decisions of the nation's most important companies are made, particularly those strategic choices that have helped define India's distinctive approach to business.

We approached a hundred fifty of the largest publicly listed companies by market capitalization, and we secured time with more than one hundred of their executives. We asked what leadership qualities they saw as most vital to their success. We probed how they worked with their boards of directors, what their directors brought to the table, and where they saw convergence with or divergence from Western practices. We inquired about their methods for recruiting talent and managing teams, and asked what lasting legacies they hoped to leave behind when they stepped down one day from their executive suites.

We cast our net broadly, interviewing executives who produced steel, managed airlines, and manufactured pharmaceuticals; those who were entirely self-made, the Horatio Algers of Indian business; and those whose company fortunes were inherited, the Fords and Rockefellers of Indian dynasties. Among those we interviewed are Reliance Industries chief executive Mukesh Ambani, ICICI Bank CEO Chanda Kochhar, Bajaj Auto chairman Rahul Bajaj, Infosys Technologies chairman Narayana Murthy, and even the former and now disgraced and imprisoned Satyam CEO, Ramalinga Raju. We have sought to let Indian business leaders speak for themselves, to characterize their leadership experience and philosophy in their own words as very well-placed participant-observers. All are immersed in the phenomenon in ways that outside observers can never be. Nine of those who are living and defining the India Way—its active proponents and daily reinventors—are displayed in figure 1-1, and the others are described in appendix B.[8]

"We Think in English and Act in Indian"

The essence of the India Way is embodied in the thinking and perceptions of the business leaders themselves. We "think in English and act in Indian," observed R. Gopalakrishnan, the executive director of Tata Sons, the holding company of the Tata Group, a set of companies dating back to 1868—some ninety-eight enterprises in all, employing 290,000 and booking annual revenue equal to 3.2 percent of the nation's GDP. By comparison, Wal-Mart Stores, America's largest company with more than 2 million employees, drew annual revenue in 2007 equivalent to 2.7 percent of the U.S. GDP.

"For the Indian manager," Gopalakrishnan explained, "his intellectual tradition, his y-axis, is Anglo-American, and his action vector, his x-axis, is in the Indian ethos. Many foreigners come to India, they talk to Indian managers, and they find them very articulate,

FIGURE 1-1

Business leaders living and defining the India Way

Indian business leaders (left to right, top to bottom): **Mukesh D. Ambani,** *managing director of Reliance Industries;* **Rahul Bajaj,** *executive chairman of the Bajaj Group of companies;* **R. Gopalakrishnan,** *executive director of Tata Sons;* **Chanda Kochhar,** *CEO and managing director of ICICI Bank;* **Anand Mahindra,** *vice chairman and managing director of Mahindra & Mahindra;* **N. R. Narayana Murthy,** *the joint chairman and chief mentor of Infosys Technologies;* **Kiran Mazumdar-Shaw,** *executive chairman and managing director of Biocon;* **Azim Premji,** *chairman of Wipro; and* **Malvinder Mohan Singh,** *managing director and CEO of Ranbaxy Laboratories*

Sources: Ambani—The India Today Group/Getty Images; Bajaj—Bajaj Auto India; Gopalakrishnan—Tata Sons Ltd.; Kochhar—ICICI Bank India; Mahindra—AFP/Getty Images; Murthy—The India Today Group/Getty Images; Mazumdar-Shaw—Biocon Ltd.; Premji—Wipro Technologies; Singh—Religare Enterprises/Fortis Healthcare. Used with permission.

very analytical, very smart, very intelligent—and then they can't for the life of them figure out why the Indian manager can't do what is prescribed by the analysis."

Compared with the West, he said, Indian executives are more respectful of seniority, government, and tradition. They rely more upon their intuition than their Western counterparts. Viewpoints are indirectly expressed; silence is sometimes golden. A European executive who had recently met with the Indian prime minister marveled at how quiet the nation's leader was—but also how powerful his words were when finally spoken. Compare that to the clamor of a gathering of the Business Roundtable—the lobbying arm for the chief executives of America's largest corporations—and you'll have some idea of how different "acting in Indian" can be.

The emergent Indian model revolves around basic questions that all companies face whatever the national setting: How can they best compete? What steps are required to prosper in a highly competitive marketplace? Are there sustainable advantages? Such questions go to the very heart of business strategy and often evoke similar responses from business leaders almost everywhere.

One of the distinguishing aspects of the India Way, however, has been the capacity of the nation's business leaders to find a creative advantage where no one else was looking. They have often built and followed structures and strategies radically different from the Western norm, though the practices that have flowed from those decisions have frequently proved applicable to business in other markets, including the United States, even if the applicability has not yet been widely recognized. The Tata Nano, the pint-size car built by Tata Motors—India's largest maker of automobiles and trucks, with 60 percent of the market—is a case in point. In its development can be seen the defining themes of acting in Indian.

Throughout the 1990s and 2000s, U.S. car makers, the global industry's most established incumbents, directed their attention to trucks and sport-utility vehicles (SUVs), and indeed, the best-selling vehicles for American companies for many years were full-size trucks, not cars. This strategic focus derived from sophisticated business analysis driven by marketing information on both consumers and competitors. Market analysis had revealed less immediate competition in the truck and SUV segments than in conventional cars since Japanese auto producers, the most important foreign makers in the American market, were still working their way up the value chain from autos to trucks. Producing trucks and SUVs was thus a market segment that offered the opportunity for the greatest immediate profit margins.

At the same time, Tata Motors was moving in the opposite direction, pushing ever deeper into its traditional market segment of small inexpensive cars. This is the most competitive, lowest-profit-per-car segment in the world auto industry, one that runs up directly against the strongest Japanese competitors. Still, Tata Motors decided to stay with its existing customer base. Realizing that India's mass market hungered for even lower-cost transportation, Tata set out to engineer an automobile whose price would be not just marginally lower than the lowest-end existing products but radically lower, not 10 percent but 75 percent below the lowest-end. Tata Motors knew that it would have to do the engineering largely on its own, without the benefit of the research and development that one might find in universities and government laboratories in other countries. It knew, too, that, like all its products, the Nano would have to be developed on a shorter life cycle. "We can't have forty-eight or thirty-six months to bring out the new products," offered Tata Motors executive director for finance Praveen Kadle; now it's just "twenty-four or eighteen months."

With all that in mind, Tata Motors swiftly designed the Nano from a clean sheet of paper to meet what appeared to be an impossibly low price point: 100,000 rupees per car, about $2,500 at the time. The sticker price of the Nano, presented as the world's most inexpensive car when unveiled in January 2008 by Ratan Tata, chairman of the Tata Group, was to be on a par with the cost of a DVD option in luxury Western autos.[9] (See figure 1-2.)

How could Tata sell the Nano at less than half the price of its closest competitor in India, the Maruti 800? The answer was not in any

FIGURE 1-2

The Tata Nano

Source: Tata Motors Corporate Communications/Wharton. Used with permission.

radical technological innovation, but in a completely new design based on what some analysts have dubbed *Gandhian engineering* principles—deep frugality and a willingness to challenge conventional wisdom—and a single-minded determination by Tata's top managers to work through the many constraints and challenges of operating in the Indian environment. They designed everything in the Nano from scratch, and they deleted many features that were taken for granted by car makers, including air-conditioning, power brakes, and radios. Although the Nano is smaller in size than the Maruti 800, it offers some 20 percent more seating capacity as a result of an intelligent design that moved the wheels to the extreme edges of the car. By using an aluminum engine and lightweight steel, the designers were able to build a car that was significantly lighter than anything else on the road with four wheels and could achieve a fuel efficiency of 50 miles to the gallon.

The Nano's other important feature is its modular design. Kits of components are to be sold en masse for assemblage and distribution by local businesses. Ratan Tata has talked about "creating entrepreneurs across the country that would produce the car." That, he said, is "my idea of dispersing wealth."[10] Tata even anticipated providing the tools for local mechanics to assemble the car in existing auto shops or new garages created to cater to rural customers. Termed *open distribution innovation* by *Business Week*, the method could create not only the world's least expensive automobile but also its largest-selling one. For proponents of the "bottom of the pyramid" approach who stress the importance of developing innovative models to tap the vast potential of the lower end of emerging markets, the Nano would seem to be the answer to a prayer: a cheap but sturdy product that could spawn a whole network of support businesses.

To be sure, production and distribution of the Tata Nano ran up against a host of constraints and challenges, from safety concerns (readying the car to meet British standards, for example, would double the price) to environmental and political ones: in October 2008, violent protests forced Tata Motors to abandon a controversial production site in the Indian state of West Bengal. Add to those problems the economic woes emanating from a global financial crisis, and realizing the Nano's full potential will depend much upon the continuing resilience and tenacity of Tata's top management—but, of course, those are the very skills that brought the car into existence in the first place.[11]

Ratan Tata created an entirely new class of car targeted at the great multitude of Indians who could not afford to buy a conventionally conceived automobile. Getting there was a matter of "pushing the organization to think very differently," said Satish Pradhan, executive vice president for group human resources at Tata Sons. The class of car also targeted the competition. "Tata Motors has built up a position," said Gopalakrishnan, "where international car companies are not able to compete with us." And that, in essence, is a large part of what the India Way is all about: a strategy of focusing the energy and attention of company managers on the hard and persistent needs of their customers, achieving outcomes that break through traditional standards of products and services.

The Promise of the Book

The insights offered by our diverse group of Indian business leaders is the spine of this book and the foundation for our fleshing out of the India Way. We have added our own voices as well, our own interpretation of what they collectively said and implied. The four of us, all colleagues at the Wharton School of the University of Pennsylvania, have long studied U.S. companies and managers, authoring a range of articles and books on American business and its leaders. But two of us also grew up and studied in India; a third spent the better part of two childhood years there; and all of us have frequently traveled to India for teaching, research, consulting, board meetings, and family visits. With this dual heritage, we have drawn on our joint experience to examine what is unique about Indian business leadership and to better understand what can be usefully learned by Western managers and executives.[12]

As directors of three Wharton research centers—the Mack Center for Technological Innovation, the Center for Human Resources, and the Center for Leadership and Change Management—we have also drawn upon diverse information networks and funding sources in preparing this account. In collaboration with the National Human Resource Development Network, India's premier human resource organization, we gained ready access to the highest circles of Indian business. And as faculty members, we have extensive contacts with the companies and executives that are at the heart of the India Way. We are also personally familiar with a broad array of American, European, Latin, and Asian companies and executives that serve as useful points of comparison. In building our portrait, we have drawn as well on a host of academic and industry studies of Indian business leadership. Our project was facilitated by India's long-standing democratic and Anglo traditions that make the experience of Indian business leaders exceptionally accessible and applicable to Western management.[13]

If business leadership around the world is converging, we have concluded, it may come to be as much on Indian terms as on those from the West. Company managers everywhere can usefully learn from India's example the power of cause, culture, and consultation; the advantage of creative value propositions and rapid decision making; the value of employees as assets instead of liabilities; the utility of building for the era, not only the quarter; the benefit of company loyalty over shareholder value; and the advantage of national mission over private purpose.

The principles are not so unique to the Indian context that they could work only there. Simply put, if Indian business leaders can build their distinctive methods so rapidly, over just the past two decades, and if they can learn to manage diversity so effectively in one of the world's most complexly diverse societies, other business leaders in other countries can surely do so as well. The model in the pages that follow is there and waiting. We begin with the nation's decision in the early 1990s to liberalize the economy and dismantle the license raj, a foundation for so much that has emerged. We then turn to the principles by which Indian business executives manage their people, lead their firms, define their culture, create their value propositions, and draw upon their governing boards.

Whether it is a good moment to invest in the subcontinent, we leave to those more versed in the ways (and caprices) of financial markets. What we do believe wholeheartedly is that the time is both ripe and right to better understand what is driving the Indian economic powerhouse: that blending of practices we call the India Way.

CHAPTER TWO

The Way to the India Way

*Economic Reforms Drive
Development of New Capabilities*

TATA GROUP, the holding company of one of India's largest conglomerates, had adapted to and actually prospered from the stifling regulatory environment that enveloped Indian business firms in the 1980s. The business context was a far cry from free-market philosophies taking hold in the United States under President Ronald Reagan and in the United Kingdom under Prime Minister Margaret Thatcher.[1] Yet the firms of the Tata Group had learned to navigate, even master, a world of state constraint and sluggish growth.

Then came a set of watershed economic reforms in the summer of 1991, opening a new world of far less domestic regulation and far more international competition. Suddenly, the very context to which

Tata firms had adapted so well—they were among India's most successful companies at the time—underwent dramatic change. Either Tata firms would have to learn to adapt to the new environment, or they would not survive the more open, more combative marketplace. Inevitably, anxieties among the holding company's senior executives soared.

At about the same time, Ratan Tata, great-grandson of Tata Group founder Jamsetji Tata, had moved into the executive chairman's office of Tata Sons. Several years later, when one of us visited him at Tata headquarters at Bombay House in Mumbai, it was very evident that he had his hands full. He was seeking to rein in several companies of the far-flung Tata empire that had become too independent at the very same time that all of his companies were faced by the far more uncertain and demanding marketplace.

What followed in the next decade and a half has been nothing short of extraordinary. Ratan Tata and his executive team sold off or shut down some of the least viable enterprises and then transformed the others, reconfiguring and realigning them to face the pitched competition that soon emerged from both domestic start-ups and foreign intruders. Tata Steel, for example, entered the 1990s with a mediocre record of efficiency, but a decade later it emerged as one of the lowest-cost steel makers in the world. Tata Consultancy Services, Tata Motors, and other Tata brands also emerged as world-class players.

In the assessment of Tata Sons executive director R. Gopalakrishnan, whom we had interviewed both for this book and prior to its inception, the apprehension that plagued managers at Tata and other major companies early in the 1990s had been gradually replaced by an abiding self-confidence among those who managed them. Business leaders were proving to themselves that they were able not only to hold their own against leading foreign challengers but to outperform them.

Though hardly evident at the time, one of the most enduring impacts of the economic reforms of the early 1990s was to force Indian firms to develop world-class capabilities if they were to survive and prosper. Simply put, the forced exposure to open competition forced

the issue. Tata Consulting Services, for instance, had relied prereform primarily on low labor costs; postreform, the firm came to appreciate that it would have to add quality service in order to retain its
customers. As is sometimes now said of the Indian software industry,
"The clients came for lower costs, but stayed for higher capabilities."

After completing an MBA degree at the Indian Institute of Management, Ahmedabad, one of us began our career at one of the Tata
Group companies, Voltas Ltd. Already in the 1970s, it was evident
from the inside that the reputation of Tata firms for being well managed and untouched by corruption was deserved. It was also clear
that the Tata leaders were strongly committed to a broader agenda
of contributing to Indian society, one of our four core components
of the India Way: broad mission and purpose. Indeed, two-thirds of
the profits of the Tata Group were annually channeled into its
charitable trusts.

A second aspect of the India Way—holistic engagement with
employees—was also readily seen in the culture of most Tata companies. The employment relationship was widely understood to be
for the long term while still contingent upon satisfactory performance. To be sure, some of this may have derived from the paternalism of an earlier generation of business leaders in India, but it was
also anchored in an emergent Indian business ethos that viewed
companies as "one big family."

The inflection point for Indian business and the appearance of
the full India Way can thus be traced to India's economic reforma-
tion of the early 1990s. In this chapter we explore how the altered
business context shaped its emergence. A brief assessment of the
cultural roots of the India Way can be found in appendix C.

The Pre-1991 Business Context

The miracles of the Indian economic miracle have been many. One:
the nation built its economic juggernaut on one of the most diverse workforces in the world. The country recognized no less than

eighteen official languages, and each major state insisted on its own regional language in schooling. When one of us attended a public school at the age of ten in the state of Maharashtra, the languages of instruction were not only English and the official national language, Hindi, but also the regional tongue of Marathi.

The country was also divided among six major ethnic groups, scores of smaller ones, and an invidious caste system that has yet to disappear completely—in many rural areas, the local culture still esteems Brahmins at the top and scorns "untouchables" at the bottom. The contrasts between wealth and poverty were extreme as well: luxury condos rose amid squalid slums, and speeding Mercedeses narrowly missed hoards of homeless sleeping along roadsides at night. And though the West sees India as a great Hindu civilization, it is also home to the world's second-largest Muslim populace. That this diverse people—dwarfing in demographic complexity any other major economy—banded together in business and beyond is testament to the power of the Indian formula.

What was truly remarkable, though, was what business had to overcome to launch almost two decades of breathtaking growth. For more than forty years after India gained its political independence from the British in 1947, a second raj, commonly referred to as the *license raj*, imposed Kafkaesque barriers in front of every business action or decision. Bajaj Auto was prohibited from making more scooters than its license permitted; Bombay rickshaw drivers were required to own their own vehicles; the use of red or green ink—rather than blue—was limited to senior civil servants. Manufacturers found that closing a money-losing factory could require a decade's journey or longer through the bureaucratic maze.

Government inspectors and regulators had also been evident at every turn, and proved executioners at some. Gurcharan Das, chief executive of Procter & Gamble's India operation, recalled, "In my thirty years in active business in India, I did not meet a single bureaucrat who really understood my business, yet he had the power to ruin it."[2] Nor did the bureaucrats appreciate the deplorable conditions that their controls had helped create. India's highways, power plants, shipping ports, and communication links were notorious for their inadequacies, inefficiencies, and frequent unavailability. Delays of six months or sometimes years for a telephone landline had long been a recognized cost of opening a new office.

Inspired in part by Soviet-style economic theory and practices, the Indian government nationalized whole industry groups after 1947 and then the banks in the mid-1960s. It also constructed towering tariff barriers to prevent competition, but the government's reach extended far beyond the companies it directly controlled. The license raj effectively nationalized even those companies and industries that were allowed to operate under private ownership. As happens in all-powerful bureaucracies, corruption was rife, and bribery commonplace. Inevitably, too, a staggering percentage of the effort put forth by both private- and public-sector companies was directed toward mollifying and cajoling the authorities in New Delhi.

Stifling Regulation, Little Capital

For many of the senior generation of current Indian business leaders, the license raj and the political climate that spawned it remain a formative experience. To ICICI Bank's K. V. Kamath, India's decades of state-planned economic policies—originally designed to balance both equitable and sustainable expansion—were primarily successful at hamstringing businesses and severely limiting options for company growth. One example: the heavily regulated financial markets provided very few suitable investment options for Indian companies. "Accelerated development required capital," Kamath said, but because of the restrictions, it was simply not forthcoming from the private sector. Although India's web of controls may have been well intentioned, designed in the ideal to lift as many people as possible out of poverty, the result, Kamath recalled, was a business environment with stifling regulation and little capital.

The state-dominated approach remained India's accepted practice until the late 1980s, when limited attempts to transform the economy were tested. "The first winds of change" were felt, Kamath recalled, when the government sought to moderate some of the rigidities in the economy and to encourage the use of technology. Business leaders themselves were becoming increasingly distressed by the economic boom going on elsewhere in Asia—in Korea, Singapore, Taiwan, and even Indonesia and Malaysia. "The emergence of the Asian tigers revealed both the opportunity that the economy had missed and also the flaws in the old approach to economic management," said Kamath.

Rana Kapoor, chief executive of Yes Bank, remembered the Asian tigers as an appealing economic model that should have been heeded sooner. "The need for a policy shift had become evident much earlier," he said, as countries in East Asia achieved their high growth and reduced poverty through policies emphasizing product exports and the private sector.

Rajat Nag, managing director general of the Asian Development Bank, added that by 1991, China's growth story was adding still another stark contrast with that of India. "In China, reforms were already under way for more than a decade, and results were beginning to show," recalled Nag. "Even if the Indian policy makers were reluctant to admit so publicly, they began to realize the country's policy environment was inadequate and inappropriate to break out of the Hindu growth rate."

The Reforms of 1991

For several years after independence, India's gross domestic product had grown at annual rates of just 2 percent to 3 percent, but in real per capita terms, the growth was closer to zero since the population had been expanding at a comparable pace. There were exceptional moments—the late 1980s, for example, when the national economy spurted briefly at better than 10 percent—but, for the most part, four decades of the license raj and other constrictive government policies and practices had yielded an economy that was barely inching along.

That was part of the incentive to change. Part, too, was geopolitical: by the early 1990s, the Soviet Union, long a large and reliable trading partner of India, had collapsed. The Berlin Wall came down in 1989, and German reunification followed; and the Soviet Union disbanded in 1991. Though India was far removed from the Iron Curtain, the Soviet dissolution called into question the wisdom of the approach to business it had adopted since independence, a version of state-centered socialism with the central government playing a major role in most economic matters. Now, India found itself without a key trading partner, and its socialist precepts without an international anchor.

To add insult to injury, the first Persian Gulf War, launched in January 1991 by a United Nations coalition of armed forces from a dozen nations, led to a suspension of oil supplies from Iraq to its contractual partners, including India. With energy prices spiking, India was forced to buy its petroleum on the open market, depleting its cushion of hard currency reserves within weeks. At one point, India had only a few days of foreign exchange reserves available.

"The country was literally going broke," remembered Asian Development Bank's Rajat Nag, forcing the Indian government to pledge its gold reserves as collateral with the Bank of England. Sanjeev Sanyal, formerly chief economist at Deutsche Bank, Singapore, similarly saw the depletion of foreign currency reserves as the tipping point that finally forced the long overdue reforms of the Indian economy. "The old socialist system simply collapsed under its own weight," recalled Sanyal. "It was not due to a change of heart in the intellectual or political elites. In the face of four decades of failure, the elites remained loyal to the 'Nehruvian' vision of isolationism and bureaucratic control. We opened up because we were forced to do so."

Breaking Away

The turning point from the Hindu growth rate to the present success story of India came in 1991 with a radical reduction in the role of the state. The economic reforms were initiated by Indian prime minister P. V. Narasimha Rao, though the critical role in bringing them about belonged to his finance minister (and later prime minister) Manmohan Singh, assisted by commerce minister (and later finance minister and then home minister) Palaniappan Chidambaram.

Contemporary accounts by government agencies sometimes tend to showcase the results of the reforms while downplaying the necessity that propelled them. The Web site for the Investment and Technology Division of the Indian Ministry of External Affairs, for example, offered that, the "reform process in India was initiated with the aim of accelerating the pace of economic growth and eradication of poverty," and it did so through an emphasis on "gradualism and evolutionary transition rather than rapid restructuring or 'shock therapy.'"[3]

But whether necessity or prescient decision making held the upper hand—and some combination of the two was most likely at play—the Indian government leadership engineered what became a radical departure from the past. The impact was profound: in the accurate words of the Investment and Technology Division Web site, the reforms "unlocked India's enormous growth potential and unleashed powerful entrepreneurial forces," and they did so across a broad business front.[4]

In the industrial sector, massive deregulation loosened what had been a virtual bureaucratic death grip. Prior to the 1991 reform, eighteen industry groups—everything from iron and steel to mining, air transport, and electrical production and distribution—had been under the thumb of government control. After the reforms, only defense firms, atomic energy, and railway transport remained under central authority.

Prereform, trade policy meant high tariffs and import restrictions as well as outright bans on the import of manufactured consumer goods; licensing requirements led to epic delays and widespread corruption. Import tariffs ran as high as 400 percent, three-fifths of the tariffs ranged from 110 to 150 percent, and only one-twentieth fell below 60 percent. Postreform, import licensing was reduced for consumer goods and mostly abolished for capital goods, and the

average tariff rate was reduced to 25 percent. India moved to a flexible exchange rate based on a basket of currencies, and the Indian
rupee steadily appreciated against the American dollar. By 2001, a
decade after the reforms were first launched, restrictions on imports
of manufactured consumer goods and agricultural products were
abolished altogether.[5]

Financial-sector reforms, similarly, were driven by an emphasis on
transparency, liberalization in interest-rate and reserve requirements, and adoption of international financial-market standards.
In large part because of these reforms, the Indian financial structure
became strong, diverse, efficient, competitive, and—as was evident in
the face of a withering global financial crisis in 2008–2009—relatively
resilient.[6]

Morphing into Something New

No one would argue that the old, bad ways spawned by the license
raj and state control were eradicated totally by the reforms of 1991.
Bureaucracy and palm greasing are still endemic in India's political
and economic life. Indeed, a national poll of some one thousand large
public and private organizations conducted in 2007 found that 80 percent of the organizations identified fraud as a continuing problem for
business, and 60 percent had experienced fraud in their own organization during the past two years. The most common forms: kickbacks,
bribery, and theft.[7] Nor can the great success of so many Indian businesses in recent years be credited entirely to the reforms. The story of
India's dramatic economic shift from the slow-going past to a fast-
moving present is a complex and multifaceted one, but the 1991 reforms do constitute *the* major divide between then and now, and their
impact cannot be overstated. In many ways the emergence of the distinctive synthesis that we have termed the India Way can be traced to
firms' capitalization on a host of novel business opportunities whose
outlines gradually became evident in the post-1991 regime.[8]

Some preexisting firms morphed into new and different incarna-
tions in the wake of the reforms: one of India's premier information

technology firms, Wipro, had begun in 1947 as Western India Vegetable Products Ltd., a cooking-oil provider. Others came fresh out of the gate. Though incorporated in 1981, Infosys Technologies, another of the country's major IT firms, with more than a hundred thousand employees in 2008, hadn't gone public until 1993. A few firms had operated for more than a century: the State Bank of India was founded in 1806. Either way, old or new, in less than two decades, many enterprises had become domestic powerhouses, with some even quite competitive with the best in the West.

Though many companies in Singapore and the United Arab Emirates also expanded at torrid rates in their growing economies until the recession of 2009, the flourishing of Indian business was on a scale and at a pace with little precedence except for the near simultaneous growth of Chinese enterprise following that country's 1980s' economic liberalization. Figures 2-1 and 2-2 paint the picture

FIGURE 2-1

Annual rate of increase in India's real gross domestic product, 1961–2008

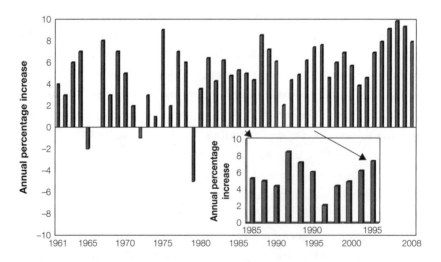

Sources: International Monetary Fund, World Economic Outlook Database, April 2008; and World Bank, Doing Business 2008: India (Washington, DC: World Bank, 2008), http://www.doingbusiness.org/.

FIGURE 2-2

Indian foreign exchange reserves, 1951–2008

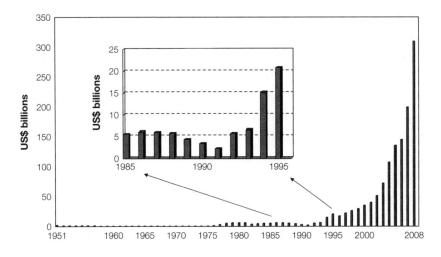

Source: Reserve Bank of India, *Report on Foreign Exchange Reserves*, 2008, http://rbidocs.rbi.org.in/rdocs/
AnnualReport/Docs/86606.xls.

better than words. Prior to the 1991 reforms, the nation's economic
growth had been an up-and-down affair, with high-growth spikes
(the late 1980s, when much of Asia was booming) offset by near-flat
and negative years. For the first seventeen years postreform, the
growth was always positive on an annual basis, and mostly robust.
Similarly, India's foreign reserves, nearly exhausted following the
oil crisis of 1991, soared in the postreform years as foreign direct
investment and foreign institutional investment came pouring into
the Indian market.[9]

At the Center of the Reforms

As useful a scorecard as economic statistics can be, the true impact of
the 1991 reforms can best be assessed by those who were at the center
of the storm. The Indian business leaders who experienced the
reforms were almost universal in deeming them to be *the* foundation

for much that was to come to define the India Way. As Manoj Kohli, CEO and joint managing director of Bharti Airtel, described it, the "bold reforms to unshackle the Indian economy from the controls of Inspector Raj" in 1991 marked "the 'economic independence' of India after the political independence in 1947."

For Infosys's Narayana Murthy, the positive effect of abolishing licensing in most industries was matched by a new government encouragement of foreign businesses to operate in India. With 100 percent foreign ownership allowed for the first time in the high-technology sector, companies like IBM, Microsoft, and Sun Microsystems invested in India and helped create a foundation for India's technology boom. Equally important for making Indian companies like Infosys internationally competitive was the introduction of current account convertibility, which allowed Indian companies for the first time to open offices abroad, hire employees abroad, travel for business abroad, and engage consultants from abroad.

Financial-sector restructuring, especially the 1992 Security and Exchange Board of India Act, also proved important. Reforms in the stock market, recollected Humayun Dhanrajgir, chairman of Emcure Pharmaceuticals, swelled investor confidence and brought about a newfound willingness to acquire equities. And currency convertibility, duty reduction, and special economic zones also helped enable businesses to take advantage of international trade that began to accelerate in the 1990s.

Elimination of still another public lever—the controller of capital issues—was critical as well. This New Delhi–based office with oversight responsibilities for the Bombay-centered emergent public-equity market had held the power to determine prices for initial company offerings to the investing public. Insisting on very low premiums over book value when companies went public, the controller often forced new companies to give away much of their equity in exchange for comparatively little capital. Going public had thus proved costly, and the abolition of its control and the resulting free pricing of initial public offerings introduced a major new incentive for entrepreneurs setting out to build new enterprises.

Kindling Indian Entrepreneurship

India has a long-standing and powerful tradition of Indian entre-preneurship, especially evident among members of prominent mer-chant groups. The Marwaris, for example, hailing originally from the Marwar region of central and western Rajasthan, carry a tradi-tion of entrepreneurship going back hundreds of years, and today they stand at the forefront of many Indian firms. Lakshmi Mittal of ArcelorMittal, the largest steel-making firm in the world; Kumar Birla of the Aditya Birla Group, a $29 billion conglomerate involved in everything from cement to finance; and Rahul Bajaj of Bajaj Auto, one of the world's largest makers of two-wheelers, are all Marwaris.

For many business leaders, the greatest single impact of the re-form process was the unleashing of what they saw as India's latent entrepreneurial energies. In the words of K. V. Kamath, "The land-scape of Indian business underwent a sea change." With "financial capital being more easily accessible, and technology and knowl-edge capital emerging as key drivers, many new-generation entre-preneurs began to make their appearance on the business scene."

Amit Chandra, managing director of Bain Capital Advisors in India, likewise saw the reforms' greatest success in "kindling the In-dian entrepreneur's spirit." Although many Indians already had proven business talent and experience, they were invigorated by lib-eralization's possibilities. "After having been shackled for a couple of decades by overly suppressive and retrograde government policies," he remembered, "our businessmen had their first real shot at compet-ing on the basis of relatively free-market principles." The resulting surge in business activity came with frequent mistakes since so many business leaders were venturing onto uncharted territory; but, Chandra noted, they were ready to take the risks and acquire new mastery through trial-and-error experience. "Our entrepreneurs learned fast," he said, and in doing so they "laid the foundations for a lot of world-class companies."

In learning to make do and even do better with less-than-stellar public provisions, business leaders and others have helped to embed an innovative attitude in the national psyche.[10] When Atul Gawande, the Boston-based surgeon and best-selling writer, visited a hospital in rural India, for example, he found that despite the appalling conditions faced by the surgeons—few instruments, deplorable sanitation, overwhelming patient flows—they "persisted in developing abilities that were a marvel to witness." An ingenuity born of necessity had turned them into instructors for the West. "I had gone there thinking that, as an American-trained surgeon, I might have a thing or two I could teach them. But the abilities of an average Indian surgeon outstripped those of any Western surgeon I know."[11]

Latent Demand and a Ready Workforce

As important as creating a new climate was for India's business transformation, the reforms could not have succeeded without emergent business leaders learning how to capitalize on the new conditions. Ravi Uppal, formerly chairman of ABB in India and now managing director and CEO of Larsen and Toubro Power (L&T Power), saw the reforms as pushing the private sector into "full blossom." As the reforms kicked in, entrepreneurs found that they could maneuver more readily to take advantage of the Indian economy's new opportunities. "A lot of latent demand came to the fore, resulting in phenomenal growth of market size," recalled Uppal. The Indian economy fast transformed from a "supply-led one to being demand and market driven."

By way of example, Infosys's Narayana Murthy early recognized that the sharp reduction in import tariffs had dramatically lowered his company's operating costs and fundamentally improved the competitive advantage of Indian businesses in software development. Infosys suddenly faced "zero friction" in doing business, he recalled, since he no longer had to frequent New Delhi for endless approvals and licenses. Duties on computers were reduced to 35 percent and on software to 0 percent—down from 150 percent before the reforms. And the cost of data communications dropped by a factor of ten times.

As entrepreneurs learned to build on the opportunities opened by the reforms, they also discovered special advantages that were specific to India—above all, the country's trained and eager workforce. K. V. Kamath observed that as firms looked for business beyond India's boundaries, they learned that India's vast middle class provided an invaluable resource. "The entrepreneurs were keen to put the law of comparative advantage to work and leverage the large, educated, and relatively cheap workforce to establish India as a key player in the global economy," he said. In doing so, they "focused on productivity, sound financial structures, and cost efficiencies, and invested in technology and human resource development to build world-class companies, competing in a global context."

Anand Nayak, head of human resource development at ITC Ltd., told us that information technology companies in particular were able to take advantage of the skills inherent in a large pool of skilled manpower that was also fluent in English, especially since Western companies were simultaneously being pressured by investors and the financial markets to lower operating costs. In effect, the added cost competition imposed by globalization forced American and European corporations to offshore both services and manufacturing to Indian companies that were eager and ready to embrace it.

Atanu Dey, chief economist at Netcore Solutions, said that the 1991 reforms proved critical in steering Indian firms toward seeking advantages distinctive to the Indian context. They found a competitive edge from lower labor costs relative to the more developed countries, from learning to operate in an environment where demand was extremely price sensitive, and from the scale economies inherent in India's vast population.

A Blank Slate

Although Indian firms at first imported technologies, foreign managers, and global consultants to take advantage of the newly opened opportunities, in time many came to invent their own ways of doing so, laying the groundwork for the India Way. The nation's well-educated but unseasoned workforce provided a fresh but largely blank-slate foundation as business leaders sought to devise their own solutions. "In an ironic way," said Blackstone's Akhil Gupta, "India's underperformance of the past has come as a blessing." Companies were able to "leapfrog into the latest technology," recalled Gupta, "since the burden of legacy systems was very little."

At the same time, foreign companies and investors were streaming into India, with foreign ownership of Indian companies limited at first to 51 percent but gradually increased to 100 percent. Foreign competitors were soon everywhere, further challenging domestic firms to improve their operations. Business apprehensions were widespread at first. "When reforms were initiated in 1991," remembered Deutsche Bank's Sanjeev Sanyal, "there were fears that multinational companies would take over the country."

Indeed, many Indian companies found themselves having to rethink their way of doing business, as international firms arrived with superior methods. Some firms sought to delay the foreign invasion, but most concluded that they had little choice but to embrace the new regime. As Sony Entertainment Television's Rakesh Aggarwal recalled, "The open trade and investment policies forced the Indian firms to improve their competitiveness by upgrading technology—as in the case of the auto industry—and by seeking international partnerships for capital, market access, and technology." Car buyers, for instance, had found little choice in the nation's closed auto market. With international brands largely barred, Hindustan Motors produced its Ambassador car, based on antiquated 1950's British automotive technology, with only the most minor annual tweaks. Buyers still lined up at Ambassador showrooms since they were often the only place to buy a car. Once real consumer choice was introduced, however, car makers had no option but to come up with more creative value propositions. As they restructured their operations to meet the foreign challenge, many business leaders found that their anxieties proved unfounded. "Once the country was opened up," recalled

Sanjeev Sanyal, "we discovered that we could compete with any-one." At "last, we were rid of the ghost of the East India Company," he said. "Instead of fearing multinationals, we are building our own."

Getting Government Out of the Way

The license raj had penalized companies for "excess production"; now business leaders increasingly found that they could compete only with production economies of scale. Manufacturing facility sizes and locations were no longer determined by political interests and bureaucratic rules, but by the simple imperatives of staying competitive.

Rajat Nag, managing director general of Asian Development Bank, observed that the Indian government's implicit message that business leaders were on their own was hard to miss. "Fundamentally, the reforms told Indian organizations and entrepreneurs that the government would no longer protect or mollycoddle the nonperformers through a maze of government protection and bureaucratic hurdles. The Indian firms were told they would be on their own to succeed or fail in India." For better or for worse, said Nag, Indian business was no longer restrained but also no longer protected by the government: "The government would be out of the way!"

In the background, the visible success of many expatriate Indians in Western companies and societies provided a confidence booster. So did the early success of India's information technology companies like Tata Consultancy Services, Infosys, and Wipro. As companies learned to navigate the more open conditions created by the 1991 reforms, their leaders developed their own experience-based self-assurance. And with that, they began to demand more of their own employees. "The dynamics within organizations" became "far more contractual than social," recalled Sushanta Banerjee of Samuday Psycon, a New Delhi–based organizational-development consulting firm. Company executives were "perforce becoming more performance conscious and indeed time conscious."

Rising Status

As business leaders across India came to think differently and to run their companies differently, they also came to be perceived differently by the Indian public. During the early years of India's independence, business had even been viewed by many as a faintly disreputable pursuit. Enterprise leaders were considered not fully deserving of trust, akin to Britain's historic disdain for manufacturing managers.[12] But the end of the license raj helped eradicate that vestige as well.

Rahul Bajaj, chairman of the Bajaj Group, said that many of his executive brethren became visible figures in India, acquiring a public status unimaginable in India's license raj era and largely unknown in the United States. The nonbusiness media increasingly featured business leaders and their achievements. In a kind of virtuous circle, the widespread admiration for well-known business leaders further reinforced their leadership commitment. "The rapid growth achieved by those who realized the opportunities created success stories," recalled Bajaj, and those accounts served to spur others. "Every member of a successful organization," concluded Bajaj, felt "enthused by this public recognition."

Government and Business, Not Government Versus Business

The 1991 reforms had also inverted the relationship between business leaders and government officials. Prior to the economic restructuring, the relationship had been mostly a one-way street, with company owners and managers playing the role of supplicants and government functionaries acting the part of semibenevolent autocrats. While many Indian business leaders said that more change in that relationship was still essential, the reforms had fundamentally altered the way that the public and private sectors looked upon one another.

One of the most common words that business leaders used in our interviews to describe the altered relationship was *respect*. In contrast to the years of state control over business licensing, when industry leaders devoted much time to gaining the favor of government ministers, now there was, in the words of Infosys's Narayana Murthy, a "newfound respect for business and business leaders in government circles." Consequently, "businesspeople do not crawl when they are asked to bend; in fact, they refuse to bend." Public officials no longer looked on business with disdain, nor did they any longer profess, recalled Murthy, that "profit is a sin and poverty is a virtue."

A supplicant–benefactor relationship gave way to a working partnership. "Indian businessmen are now more confident of dealing with government on equal terms and on the basis of a mutually beneficial relationship," Bain Capital's Amit Chandra told us. "As good economics has become good politics, business leaders now have a much more open dialogue with the government" on both policy and execution. The altered relationship stemmed in part from the fact that company prosperity now depended far more upon executive performance than government patronage, and national prosperity depended more upon company performance than government edict.

"Success breeds respect," said Netcore Solutions' Atanu Dey. "The government knows that eventually the private sector will pull India out of poverty," he said. "In the end," he concluded, "the government does not actually generate wealth. At best, it can make the conditions conducive to wealth creation by the private sector."

With less need to curry favor with government, business leaders could invest more energy in creating sustainable enterprise. "The most important behavioral change that emerged," said Bain Capital's Amit Chandra, "was that business leaders realized that the key to creating sustainable value was to spend less time in Delhi, doing rounds of the corridors of power, and more on thinking about competitive advantage, operating excellence, customers, employees, and shareholders." Instead of public officials holding the key, the "discerning consumer now will dictate who succeeds in the marketplace," said Emcure's Humayun Dhanrajgir. "No longer is it possible for Indian manufacturers to sell shoddy goods in the market."

Private Enterprise, Public Purpose

Eventually, business came to be seen as a cornerstone in achieving the country's broader social goals. "The Indian leaders, today, are far more involved and play an active and influential role in the nation's long-term economic planning process along with the government," observed Bharti Airtel's Manoj Kohli, giving rise to a partnership. "The government," concluded Kohli, "is also far more responsive to industry needs."

The public-private dialogue even reversed direction, with Indian business leaders often consulted not only on economic affairs but also on social matters. The latter stemmed in part from government recognition that it could not resolve many of the nation's social ills over which it had held exclusive responsibility. Public figures came to expect that private enterprise would lend a hand, especially in times of national crisis. Even a decade ago, asking Anil Ambani to remain visible in Mumbai after the 26/11 attacks there would have been unlikely. So, too, would asking Infosys cochair Nandan Nilekani to direct a national initiative to create a unique identification number for everybody. Indeed, before the 1991 reforms, either request would have been unthinkable.

Jumping into the Public Dialogue

Many Indian executives preemptively engaged themselves and their companies in tackling societal shortcomings even without government entreaty, investing in medical clinics, employee housing, and community services. They also thrust themselves into the public dialogue over the nation's social goals, a move welcomed in a way that would have been unknown before the reforms. "The government for its part has been more willing and receptive of the voices raised by industry," recalled K. V. Kamath, especially "if they come from iconic figures who have exhibited an ability to rise above their business interests and drive an agenda for reform on a larger canvas."

Indeed, public purpose had become a calling for private enterprise, in the words of ITC's Anand Nayak: "Indian enterprises realize their responsibility as economic organs of society, and many of them believe that in the ultimate analysis, they are accountable to society."

Nearly two decades after the 1991 reforms began dismantling the regulatory architecture, the most lasting impact may well be in business leadership itself, the daily behavior and enduring mind-sets of those who presided over the nation's largest enterprises. For many of them, the calling became collective, not just corporate.

We had an opportunity to witness the change firsthand when three of the authors joined a meeting in 2006 with a dozen chief executives of major Indian firms who had been invited to advise Wharton about the content of its executive-education programs in India. Their commentary spontaneously turned to what business leaders needed to do to rebuild the country—not just their own companies—for the coming generation. It seemed a sharp contrast to the focus on profit margins and shareholder returns that we had heard referenced so often in such meetings across many parts of the world.

Beyond the Four Purusharthas

Business leaders in India have, almost as a matter of tradition, been deeply involved in nation building. The original patriarch of the Birla Group, Ghanshyam Das Birla, was an avid supporter of India's freedom struggle prior to independence from British rule in 1947. Mahatma Gandhi was a frequent houseguest of Birla; Birla advised Gandhi on economic policies; and the Congress Party, which inherited the mantle of running independent India, received financial support from the Birla Group. Perhaps this was no more than an illustration of the Hindu view of life, with its emphasis on pursuing the four *purusharthas*, or four desirable aims of human life: *dharma, artha, kama,* and *moksha,* the goals, respectively, of righteousness, wealth, desire, and, finally, salvation or liberation.

But the service calling was not confined to Hindu business leaders either. The Tata Group was founded by Jamsetji Tata, a Parsi, whose Zoroastrian ancestors had fled persecution centuries earlier in what is current-day Iran, eventually finding refuge and thriving in India. He is often regarded as the father of modern Indian industry, among the first in the nineteenth century to bring the industrial revolution to India. A set of charitable trusts—the oldest dating to 1892—now owns two-thirds of Tata Sons, the holding company of the Tata Group, and income from the trusts is regularly plowed back into Indian society. Jamsetji Tata's pledge of half his wealth—£200,000—in 1898 led to the creation of the Indian Institute of Science in Bangalore, predating Andrew Carnegie's endowment of $1 million to establish what is now Carnegie Mellon University. Tata Group philanthropy would later help create a range of other leading institutions, including the Tata Memorial Center, Tata Institute of Fundamental Research, Tata Institute of Social Sciences, the recent JRD Tata Ecotechnology Center, and the upcoming Tata Medical Center.

Social Performance, Not Financial Performance

The stress on public purpose, not just private gain, was evident as well in most of our interviews with the Indian business leaders. Over the course of a lengthy discussion with Reliance Industries' Mukesh Ambani, for instance, he rarely dwelled on increasing his firm's financial performance. Instead, he focused on what he saw as the pressing need for the Indian economy to create at least 10 million jobs annually to absorb the burgeoning number of young people entering the workforce—and the critical role that Reliance Industries must play in achieving the job growth. Similarly, in one of our interviews with K. V. Kamath, the bulk of his remarks were devoted to arguing for India's need to develop vocational skills for millions of young people that would make them more employable. Earnings per share and total shareholder return were most notable for their complete absence in the conversation.

Counterpoint

In the wake of the watershed reforms of 1991, Indian business became far more attractive to international owners and investors. Foreign institutional and direct investment grew rapidly, rising by a factor of almost 15 times from $4.9 billion in 1995–1996 to $63.7 billion in 2007–2008.[13] The value of Indian exports was up by a factor of 2.5 from 2004 to 2008. A host of surveys confirmed that India had become one of the most favored destinations for direct investment, behind China, but ahead of the United States. India's foreign exchange reserves rose from less than $1 billion at their bottom in 1991 to more than $300 billion at the peak in 2008. Most leading investment banks and private equity firms established a significant presence in India. The market capitalization of publicly traded Indian firms at one point exceeded the country's gross domestic product.[14]

Some areas of business particularly thrived under the new regime. Information technology and software services soared. The deregulation of the telecom industry and radical declines in the cost of voice and data services stimulated an explosive growth in wireless communication. Business process outsourcing and subsequently a host of other outsourcing arenas became signature areas of rapid growth. Manufacturing firms soared as well. Companies like Sundaram Fasteners and Bharat Forge emerged as top-notch players in automotive components and castings. Indian pharmaceuticals played an increasingly visible role in the discovery and manufacturing arenas. And Indian producers in time became international acquirers, able to compete with the best of enterprises operating well beyond the boundaries of India. Tata Steel purchased the Anglo-Dutch Corus in 2007 for $12 billion; aluminum producer Hindalco Industries bought the Canadian aluminum maker Novelis the same year for $6 billion.

In collaboration with Steven Spielberg's DreamWorks, Reliance Entertainment in 2008 invested $1.2 billion in a new U.S. film company; and Tata Motors acquired the marquee auto brands Jaguar and Land Rover from the American Ford Motor Company in 2008 for $2 billion.[15] The passage of time will reveal whether all of these moves were equally wise, and it may turn out that the acquiring firms in some cases paid too much for the assets. But that this happened was unprecedented.

Winners and Losers

All of this is part of the miracle of the Indian miracle, and central to the India Way. But change at this scale has losers as well as winners. For many Indian companies, the postreform experience proved wrenching. A number of firms that were well adapted to the relatively closed pre-1991 marketplace abruptly found a far more challenging competitive landscape, and many proved unable to master the new rules. A group of Indian firms known as the "Bombay Club" led an effort to roll back the reforms, though without much success. As noted earlier, fears abounded that powerful international firms would steamroll the local competition and capture the Indian market.

Even some of the most successful business players remained reluctant to boast about their and the nation's seeming triumphs. Despite their own company's growth, Indian fissures still ran deep, the infrastructure remained flawed, and poverty was pervasive. The Asian Development Bank's Rajat Nag cautioned against what he saw as "the emergence of the 'two faces' of India," the poor and the rich. Blackstone's Akhil Gupta warned against two of what he termed the nation's three faces: India's "glorious past"; its "decaying civilization due to its caste, corruption, and superstition"; and its "resurgent" present. Further reforms of the economy and still greater openness were critical, in Gupta's view, if the third, resurgent face was to dominate.

Infosys's Narayana Murthy concurred that still further reform was critical to sustaining both business growth and social prosperity.

That reform, he believed, should be extended to all social arenas, including education: "We have not liberalized our education sector even after almost twenty years of economic reforms," he warned. "I am afraid we will pay a huge price for this." The same could be said for the country's failure to bring sufficient efficiency, transparency, and accountability to public agencies; for the cities' failures to overcome urban squalor, congestion, and gridlock; and for the countryside's failure to mitigate its grinding poverty, adult illiteracy, and early mortality.

Yet another distinctive thread running through the business leaders' commentary—and still more evidence of the uniqueness of the India Way—was the manner in which they embraced India's enduring tribulations. Rather than just "externalities" whose cost must be factored into their business model, executives deemed countrywide problems part of their own obligation to address. Though much of India's business promise had been unlocked by the reforms of 1991, far more societal promise is yet to be realized. In the cautionary words of K. V. Kamath, "It cannot be denied that India, given the huge resources it has at its command—both natural and human—has been relatively slow in unlocking its own potential." That was not just a challenge for government, he said; business would have to do its share. Reducing "existing inequalities that continue to render a large number of our people powerless to improve their lives is something we have to focus on."

The Indian Ethic and the Spirit of Capitalism

Late on the afternoon of New Year's Day, 2000, as the shimmering sun sank into the Arabian Sea, one of the authors stood before the storied Somnath Temple in Veraval, Gujarat.[16] The history of the temple provoked the question of what might have been. In AD 1026, a Muslim invader from current-day Afghanistan, Mahmud of Ghazni, sacked the temple, carrying the plunder back home in long caravans. Over the next seven centuries, the local populace would rebuild the temple again and again in the wake of its repeated destruction by invader after invader.

For nearly a millennium, the Indian subcontinent experienced repeated conquest, political subjugation, and economic exploitation, culminating in the rule of the East India Company and the British Crown from about the mid-nineteenth century through 1947. Brief periods of cultural flowering and political openness, such as the reign from 1556 to 1605 by the Mughal Emperor of India, Akbar the Great, had occasioned only temporary relief. Even the removal of the British Raj hadn't removed the onerous conditions under which Indian business had so long operated.

Standing there in front of the temple, one wondered how much stronger a platform Indian companies might have enjoyed over the past two decades if they had been as free to prosper before the 1991 reforms as afterward. European and American enterprise had already enjoyed more than two centuries of political sovereignty and business independence. The India Way had been building over millennia, but the unshackling of Indian enterprise and the following success was still barely in its teens. Yet in less than two decades, Indian companies had managed not only to overcome a thousand years of dependence; they had caught up with some of their better-known Western competitors in some industries.

Newfound Confidence

The confidence with which the country's business leaders have now set sail has been all the more reinforced by events that symbolize similar success in other realms—in achieving what had not been done before and achieving it by global, not just domestic standards. Indian grand master Viswanathan Anand defeated Russia's Vladimir Kramnik in 2007 to become World Chess Champion, and then successfully defended his world title again in 2008. Late the same year, India successfully inserted a spacecraft—Chandrayaan-1—into lunar orbit and then landed a probe on the moon's south pole, doing so at a fraction of the cost of comparable Western missions, and making India only the fourth country to place its flag on the moon. Even Hollywood had capitulated to the juggernaut from the subcontinent, awarding the 2008 Oscar for Best Picture to an Indian film, even if it was directed by an Englishman, which straddled the nation's many divisions: *Slumdog Millionaire*.

Virtually all the Indian business leaders we interviewed conveyed a sense of newfound confidence in both private enterprise and national purpose. "Several bureaucratic myths have been shattered" by the postreform India Way, said Narayana Murthy, including the folklore "that policies that worked in small quasi-democratic nations will not work in India; that removing restrictions on foreign exchange will drain away the entire foreign exchange reserves; that the Indian businessmen are crooks and any freedom given to them will be misused; that any reduction of tax rates will not result in enhanced tax collection; and that [multinational corporations] will not work for the betterment of the country."

With those myths relegated to the past, business leaders could now play a prominent role in social growth to parallel and build on their proven role in economic growth. Bharti Airtel's Manoj Kohli offered a vision shared by many: "My view is simple. Look at the way we made the Indian telecom sector a shining example of India's success story. Likewise, we need to identify other key sectors, such as power, roads, manufacturing, agriculture, health, and education, and work with similar passion and energy to turn them around. Let no house or factory be without power; let no village be without roads; let our manufacturing prowess match China; let another green revolution take off; let there be schools and colleges in every corner of the country and basic health facilities in each village. This is my dream for the India of the future."

While the turning-point events of 1991 and beyond established a new commercial stage, Indian company leaders of necessity had to write their own performance scripts. Educated abroad and steeped in business best sellers, many were well familiar with the tenets of

Western management, but as they confronted the challenges of running enterprises in their own market—newly competitive, highly turbulent—they found themselves devising the India Way, not by drafting a manual from a set of preexisting precepts but rather through inventing pragmatic solutions to tangible problems and learning as they went.

As we reported in the first chapter, four defining qualities emerged as the Indian executives have built their way: broad mission and purpose, improvisation and adaptability, creative value propositions, and holistic engagement with employees. We see the logic of these features play out repeatedly in five areas that characterize how companies operate: *people management*, *executive leadership*, *competitive strategy*, *company governance*, and *social responsibility*.

We begin with a focus in the next chapter on the first, people management. Indian business leaders give great emphasis to a broad-spectrum engagement with their employees, seeing them as assets to be developed, not costs to be cut. We then turn in the following chapter to the second area, executive leadership, where improvisation and adaptability prove particularly important.

With the workforce and the top team in place, trained, and engaged, the Indian executives also focused on building the capabilities required for leading large-scale enterprise. In chapter 5, we focus on the third area, competitive strategy, and look in particular at how India's business leaders have combined organizational architecture, company culture, and innovative approaches to markets and customers into creative value propositions.

While the governing board has traditionally served a largely monitoring function in Western enterprise, we find that directors play a broader role among many of the Indian firms, and leaders of those firms in turn play a broader role in Indian society. The fourth and fifth areas—company governance and social responsibility— are the central concerns of our final two chapters, and there we see full expression of the India Way's broad mission and purpose.

We believe it is worth looking in some depth at each of these five areas—people management, executive leadership, competitive strategy, company governance, and social responsibility—both to see how the India Way plays out on its own ground and to judge what aspects of it might be usefully employed in other venues. Our research and our extensive interviewing have convinced us that the West has much to learn from modern Indian business practices. We hope *The India Way* will open eyes the world around.

Managing People

Holistic Engagement of Employees

NONE OF THE INDIAN BUSINESS leaders we interviewed claimed that their company succeeded based on his or her own cleverness or even on the efforts of a top team. Almost without exception, Indian business leaders—and the industry analysts and business journalists who follow their companies—described the source of comparative advantage as coming from deep inside the company, from new and better ideas, superior execution, and the process of *jugaad* that gets things done. And these outcomes, in turn, were traced to the positive attitudes and behaviors of employees. The obvious conclusion: the source of the distinctiveness of the India Way and the ability to focus the business on solving hard problems rests heavily on the management of people, on the holistic engagement with employees.

Motivated and committed employees hammer away at problems and persist until they find creative solutions and workarounds that solve tough problems. That seems straightforward. But what makes them want to do that? As noted in chapter 1, having a sense of mission and social goal for the organization helps employees see a purpose in their work that goes beyond their immediate self-interest, beyond the achievements of the firm and its owners. Typically, that sense of mission extends to helping India and its citizens. The Indian firms included in our research motivated employees at least in part by connecting their work to these broader social goals—improving phone service for rural customers, expanding access to health care by lowering its cost, enhancing the competitiveness of the overall Indian economy. This sense of mission tapped into what organizational psychologists call *task significance*, seeing the link between the sometimes small tasks they perform and the bigger goal. President Lyndon Johnson loved to tell the story about asking a truck driver working at NASA in the 1960s what his job was. The driver's response: "I'm helping to put a man on the moon." *That's* task significance.

Beyond the sense of mission lies the management of employees. Indian companies, we found, built employee commitment by creating a sense of reciprocity with the workforce, looking after their interests and those of their families, and implicitly asking employees to look after the firm's interests in return. To translate commitment into action, the business leaders went to extraordinary lengths to empower employees in a way that often conflicted with historical norms, giving them the freedom to plunge into problems that they encounter and create their own solutions. Then they devoted a great deal of executive attention and resources to the practices that support this approach, such as finding the right people to hire, developing them internally, and improving morale. Business leaders directed their attention to building organizational culture, which shows employees how to perform, and to demonstrating the connection between employee competencies and business strategies.

This is the inside picture of the India Way. In addition to instilling a sense of mission, management practices help produce the engagement and motivation that allows the organizations to be persistent and innovative. While the companies we studied all focused intensely on hiring, they did not try to compete simply by winning a "war for talent" by hiring "stars" from the labor market. Instead, they leveraged existing human resources through extensive investments in the competencies of employees and in developing them for careers inside the firm.

It would be a mistake to assume that these Indian companies have relied solely on "soft" practices like culture and commitment. Our research revealed that they are sophisticated about other human resource practices as well. Extensive diversity programs, for example, were common as a means to reach a broader labor market. We also found more sophisticated systems of workforce planning and of performance management than are common in the United States. We can see these differences in part with comparative data and by comparing similar companies in the two countries. Where American companies focused their human resource attention more on cost reduction, Indian companies saw their employees more as capital investments that should be supported and managed.

Engaging Employees at HCL

To see the connection between how employees are managed and how Indian companies compete, consider the case of IT services giant HCL Technologies. With fifty-five thousand employees spread across eighteen nations and a broad array of international clients including Boeing, Cisco, and Merck, HCL nurtures its basic DNA by tying long-term business approaches to principles for managing employees. HCL was founded as a computer hardware company in a garage in 1976 and flourished in the early 1990s when the Indian government was still restricting access of multinational competitors to the domestic hardware market. Thus protected, HCL was among the early leaders in Indian IT, offering the highest salaries to attract the best talent. Whether the company would have been able to compete with multinationals, however, was not yet obvious.

Vineet Nayar, a young HCL engineer, was thinking about leaving for a more entrepreneurial environment when he was offered the chance to be an "intrapreneur" in the information networks area. The Comnet subsidiary that he helped create soon became the tail that wagged the dog as HCL moved from the hardware business to software. The division's distinctive approach to its market, its business strategy, was to empower each individual employee to meet customer needs. To achieve that, Comnet combined an entrepreneurial business environment with extensive investments in employee development and training. Without really knowing it at the time, Nayar was incubating the personnel strategy he would later apply to the entire company.

Employee First, Customer Second

Nayar became CEO of the overall HCL company in 2005 and confronted a market that had become global just seven years earlier, when the government lifted its protections for Indian hardware companies. The growing end of the IT industry was clearly in IT services and software-driven solutions, not hardware. The biggest players in the international marketplace were competing based on scale, using classic "scientific management" and engineering approaches where the same employees delivered the same solutions and where projects were broken down so that cheaper, lower-skilled employees could do the easy parts in order to drive down costs. HCL decided to go a different route. The company opted to move away from the low-cost, high-volume business and instead ascend the value chain by getting closer to existing customers and better meeting their unique needs, another example of the innovativeness and adaptability that are part and parcel of the India Way approach to business strategy.

Nayar began by pulling together groups of younger employees to work on a theme that would reenergize the company and signal both a new way of operating in the product market and a new way of managing internally. The motto they created for their mission—"Employee First, Customer Second"—was meant to shock people and get their attention, but it also reflected the basic alignment between employee management and business strategy that we see across Indian companies. The idea was to give the employees whatever they needed, including autonomy, so that they could meet the unique needs of customers in the field (see "Employee First at HCL").

An Inverted Pyramid

The corporate pyramid, broad at the base and slender at the summit, with decision-making authority concentrated at the top, has long been the very definition of company organization. Virtually all organizational charts place a CEO box at the top, with ever-widening layers arrayed below. A select few reach the highest offices, and their job is to hold the lower levels accountable for results. But HCL Technologies, metaphorically speaking, sought to invert that pyramid by making, as Vineet Nayar told us, "our managers accountable to our employees."

One tactic was to encourage employees to submit electronic "tickets" on what needed to be changed or fixed, even the very personal, which ranged from "I have a problem with my bonus" to "My boss sucks." Employees posted comments and questions on a "U and I" Web page, with Nayar himself publicly answering some fifty questions a month. An even more unusual tactic was to require 360-degree feedback on the fifteen hundred most senior company managers worldwide, including the chief executive himself. Employees had the option of evaluating not just their boss but also their boss's boss and three other managers. And the 360-degree feedback, including the CEO's, was posted on an intranet Web site within several weeks—for all employees to see, all of it, the good and the bad. Nayar led the way, and soon all the executives posted their own 360-degree feedback assessments by others online as well. As he told us, "Our competitive differentiation should be the fact that we are more transparent than anybody else in our industry, and therefore the customer likes us because of transparency, employees like us

Employee First at HCL

Vineet Nayar, HCL's CEO, told us that "people are a very important component of an Indian CEO strategy," which is
based on "people development and long-term engagement
of people." He outlined an approach at the company where
serving the customer starts by taking care of the employees
who service those customers. Here's what the company says
about this approach:

> Employee First: The service industry, from fast food to
> business consulting, has long lived by the mantra that
> serving the customer is the only thing that matters. As
> a result, customer need is placed above all others—often
> at the sacrifice of employees, managers and administra-
> tors. HCL Technologies, one of India's fastest growing
> IT services companies, has embraced a new strategy—
> Employee First—that places the needs of employees before
> the needs of customers. This seemingly counterintuitive
> strategy has provoked a sea-change at the company and,
> believe it or not, greater customer loyalty, better engage-
> ments, and higher revenues.

because there are no hidden secrets. So we built transparency." The
idea of performance improvement became more broadly acceptable,
and the heightened personal transparency at the top served to reduce the sense of vertical separation.

The main point, Nayar said, is "if you are willing to be accountable
to your employees, then the way the employee behaves with the customer is with a high degree of ownership." At HCL, Nayar contended,
"command and control" is giving way to "collaborative management."
To that end, he has pushed for ever "smaller units of decision makers

Given the pace of industry growth and its dependency on headcount, attracting, retaining, and motivating talent is the top challenge for the industry. The traditional approach viewed employees as commodities and placed emphasis on deploying entry-level talent and a factory-like approach for project execution. There were no unique engagement strategies centered on the employee . . .

To make the Employee First concept work, HCL launched a variety of internal initiatives designed to both give employees more personal responsibility for the company's service offerings and a voice with upper management. HCL's enlightened approach to employee development focuses on giving people whatever they need to succeed: be it a virtual assistant or talent transformation sabbaticals, expert guidance or fast track growth, inner peace or democratic empowerment. At HCL, what we have is Five Fold Path to Individual Enlightenment. This ensures they are given Support, Knowledge, Recognition, Empowerment, and Transformation.[a]

a. The fivefold path to enlightenment references the eleventh-century mystic Gampopa, who organized Buddhist thoughts into the Mahamudra teaching; HCL Technology Web site, http://www.hcltech.com/employee-first.

for faster speed and higher accuracy in decisions" to provide HCL's customers with more timely and customized service.

Vineet Nayar had worked his way to the top of HCL Technologies after twenty-one years, and after his one-year anniversary as company president, he wrote all employees, "I am here as long as I have your support and confidence."[1] As much as half of his time has been spent in town hall meetings with all the company's employees, communicating this vision for the company and managing the corporate culture. He made it a personal goal to shake the hand of every employee every year, and when asked what he would like to be his greatest legacy to the company in five years, Nayar responded without missing a beat: "They would say that I have destroyed the office of the CEO." Pressed to explain, he said he sought so much "transparency" and "empowerment" in the company that "decisions would be made at the points where the decisions should be made"—that is, where the company meets the client. Ideally, the "organization would be inverted, where the top is accountable to the bottom, and therefore the CEO's office will become irrelevant." His public blogs on the company Web site included a posting in 2008 entitled "Destroying the office of the CEO."[2]

As HCL's chief executive, Nayar warned, "Don't believe that you are God's gift to mankind. I do believe that the rest of [our] people are smarter and greater [and] better than you. So as long as you go to sleep assuming that you have 48,000 smart people, you will sleep well. The day you start believing that you are the smartest, I think you will get it wrong." In 2006, *Fortune* magazine dubbed the executive team at HCL Technologies the "world's most modern management."

Trust Pay

One of the most interesting and perhaps controversial aspects of HCL's people management practices was to move away from the traditional practice in IT companies of having 30 percent of an employee's pay at risk, based on the achievement of "stretch goals" for individuals or their groups. In practice, these stretch goals are rarely achieved, at least completely, which means that the employees end up earning less than their full salary. HCL referred to its new arrangement as *trust pay*, which reinforced the idea of reciprocity: we'll pay you the full salary, and we expect you to do your utmost at all times to meet your goals. To help model this new approach, HCL created an elite Multi-Service Delivery Unit, a separate organization to tackle the most important client assignments. Competition for election into this unit was intense and involved assessments based on personality as well as business and technical capability.[3]

Human Resource Priorities

HCL focused so much attention on managing employees because its business strategy centered on their behavior. That might seem axiomatic for most companies—Indian and American—but our survey of top human resource executives found that Indian firms were far more likely than their American counterparts to closely intertwine HR management and business strategy. Indeed, as shown in figure 3-1, on every one of the twelve dimensions of engagement in organizational strategy, Indian company HR roles outstripped U.S. company ones, in the majority of cases substantially so.

Sixty-eight percent of the Indian human resource executives reported that they were closely involved in creating strategy with the other top leaders in their companies versus 44 percent in U.S. companies. In terms of implementing strategies, virtually all Indian HR heads—87 percent—said that they worked closely with the top management team, as compared with 56 percent in the United States. Particularly striking was the relatively large percentage of those in the United States who reported that they were not at all involved in these decisions, ranging from 6 to 30 percent on the twelve practices, compared with 0 to 10 percent among the Indian companies.

The Indian business executives were overwhelmingly of the view that competitiveness derived from people, not just for their own businesses but for India as a whole. As Mukesh Ambani of Reliance Industries observed, "The strength of India is really in the depth of talent that we have." Anand Mahindra of Mahindra & Mahindra noted, "It's not the lowest cost per unit of output or service that India is known for. It should be known for the lowest cost per unit of innovation because it is people plus our ability to innovate that is India's strength, and I would want our companies and our businesses to embody that." And as S. Ramadorai of Tata Consultancy Services concluded about his company's success, "It's all human capital at the end of the day."

FIGURE 3-1

Extent of human resource's involvement in the organization

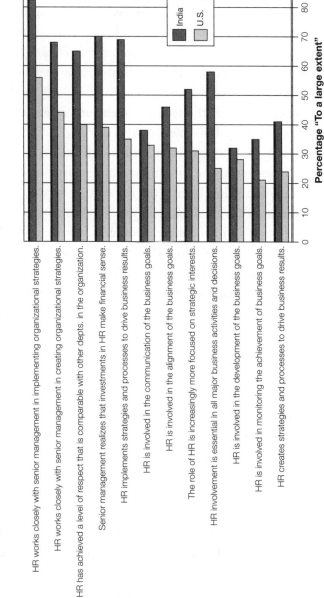

Sources: Survey of Indian companies, and Society for Human Resource Management, *Strategic HR Management Survey Report* (McLean, VA: Society for Human Resource Management, 2006).

This view extended to the leaders of all the companies. When we asked the Indian business leaders the details about their priorities for human resources in their companies, the results were consistent with an employee-centric view. Our question was open ended—executives could say anything they wanted—yet with remarkable consistency, the responses centered around four themes:

- Managing and developing talent

- Shaping employee attitudes

- Managing organizational culture

- Internationalization

Far and away the overwhelming majority of responses fell into the first of those categories: managing and developing talent. The single most commonly used phrase in this context was "employee retention," followed by "recruiting" and "developing talent" internally, the core issues in talent management. Indian business leaders by and large saw no trade-off between recruiting and development, and they expected their firms to pay attention to both.

The second most common response reflected the concern with employee attitudes. The company executives wanted their human resource functions to manage employee engagement, one of the key pillars on which the India Way operates. Managing organizational culture, a third priority, might seem at odds with the high priority executives set for themselves on shaping culture, but the clear conclusion is that they are not delegating the task to the human resource function. They embrace culture management as *their* priority, to be supported by human resources.

Compared with the United States, the most interesting finding in this area was what the business executives did not say. Among American firms, the human resource function has been continuously pressed to lower costs, to find savings in all areas of operations through outsourcing, squeezing health care savings, and the like. Indian company leaders never mentioned cost reduction as a priority for human resources. A cynic might argue that labor costs were already lower for Indian companies than for their competitors, but the costs were rising far faster in India than elsewhere, and these firms were increasingly competing with each other. Another possible explanation might be that Indian firms do not have the cost-cutting outsourcing possibilities that existed in the United States—a long-time preoccupation for American human resource executives. But that proved not to be true, either. As we see in figure 3-2, Indian companies actually outsourced the human resource operations on a par with those in the United States. When it came to recruiting, payroll, pension and retirement, and health and welfare benefits, more than a third of the companies in both countries outsourced their operations.

FIGURE 3-2

Company outsourcing of employment function

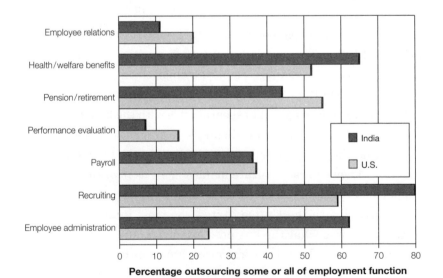

Percentage outsourcing some or all of employment function

Sources: Survey of Indian companies, and Society for Human Resource Management, *HR Outsourcing Survey Report* (McLean, VA: Society for Human Resource Management, 2004).

Another explanation for the Indian CEOs' lack of focus on employment costs might be that there was something like a natural evolution of practices with respect to managing people: as employers get
more sophisticated and advanced, perhaps they become better able to
measure outcomes so that they can focus on "hard" outcomes like
costs. The well-known phenomenon that "what gets measured gets
managed" is certainly true. Without the ability to measure factors
like costs, it is difficult to manage them. But what gets measured also
reflects the priorities of the organization: virtually anything can be
measured if one is willing to put the effort into it.

To get at this issue, we asked Indian companies about the metrics
they used to assess the performance of employees and aspects of
human resources. In the United States, metrics are often seen as a
measure of the sophistication of an HR function. The results in
figure 3-3 suggest that the Indian firms were more likely to measure

FIGURE 3-3

Company use of human resource metrics

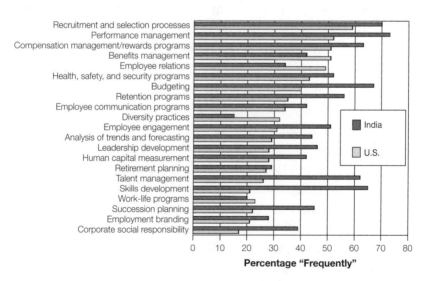

Percentage "Frequently"

Sources: Survey of Indian companies, and Society for Human Resource Management, *Strategic HR
Management Survey Report* (McLean, VA: Society for Human Resource Management, 2006).

and track human resource outcomes than were U.S. firms, suggesting that, in fact, HR functions in India were often more sophisticated than those in the United States and more able to focus attention on cost reduction. They just chose not to.

What gets measured also tells us a great deal about the priorities within companies. In this case, the differences in metrics used in the Indian and the American companies reflected the much greater interest and efforts that Indian companies placed on developing talent. With respect to simply getting and keeping the best employees, Indian companies were much more likely to track human resource performance. Regarding the recruitment and selection of employees, 70 percent of the Indian companies confirmed that they measure their performance, compared with 59 percent in the United States; regarding retention, 56 percent did so among Indian firms, but just 35 percent among the American firms.

But the biggest differences had to do with internal development: 62 percent of the Indian firms frequently tracked progress in overall talent management, compared with only 26 percent in the United States; 65 percent frequently measured the development of skills of employees versus only 21 percent in the United States; 45 percent frequently tracked the ability to promote from within through succession versus 21 percent in the United States; and 46 percent frequently used metrics to assess the development of leaders versus 28 percent in the United States. By these measures, American companies were simply less interested in employee issues altogether than their Indian counterparts—and especially less interested in developing their own talent. This reflected a much greater "hire and fire" strategy in the United States, a more arm's-length overall approach to the management of people.

Indian CEOs were not insensitive to labor cost issues, but they did not see their immediate or even long-term competitiveness as being based on labor costs. Instead, they viewed competitiveness and firm goals as moving up the value chain and doing so based on innovation and superior execution. Those outcomes were closely tied to superior talent, motivated employees, and organizational cultures that encouraged individuals to act in the interests of the company. (For a successful example of India Way human resource priorities put into practice, see "Putting People First Makes the Best Restaurant in Asia.")

A different measure of the priorities held by India Way companies comes from what they tell shareholders and the broader community about their operations. One interesting study of the annual reports in the Indian information technology industry found that the most common mention of any human resource issue—so common, in fact, that it happened on average more than once in each report—was to thank employees for their contributions. The second most common HR mention was to highlight individual employees, typically for their special contributions or sometimes for their life experiences. That was followed in frequency by mentions of employee capabilities and efforts to train and develop employees. And the fourth most common mention was to discuss contributions employees were making to the broader community, outside of their work tasks.

Equally interesting is what was not presented. Despite the fact that labor accounts for far and away the biggest component of operating expenses, human resource costs were never mentioned in these reports.[4] By contrast, the annual reports of the leading U.S. information technology companies contained nary a mention of the employees.[5]

Building Employee Capabilities

We know that India Way companies pay more attention to employee management than their U.S. counterparts, and we also know that their leaders focus on a very different set of priorities for their employees. The people management approach in these Indian companies—holistic engagement with employees and capability building, one of the four primary features defining the India Way— boils down to three distinct sets of practices. The first has to do with investments in the employees, both for current jobs and for

Putting People First Makes the Best Restaurant in Asia

Bukhara is routinely voted as the best restaurant in India, the best Indian restaurant in the world, and one of the top fifty restaurants of any cuisine in the world. And there are a lot of restaurants in that competition. Vladimir Putin is said to have wanted to eat here three times a day when he was in Delhi, and Bill Clinton, another big fan, got to make bread in the restaurant's tandoor oven and now even has a dish named after him.

The restaurant did not get its top rating because of fancy decor. The style might be described as rustic: log benches and rough wooden tables. Diners eat with their hands—no silverware. Long bibs protect the clothes of messy eaters. Bukhara takes no reservations, and crowds regularly queue up in the lounge, waiting to get in.

Nor has this restaurant achieved its distinction through innovation, offering the latest new ideas in dishes. The menu has not changed in thirty-seven years. There are many different kinds of Indian cuisines, some with sophisticated sauces, for example, that represent complex blends of unique spices. That is not Bukhara, either. It offers a decidedly simple and straightforward cuisine from the northern frontier that features mainly meats and breads, few sauces and fewer vegetables. The dishes would not surprise anyone familiar with Indian food: shrimp, chicken, and lamb marinated in yogurt and spices and cooked in a hot tandoor oven.

Where Bukhara excels is with execution. Even though the dishes it turns out are similar to what one could get elsewhere, Bukhara's are just better. Some part of this is through choosing the very best ingredients. But most of it comes from the skill of the cooks. The head chefs at Bukhara have been with the restaurant for more than twenty-five years. The kitchen is organized around an apprenticeship model where beginning employees slowly learn the craft associated with Bukhara's menu and then spend a lifetime working in the restaurant. How much could there be to learning how to prepare this straightforward menu? The answer, apparently, is a lot, because the dishes are unmatched by the competition anywhere.

The kitchen has another interesting management practice. In most restaurants, staff members cook their own meals, often grabbing them whenever they can between shifts. At Bukhara, the head chefs are the ones who do the cooking for the rest of the staff, as clear an example of acting as a guide for your employees—or "servant leadership"—as you'll ever find.

The restaurant staff works ultimately for the giant ITC corporation, but the company is smart enough to do what is necessary in terms of salaries and practices to keep the kitchen together and avoid imposing corporatewide policies that would not fit the unique context of this restaurant. There are no commissions or bonus payments for the staff for being the best restaurant in India. Instead, pride in a job well done is the key.

Anil Sharma, vice president for human resources for the ITC hotel and hospitality company, says that the company is not worried about competitors trying to copy Bukhara, despite the simplicity of its concept. Even if one of the head chefs left to start up another restaurant, taking all that knowledge with him, the system and practices in the kitchen that support the execution of the dishes would not be there, and the competitor would not be as good.

What's the lesson here? The entire business strategy of the top Indian restaurant in the world rests on the ability to perfect and then execute what is otherwise a very simple and straightforward product, something that would appear to be extremely easy to copy. And the ability to perfect and execute, in turn, is based on human resource practices that create the kind of stability and morale in the workplace that makes it possible to learn best practices, standardize them, and then pass them along.

internal promotions. The second, as we saw in the HCL case, centers on empowering employees, giving them the authority and autonomy to make decisions and solve problems on their own. And the third, where the business leaders are most personally involved, is to create and manage a culture that pushes employees to act in the interests of the organization.

Investments in Employees Begin with Recruiting

Consistent with the India Way's heavy emphasis on developing talent and making investments in employees, the firms we studied spent a great deal of time and energy making sure that they start out with the right kind of talent. Candidates who lacked the ability to make use of the training and education programs would be a poor fit. But equally important, candidates who did not have the character to respond to broader missions and who would not respond to empowerment were considered bad matches.

Because of its spectacular growth, Infosys was one of the first of the important Indian companies to take on the challenge of recruitment and selection in a sophisticated and rigorous way. Infosys expected to hire almost 10 percent of all the incoming IT recruits in India, so it had the scale to do things right. Somnath Baishya, head of entry-level hiring for Infosys, described the company's goal: "Recruit the best talent and create a professionally competent, socially conscious, happy, and prosperous team."[6] Like ICICI, Infosys early on established close ties with the schools where it wanted to recruit. When it found deficits in the quality of the recruits, it worked with the schools to improve their programs. Through Campus Connect—a program Infosys runs with three hundred engineering schools across the country—faculty members trained in part by Infosys helped teach a curriculum created by Infosys and supported by courseware the company had placed online.

The recruiting goal at Infosys was not only to find the best talent but to build the "HR" brand of the company, to create the sense that Infosys was the most desirable place to work in India. To do that, the company also targeted the parents and family of potential applicants, marketing the company and the job to them on the theory that close relatives shape the views of potential applicants in important ways. The goal was to get parents to want their kids to work at Infosys.

Looking (and Training) Outside the Box

What did the company look for? Beyond the technical skills of specific engineering recruits, Infosys valued general academic ability—what we might think of as measured by IQ. This was what it tested applicants on, not subject matter knowledge. Because the company hired only 1 percent of applicants, it needed a very large pool of quality applicants. So it began recruiting in fields beyond IT to find better problem-solving skills from a deeper pool of talent. Its Project Genesis reached out to students in smaller towns that had less access to the best education services, to offer career guidance for jobs in the IT industry as well as training to help them get there. In 2007, Infosys drew 1.3 million applications for employment.

The selection process did not stop with hiring. Once hired, new recruits moved to the largest corporate training facility in the world, just short of 300 acres outside of Mysore. The facility could handle six thousand trainees at a time, with plans to quintuple in size. The training center was designed to feel like a college campus; and indeed, when we visited, we were struck by how much the training-session rooms resembled typical college classrooms, a similarity that makes the transition from college to the company as smooth as possible. The fourteen-week training regimen included regular "exams" and assessments that the new hires must pass to continue in the program. Candidates hired from outside India received even longer training, six months, to help them adapt to the Indian and Infosys cultures. Company managers were assessed based on the percentage of new hires in their group who achieved an A grade on these tests, the number who achieved various competency certifications, and the percentage of outside or lateral hires who were rated as "good" in their first review. More senior managers were assessed based on the job satisfaction of their employees and the percentage of leadership positions that had an identified internal successor. Holding supervisors similarly responsible for the achievements of their subordinates was quite common in the United States before the mid-1980s but is now extremely rare.[7]

Working at Infosys is no picnic, however, as it also demands performance. The company maintains a forced ranking system where the appraisals are scored not only on employees' task-based performance but also on the extent to which they are keeping their own skills current. The India Way companies as a group take performance management seriously, but perhaps because of greater investments in employees or a more family-oriented culture, they also seem much more focused on improving future performance as opposed to accounting for past outcomes. Consider this description of the performance assessment and review process at the India-based global pharmaceutical manufacturer Dr. Reddy's Laboratories: "We believe a great supervisor is actually an excellent coach, not just a boss. Our performance management process, 'PerfECT', gets our managers to do just that—COACH. It is all about inspiring breakthrough thinking. It is about challenging your limits. It is about an empowering environment to get you to be at your best—ALWAYS."[8] India Way companies were also more engaged in improving and updating their performance management systems, with 81 percent reporting that they had revised their performance management and performance review programs this past year; 58 percent of U.S. companies reported a similar effort.

Hiring and Training at Yes Bank

Hiring talent is clearly a critical component of the India Way, but it is not a substitute for nurturing and developing the talent already in-house. Consider the example of Yes Bank, where employees are also considered key to the business strategy. Incorporated in 2003, Yes Bank grew at a remarkable 150 percent per year through 2007.

Not only was the bank ranked number one in India in growth; it also led in efficiency and safety of deposits.

The company's operating principles are another textbook example of "strategic" human resources. Yes Bank's competitive advantage as a late entrant into a crowded marketplace was a distinctive, high-quality customer experience. Because frontline employees deliver that experience, the bank worked hard to shape their attitudes and behaviors—*shape* them but not *automate* them. The problems customers bring to the branches of the bank are so unique that "scripting" all the appropriate responses is simply not practical. It is equally impossible for anyone but professional actors to project an engaging and friendly persona if they do not feel it, or for the management to stand over the employees and ensure that they act the right way.

All that is largely obvious, but how do you get the employees to create that right customer experience? Doing so at Yes Bank began with getting the right employees, and that started by creating a unique *employee value proposition*—a set of practices, programs, and organizational culture that attracts the right kind of employees with the right attributes. As a start-up, Yes Bank had no choice but to hire from the outside. It attracted the best and the brightest banking stars by paying top dollar and then by offering far more opportunity and responsibility than one could get at a bigger, more established bank.

Yes Bank kept an intense focus on recruiting, partnering with the best professionals in the field to find experienced hires and spot potential stars among the graduates of the leading schools. Part of the goal was also to hire for the kind of workplace diversity that mirrors the broader society and the bank's customer base, not just on ethnicity and region but on gender and age as well.

Yes Bank also built strong relations with a select group of universities to help spot the best students and begin growing talent from within. It engaged students in internships, which led to full-time jobs, before the candidates even got to the job market. Then it offered extensive training and development programs, including job

rotation to build cross-functional skills. By themselves, these investments are not unusual, but programs of internal development are
very atypical among companies that rely so heavily on outside hiring.[9] The success of Yes Bank offers compelling evidence that you
can do both.

Training and Development Follows

Once they get the right candidates, Indian companies pour on
the training. One study of practices in India found that the IT industry provided new hires with more than sixty days of formal
training—about twelve weeks. Some companies did even more:
Tata Consultancy Services, for example, had a seven-month training program for science graduates who were being converted into
business consultant roles, and everyone in the company got fourteen days of formal training each year. MindTree Consulting, another IT company, extended its orientation period for new hires to
eight weeks, combining classroom training, mentoring, and peer-
based learning communities. Even relatively low-skill industries
like business process outsourcing and call centers provided something like thirty days of training, and retail companies required
about twenty days. Systematic data on training among U.S. companies is hard to come by, but the available statistics suggested that 23
percent of new hires received no training of any kind from their
employer in the first two years of employment, while the average
amount of training received for those with two years or less of
tenure was just thirteen hours within a six-month period.[10]

Satyam is now embroiled in financial malfeasance, but the story of
how it went from nothing to a giant business based on the skills of its
employees is instructive. Now-disgraced founder and chairman of
Satyam B. Ramalinga Raju told us how: "In the past fifteen years, we
have seen enormous change take place [in outsourcing], and we have
had to reinvent ourselves half a dozen times. Customers are no longer
satisfied with the services they can access from the global systems integrators. This means adopting business models that are conducive

to distributing leadership and empowering the people who are inter-facing with the stakeholders." To that end, the company embarked on extensive programs to develop the skills of its employees with a model it called *full lifecycle leadership*, enabling employees to solve customer problems on the ground.[11] Satyam received the American Society for Training & Development's 2007 award for the best com-pany at training developing talent based on this model.

After the Second World War, U.S. companies also had pioneered extensive training programs. Back then, American companies could be confident that they would harvest most of the skills they devel-oped: the job market was tight, so companies had to train to get what they needed. But turnover was kept relatively low through union-based seniority systems and other practices. Indian compa-nies today have much the same motivation—a shortage of specific skills for a rapidly changing world—but they cannot be nearly as certain they will benefit from the specific talent they develop: esti-mates put employee turnover in the Indian corporate sector at close to 30 percent. While American employers today face far more mod-est turnover rates, they have largely abandoned investments of all kinds in employees, especially managerial development, for fear that such investments will simply be lost if employees leave. The fact that Indian companies have opted for the longer-term strategy of investing in employees despite the high turnover rates says a great deal about the commitment to employees in the India Way (see "Pantaloon Versus Wal-Mart" for one example).

Developing Leaders and Building Capabilities

Training is designed to help employees perform better in their current job. Development is the far more risky process of helping prepare candidates for new and more challenging duties, particu-larly management and executive roles. The Indian business leaders we talked with were interested to a person in developing their em-ployees into executives and potential leaders for the firm. Indeed, all the companies examined in this study had extensive programs

Pantaloon Versus Wal-Mart

Comparing India's biggest and fastest-growing retailer, Pantaloon Retail (India) Ltd., and Wal-Mart, the largest retailer in the United States and, indeed, the world, provides a useful window into the different choices that businesses make about training employees and how those choices affect business strategy. New recruits at Pantaloon for frontline jobs received six weeks of training, including five and one-half days in residence at a company training center followed by five weeks of on-the-job training directed by local store managers. As Kishore Biyani, Pantaloon's chief executive, told us, "We run a program in the organization which everyone has to go through, called 'design management,' which basically trains people to use both sides of the brain," both "the visual and esthetic side and the logical rational." After that, store staff received a week of new training each year.[a] Training is one way the company develops a shopping experience more suited to customers.

Wal-Mart's store employees had an orientation program; and cashier positions, the most challenging of frontline jobs, had eight days of training. Other employees received substantially less. Training thereafter was rare, typically limited to dealing with new technology or initiatives when they are introduced. Little surprise, then, that Wal-Mart competes based on cost, in part through the use of technology but also by keeping labor costs as low as possible, while Pantaloon competes at least in part on customer service.

a. Vivek Wadhwa, Una Kim de Vitton, and Gary Gereffi, "How the Disciple Became the Guru: Is It Time for the U.S. to Learn Workforce Development from Former Disciple India?" working paper, School of Engineering, Duke University, Durham, NC, 2008.

for promoting internal candidates to the executive ranks. Most all had development centers at least equivalent to virtual corporate universities. In terms of metrics, 46 percent of the Indian companies tracked leadership development using formal measures versus 28 percent among U.S. firms.

Wipro's detailed and sophisticated executive development program covered roughly a thousand managers and executives, each of whom were assessed against twelve leadership measures and then compared with the overall scores in the firm. Every leader was placed into one of three performance/potential categories based on those comparative scores: A (top), B (middle), or C (bottom). The top three hundred leaders were then reviewed with the company chairman in a process that extended over five days. From those reviews, the company created a developmental plan for each candidate that included coaching, training, and rotational assignments. The process created a pool of candidates designed to meet anticipated vacancies in the next few years.

On the surface, this might sound no different from what one would see in the largest and oldest U.S. corporations (although precious few companies still do this), but Wipro added another feature that was quite distinctive. It tracked candidates outside the firm, those they would like to attract at some point, keeping up with their development elsewhere and planning for the point where vacancies inside Wipro would create an opportunity to recruit them.

Development programs like these were not limited to entry-level candidates. Dr. Reddy's Laboratories put all its outside hires, including those with substantial experience, through a one-year training program that included ten weeks of assignments abroad as well as a culminating cross-functional project presented to the top executives.

Figure 3-4 reports on the employee development programs of Indian and American companies. While companies in both countries reported reasonably high incidences of various development initiatives, the Indian group in most cases reported more extensive use. This was particularly so for leadership training (90 percent in

FIGURE 3-4

Employee development methods

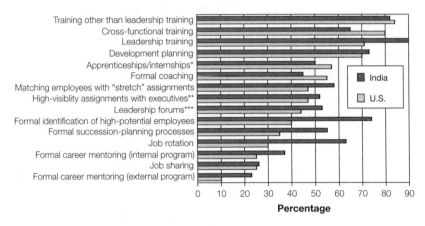

*To assess potential future hires. **E.g., executive task forces. ***E.g., opportunities for individuals to meet with senior executives in organized events or semiformal settings.

Sources: Survey of Indian companies, and Society for Human Resource Management, *SHRM/Catalyst Employee Development Survey Report* (McLean, VA: Society for Human Resource Management, 2007).

India versus 71 percent in the United States), identification of high-potential candidates (74 percent in India versus 40 percent in the United States), and job rotational assignments to build cross-functional skills (63 percent in India versus 30 percent in the United States). These were all initiatives that embody significant commitments of executive time and company money—powerful indicators of the priority that Indian companies gave to developing talent from within the company.

Further evidence of exactly where the link between employees and strategy plays out came from another survey question that asked about the importance of employee learning—training and development broadly defined—and how it is useful to the business. The results are displayed in figure 3-5.

By far the most important purpose of employee learning in the Indian companies was in building capabilities for the organization—that is, building the basic attributes that the business uses to compete, such as the innovation and customer problem solving at HCL

FIGURE 3-5

How the learning function provides stategic value to the organization

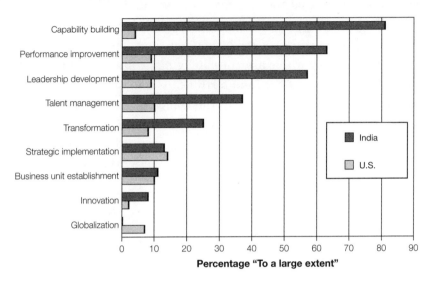

Percentage "To a large extent"

Sources: Survey of Indian companies, and American Society for Training & Development, *C-Level Perceptions of the Strategic Value of Learning* (Alexandria, VA: American Society for Training & Development, 2006).

Technologies or the superior customer service experience at Yes Bank. Four in five Indian human resource executives reported that capability building was an important purpose for employee learning, while a meager 4 percent of their American counterparts said the same thing. In fact, capability building ranked next to the bottom on the list of U.S. outcomes, a stunning difference.

In general, the American executives rarely saw learning as serving strategic-level goals for the organization. The outcome that American executives reported most frequently as the purpose of employee learning was to better execute existing strategies: "learning," in short, really was mostly training, designed to improve performance on existing tasks. Even then it was only embraced by 14 percent of respondents.

The Indian business leaders were aware that building a competitive edge through employee competencies was not guaranteed or an easy thing to pull off. As Deepak Parekh of Housing Development Finance Corporation Ltd. (HDFC) said, "Unless people in organizations are mobilized and energized on a sustained basis in support of business priorities, success can be elusive." Yet the very difficulty of this central task might explain the generally greater esteem in which the whole area of managing people is held in India. Overall, 65 percent of the Indian HR heads said that their function had the same level of respect in the company as other functional areas like finance and marketing versus only 40 percent in the United States (see figure 3-1). Some of the executives went further. "If you ask me," said Ravi Uppal of L&T Power, "the CEOs of companies today should be the HR managers."

Culture and Commitment: We Are Family

When asked about their overall priorities as the top executive, the business leaders we surveyed obviously had a lot of items they could list. It might not be a huge surprise to find that their number one priority was setting strategy, but number two on the list is something of a shock: keeper of organizational culture. And number three is even more surprising: acting as a role model or teacher for the employees.

The number two and three priorities together are efforts to harness the norms and values inside the organization—culture—that shape the attitudes and behaviors of the employees. Especially in the absence of formal rules and direct supervision, culture tells people how they should act and respond to new circumstances, especially when no one is watching. The business leaders saw the need for culture to extend their personal leadership and convey their company strategy far beyond their own individual presence. They viewed culture as a magnetic force that would align even the most remote of their managers' needles. Many of the business leaders stressed the powerful importance of an organizationwide mindset that valued performance, focused on customers, and identified with the firm's mission.

Here again, the lack of legacy burdens helped the executives execute this aspect of the India Way. Many of the business leaders whom we interviewed had virtually clean slates on which to write. Bharti Airtel, India's largest mobile telephone carrier, had been operating for a little more than a decade, and as CEO and joint managing director Manoj Kohli saw it, it was now the critical time to confirm the culture. As "parents we know that when a child is ten, it is the time to build character, build values, build the core values of a child—or of a company." If "we don't inculcate deep-rooted values now," he concluded, "the character of this child will never be built for the long term."

Role Modeling

Employees learn about organizational culture by seeing what gets rewarded, noting priorities when strategic choices have to be made, and observing how company leaders behave. Managing culture therefore cannot be a staff function; it has to come from the top. And it is impossible to manage the culture of an organization unless the top leaders recognize that they are being watched carefully and are of necessity teaching through example. Psychologists refer to this as *role modeling*, where individuals consciously or subconsciously copy the behavior of those they look up to. And what makes for an effective role model? Someone who is attractive in having positions of influence, especially power over individuals; someone who seems to have come from a similar set of experiences, such as manager who has advanced in one's own company.

The business leaders in our study implicitly understood the power of modeling behavior. Why else would they have placed such a high emphasis on being a guide or teacher for employees, ahead even of being a representative of shareholder interests? It is hard to imagine American executives saying that they thought serving as a personal guide or teacher for employees was more important than serving shareholder concerns.

When asked why "keeper of organizational culture" was his number one priority, Azim Premji of Wipro responded, "because any company, which is growing at 30 percent plus, is highly people inten-sive. In trying to localize more and more to the various geographies, we need a common face with the customer. Maintaining that culture or building that culture is an absolutely key priority of a CEO. He must walk the talk." In Premji's view, a strong, common set of values and norms is the glue that keeps employees operating in a consistent fashion, even when the company itself is large and geographically dispersed.

Subodh Bhargava, chairman of Tata Communications, offered a similar account. Amid all the course corrections, even strategic changes, of the last twenty-five years, values and vision, he said, al-ways served as the "first anchor" to keep the company operating in a consistent direction. Proshanto Banerjee, former chairman and man-aging director of Gas Authority of India Ltd., spoke for many when he said that he had worked hard to ensure that his employees could "see the larger picture in which they were operating, understand the importance of the company that they were working for, and feel strongly about its purpose and develop a certain amount of pride."

While each company represented a unique blend of cultural facets, virtually every business leader whom we interviewed said culture was rooted in commonly shared values of how the company should operate and the goals for which it should strive, and extended from shop-floor conversation to executive-suite decision making. Among those shared values, two particularly stood out during our interviews with Indian chief executives: a relishing of risk and a fervent customer focus. Narayana Murthy offered a suc-cinct description of the culture he wanted at Infosys: creating an environment where people are tired when they leave work but come back with enthusiasm the next morning.

Culture As Family

The norms and values that form the culture of most of the India Way companies envelop the entire workforce into a sense of family with requisite obligations. In one sense, this is reminiscent of the "organization man" approach common to American corporations in the 1950s, an explicit exchange of loyalty and commitment for job and economic security, but this is not a bartered arrangement to placate unions or other stakeholders.[12] It arises instead from a genuine sense of obligation to the employees on the part of the employer.

The executives that we interviewed saw serving their own workers as an important mission for their company. Narayana Murthy of Infosys Technologies spoke for many: "Indian business leaders bring a sense of family, a sense of closeness to the office. In other words, they relate to their people in a much more familiar manner—a much more affectionate and closer way than I have seen" in the United States.

When we asked the Indian business leaders about their personal legacies as leaders, one of the first responses was about transforming their organizations, but a second theme revolved around obligations to employees: empowering them, creating development opportunities, and enriching their lives. B. Muthuraman of Tata Steel put it in simple and straightforward terms: "To make people happy. That's it!"

The important advantage of this approach is that it creates a sense of reciprocity with the employees: if the executives and the company care about you and look after your interests, you should look after the interests of the company, tapping into the aspects of commitment that create high levels of performance and citizenship by employees. (Think of citizenship as how they behave when no one is monitoring them.) In keeping with this sense of commitment, India's major companies are much more likely than their American counterparts to offer workers a range of benefits that can evoke a strong sense of paternalism: on-site health-care and wellness programs, for example, plus family days and programs for balancing work and career.

Family As a Double-Edged Sword

As admirable as the culture of family and the emphasis on personal relationships that permeate Indian business life can be, it also creates challenges, especially at the management level. Vice-chairman and managing director K. Ramachandran of Philips

Electronics India noted that in Indian businesses, as opposed to Western firms, "relationships play a much larger role than black-and-white, pure objectives." With a lingering overlay of caste traditions and a concomitant deference to status and authority, the persistence of personal over professional relations sometimes shaded into a deference toward leaders per se.

Gurcharan Das—former chief executive of Procter & Gamble India—argued that some of this focus on keeping business relations within a tight community (traditionally caste, religion, and family) came about during the license raj, when businesspeople always had to break some law in order to adjust and survive under extant government regulations. For that reason, they wanted people around them who could keep secrets, people who were bound to them through other relationships.[13] This predilection to keep business relationships within existing social communities represented a challenge that Indian businesses had to address after the 1991 economic reforms, especially with their need to develop a diverse workforce commensurate with the diversity of their customer base.

The stress on personal relationships creates problems in assessing talent as well. As Subodh Bhargava explained, "One of our biggest weaknesses is that we are unable to reach scientific, reasonable assessments of white-collar productivity. [When] it comes to judging people and their capabilities and expectations, we tend to be poor judges." Bharti Airtel's Manoj Kohli added, "Emotionality is still higher than rationality," among Indian business leaders, "which is bad news because the rationality has to overtake emotionality" for companies to prosper.

Another set of dispositions that had to be overturned with the emerging India Way is the notion that superiors lead and subordinates follow, even when the former are faltering. Subodh Bhargava of Tata Communications noted that "in India we tend to be hierarchical, not just in administrative and management structure hierarchy. We are very conscious of personal hierarchy in our position. In fact, many companies have fallen by the wayside because they couldn't shed their hierarchical mind-sets."

Empowering Employees

Creating a sense of commitment through these mutual obligations would be almost cruel if the employees could not act on it for cultural, hierarchal, or other reasons. Perhaps that is why, in the past, empowerment in Indian firms was rare. Gurcharan Das remembered one business leader confessing, "In the past, I was extravagantly wasteful of talent or myopic in believing that I could do it all myself."[14] In recent years, though, the Indian business leaders we studied have worked hard to turn the theory about the advantages of empowering employees into practice. HCL went out of its way to enable individuals to solve customer problems, and Dr. Reddy's Laboratories, India's second-largest pharmaceutical company, made teamwork one of its five core values, along with a supporting value of respect for individuals regardless of hierarchy.

Jagdish Khattar, formerly of Maruti Udyog (now Maruti Suzuki) offered advice to his fellow business leaders from his own experience with empowerment. "Don't come with your own fixed views," he urged. "People within the company: throw issues to them, let them examine and come back to you with solutions. I have done it again and again. Eighty-five percent of their solutions would be what you have in mind, maybe 90 percent," but let "them go back with the impression that 100 percent of the solution is theirs. The implementation would be quick and smooth. And they will feel very proud of it, but it serves your purpose."

From "All Minds Meet" to "Single Status"

Empowerment produces not only better ideas but stronger commitment to their execution. The software company MindTree adopted a host of innovative methods for fostering ideas and execution, beginning with an entire menu of ways for the employees to give feedback to executives. Among the arrangements: monthly updates called snapshots that described the competitive environment and the state of the company; "All Minds Meet," a regular open house with the company's leadership where all questions were tackled on the spot; the "People Net" intranet, where grievances were addressed; and "Petals," a blogging site.[15] But the most unusual aspect of the MindTree approach, both in transparency and role modeling, could be found in the company's integrity policy. MindTree posted on its Web site accounts of ethical failures and violations of company policies, and the lessons the firm had learned from each.[16] The idea is that by acknowledging mistakes, especially those made by leaders, the company encourages others to admit theirs and to follow its lead in making changes.

The high-water mark for a culture of openness and flat hierarchy probably goes to Sasken Communication Technologies, which Rajiv Mody started in Silicon Valley and moved back to his home in Bangalore in 1991. The company's "single-status" policy meant that all employees, from entry level to Mody himself, were treated identically—same offices, same travel policies (coach class), same criteria for compensation (no separate executive compensation policies). While the company is known for being cheap in the area of compensation, it is otherwise extremely employee friendly, with policies that provide extensive programs for leaves, including a six-week sabbatical after four years of employment.[17]

Blowing It Up

In addition to programs of communication and feedback, most of the companies we studied had regular programs to survey and assess employee attitudes. And many openly shared the results with employees. Some went further with arrangements for addressing specific employee complaints and grievances. Tata Consultancy Services, for example, has an online system where employees submit grievances about how they have been mistreated by management.

Comparing the extent to which the Indian and the American companies track initiatives designed to enhance employee engagement provides a useful index of how seriously businesses and their leaders in both nations take the concept. In our surveying, 51 percent of the Indian firms frequently tracked these initiatives, while only 31 percent of the U.S. firms did so.[18] Kiran Mazumdar-Shaw of Biocon spoke for many in describing how her company moved empowerment into the team arena: "We have created very focused . . . groups to think strategically. The way you do that is to handpick all these people—and it has to be cross-functional groups—and get them to work in teams. It all sounds like motherhood statements, but getting people to work as cross-functional teams is very important." The final word on the importance of empowerment comes from Anand Mahindra of Mahindra & Mahindra, who offered this advice to an eventual successor: "If you do not continue to empower people as I have been doing, you are going to blow this thing up."

Summing Up

Perhaps the main conclusion about the India Way's approach to managing people is that it is integral to the way the companies compete, to their business strategies. In these companies, strategy is based on internal competencies, which ultimately come from the actions and efforts of employees. The fact that Indian CEOs give so much attention to employee issues, therefore, is not just because they want to be generous to their employees. It is because it drives the competitiveness of their businesses.

The focus on employees can go too far, some argue, especially where that focus gets confused with personal relationships. Vice-chairman and managing director K. Ramachandran of Philips Electronics India warned about the downsides of personal ties in Indian companies. They might dominate professional relations, for example, in dealing with poor-performing family members in promoter-led companies. Tata Communication's Subodh Bhargava observed, "One of our biggest weaknesses" in India "is that we are unable to reach scientific, reasonable assessments of white-collar productivity." When it comes to "judging people and their capabilities and expectations, we tend to be poor judges." Managing director

G. R. Gopinath of Deccan Aviation contrasted India and the United States: While "there is a ruthless insensitivity to anything other than financial performance" in the United States, he observed, "the danger in India sometimes is, people are not performance oriented enough. When your personal relationships get sometimes mixed up, you tend to take a soft approach."

More generally, some worry about the paternalism of Indian firms. Jet Airways' executive director Saroj K. Datta saw paternalism as a major difference between Indian leaders and their peers in the Western world. The concern about paternalism is that it may mutate into a kind of mutual dependency, with a company remaining loyal to employees and employees to the company in ways that restrict change.

Such concerns come down to taking a good thing too far. At least at present, the India Way companies seem to be striking the right balance in their holistic engagement of employees.

CHAPTER FOUR

Leading the Enterprise

Improvisation and Adaptability

IF PEOPLE MANAGEMENT constitutes a defining quality of the India Way, so too does a distinctive style of executive leadership. The unique approach derives from the India Way's
emphasis on broad mission and purpose, and it builds on the stress
on improvisation and adaptability. Business leaders think broadly
and act pragmatically, setting grand agendas and then testing
through trial and error what works and what does not. While that
approach has served Indian business leaders well, the global business community has remained remarkably unaware of its impact
and unfamiliar with its most noted practitioners.

This was evident by exception in 2001, when on a balmy May afternoon in West Philadelphia, roughly one thousand MBA students
assembled to hear a groundbreaking commencement address. For the
first time in the Wharton School's 120-year history, the graduation
speaker—by overwhelming student demand—was the chief executive

of an Indian company, N. R. Narayana Murthy of Infosys Technologies. Just six years later, this once rarest of scenarios would repeat itself, this time with Lakshmi Mittal, the chairman and chief executive of the world's largest steel company, ArcelorMittal, addressing Wharton's 2007 MBA class.

For years, Indian executives had *attended* American business schools. Mukesh Ambani of Reliance Industries and Anil Ambani of Reliance ADA Enterprises graduated from Stanford and Wharton, respectively. Adi Godrej of the Godrej Group graduated from MIT's Sloan School of Management, while Rahul Bajaj—head of India's largest maker of scooters, rickshaws, and three-wheelers—and Palaniappan Chidambaram, Indian home minister in 2009 and formerly finance minister, both earned MBAs at Harvard. Even those Indian leaders who did not attend American universities still studied the world's best practices—multidivisional management, process reengineering, and flexible manufacturing—commonly taught and developed at U.S. business schools. ICICI's K. V. Kamath, for example, learned U.S.—as well as Japanese and European—management techniques while at the Asian Development Bank in Singapore.

Why then—given the deep familiarity of Indian business leaders with U.S. management precepts, the growing Indian student presence at American business schools, and the explosive Indian economy— was it so rare to find a Murthy or a Mittal at the commencement lectern in the United States, until recently? That answer reflects a larger ideological battle—one that heavily favored American executives.

The Indian Ethic and the Spirit of Capitalism

The relationship between capitalism and the power of ideas was most famously addressed in Max Weber's *The Protestant Ethic and the Spirit of Capitalism*. Weber presented a compelling argument that the fuel of northern European capitalism came not from the magic of markets but from the religious ideology specific to that region. In Weber's telling, Protestantism prescribed that individuals should accumulate and reinvest in their material creation, generating what might now be called a "powerful synergy" between ideas—religious ethics—and capitalist growth.

Later, Weber's intellectual disciples Reinhard Bendix and Mauro Guillén offered kindred explanations for the drivers of executive behavior. In their respective books, *Work and Authority in Industry* and *Models of Management*, they argued the case for seeing business practices as a product of managerial ideologies, not just organizational necessities. Together, Weber and his academic progeny continue to remind us of the supremacy of ideas, even when we are engaged in the most material of human endeavors: building private enterprise.[1]

In recent years, the most popular and influential of these books have largely focused on American executives and their management techniques. Just as Indian business leaders were largely overlooked as graduation speakers, they did not author popular books on what constitutes good private enterprise leadership. Instead, those ideas largely came from the pinnacles of U.S. business experience—the titans who transformed fledgling enterprises into American powerhouses.

Early accounts by Alfred P. Sloan of his years at General Motors and AT&T's Chester I. Barnard defined how executives around the world thought of themselves. In more recent years, the chronicles of Lee Iacocca at Chrysler and Jack Welch at General Electric had become exemplary accounts for many managers as well. So, too, had Thomas Peters and Robert Waterman's *In Search of Excellence*, Jim Collins and Jerry Porras's *Built to Last*, and Jim Collins's *Good to Great*.[2]

For decades, Indians have been among the most avid readers of these books. Jack and Suzy Welch's *Winning* spent months on the *Times of India*'s business best-seller list and, for a time, was generally available in the country's business centers. Caught by a Mumbai traffic light, waiting drivers were often surrounded by street vendors with fresh pineapples, cheap umbrellas, and Jack Welch's books.

For all its intensity, though, this flow of ideas has tended to be a one-way conversation. Even as Indian business continued to compete successfully on the world stage, there was very little recounting of Indian managerial models. One exception was C. K. Prahalad's *The Fortune at the Bottom of the Pyramid*, showing that there was a large, untapped opportunity in servicing low-income consumers in India and that emergent business models for doing so had much to offer managers from the West.[3] Yet in mid-2008, the *Wall Street Journal* listed no best sellers on Indian business; all its titles focused on U.S. enterprise. Even more surprisingly, the *Business Standard*, India's equivalent to the *Wall Street Journal*, reported that the ten best-selling business books during the same time period included eight on American business or by U.S.-based authors, including Sloan's *My Years with General Motors*, first published in 1964, and Peter Drucker's *People and Performance*. Only one Indian title, *Business Mantras* by Radhika Piramal et al., made the list.[4]

The overwhelming influence of U.S. business leadership and precepts could be seen in the number of foreign students seeking to enter American MBA programs. From a steady trickle in previous years, foreign admissions had grown to a torrent in the late 2000s, with Indian students leading the way. Just eleven Indian students finished the Wharton MBA program in 1990; by 2008, that number had grown tenfold, well ahead of China or any other nation (see figure 4-1).[5]

The number of Graduate Management Admission Tests taken during the 2000s, a necessary step for entry to most American MBA programs, showed the same pitched trend. GMAT test taking rose during the decade by 74 percent in Asia, by 161 percent in China, and by 341 percent in India (see figure 4-2). Not all of the test takers were heading for American business schools, but they were submitting 70 percent of their test scores to U.S. programs.[6]

Different Similarities

Given these trends, it comes as no surprise that many principles of business leadership are virtually identical in both the United

FIGURE 4-1

Number of students completing Wharton School MBA program, 1990–2008

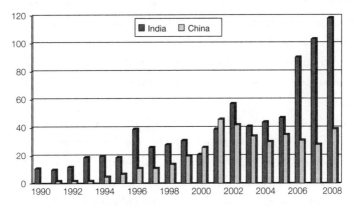

Source: Graduate Program, Wharton School, 2008.

FIGURE 4-2

Number of Graduate Management Admission Tests (GMAT) taken in India and China, 2000–2008

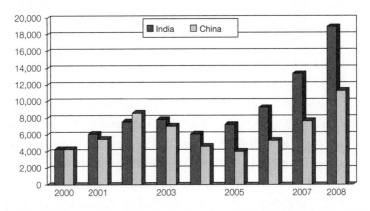

Sources: Graduate Management Admission Council, *Asian Geographic Trend Report for Examinees Taking the Graduate Management Admission Test, 2002-2006* (McLean, VA: Graduate Management Admission Council, 2007); Graduate Management Admission Council, *Asian Geographic Trend Report for GMAT Examinees, 2003-07* (McLean, VA: Graduate Management Admission Council, 2008); and Graduate Management Admission Council, *Asian Geographic Trend Report for GMAT Examinees, 2004–08* (McLean, VA: Graduate Management Admission Council, 2009).

States and India, and indeed are valued in virtually all countries.[7] Managers worldwide are looking to absorb best practices from wherever they have been developed, and inevitably, the U.S. experience has served as a major source of ideas. But while Western management principles are well known, Indian executives report they are not necessarily emulated. Rather, over the past two decades, Indian business executives have evolved their own leadership style and developed ideas that reflect a unique cultural heritage and history.

When Dale Berra, son of baseball icon (and legendary malapropist) Yogi Berra, was asked whether he was similar to his father, he replied no, their similarities were different. So it is with Indian business leaders. As similar as they are in many ways to American business leaders, their "similarities" are also different. Both sets of leaders, Indian and American, preside over demanding worlds, both bring a vision of where they want to take their enterprise, both are called on to make timely decisions, and both use much the same skill set. But at the same time, American and Indian executives have evolved distinct approaches to their positions—critical leadership distinctions that, in India's case, have helped the nation's businesses thrive. As ICICI's K. V. Kamath summed up, "Time and again it has been proved that the Western model of doing business would not be a success here."[8]

We identified the broad outlines of those "similar differences" in the opening chapter, and in this chapter we offer more specific assessment of the second of our four principal practices of the India Way. Emphasizing *improvisation and adaptability*, Indian business leaders stress sideways movements into areas with promising prospects and the building of a model of what should work by witnessing what does work. Utilizing a trial-and-error method, they draw upon the virtues of flexibility and resilience in the face of obstacles and challenges. We have found that this is also closely coupled with aspects of the fourth principle theme. Emphasizing *broad mission and purpose*, Indian business leaders also place special emphasis on personal values, a vision of growth, and strategic thinking.

Improvisation and Adaptability

Indian business leaders, we found, had no great desire to reinvent the wheel when it came to strategic thinking. For the most part, they would have been content to follow well-established Western practices, but the on-the-ground realities of establishing and nurturing companies in a dynamically changing and unique business climate left them little choice but to write their own how-to manuals. Rather than being imposed from above, their course involved making numerous operational bets, watching what worked, and then codifying the tangible successes into a more systematic framework: the trial-and-error path from good to great. In traveling this frequently tortuous and oft-changing path, they found that flexibility and resilience proved essential.

Trial and Error

Deepak Parekh, executive chairman of Housing Development Finance Corporation (HDFC), emphasized customer focus with a see-what-works approach. "Being the pioneers in housing finance in India for the middle class, we had no model to emulate," he said. "So we adopted the 'learning by doing' philosophy." Earlier in the decade, "most Indians were rather debt averse, but what we realized is that our customers didn't need just money, they needed counseling— legal and technical advice on the property they were purchasing— and we provided it in-house. Each decision, whether on product development, pricing, or office automation and office layout, was oriented towards enhancing customer satisfaction. Understanding the customer's needs was our key focus, and that's where I think we made the difference." Parekh characterized the process as iterative. His company's direction must be "strengthened and nurtured by an analytical ability that assesses emerging environments and strategic alternatives and exploits opportunities as they emerge."

Analjit Singh, cofounder and chairman of Max India, a company involved in information, health-care, and financial services, emphasized the necessity for flexible thinking as timelines shorten and tempos increase. "The time to make mistakes and learn over longer durations has been compressed," he said. "If you put a strategy in place, you've got to be open minded enough as a management team to go back to the drawing board as often as you need to tweak it." Planning, of necessity, is a work in progress, a product of what he termed *strategy-based learning.*

Is strategic thinking any less important to Indian business leaders than elsewhere? Hardly. If anything, it has become relatively more important in recent years, especially as compared with the United States. As table 4-1 shows, business leaders in both countries said they were devoting more time to just about everything.[9] However, American business leaders reported the largest time-demand increases in areas of governance issues, including regulatory, board,

TABLE 4-1

How Indian and U.S. business leaders have changed their allocation of time over the past three years

The question: "Considering your various roles as a CEO, how has your time allocation for each of the following tasks changed over the past three years? Are you spending more time, about the same amount of time, or less time on each task?"

Leadership tasks	UNITED STATES		INDIA	
	% more time	% less time	% more time	% less time
1. Regulatory/compliance issues	**98**	2	41	24
2. Reporting to the board	**72**	1	41	17
3. Shareholder relations	**58**	4	41	31
4. Setting strategy	47	9	**93**	0
5. Media relations	31	11	31	17
6. Day-to-day management	28	27	24	**55**
7. Fostering workplace diversity	26	13	21	41
8. Customer relations	22	27	**62**	7

Note: For items in bold, more than half of the executives affirmed.

and shareholder relations. Meanwhile, customer relationships were the only area seeing a net decline for American executives, while such relationships represented the second-greatest increase in demand for Indian executives, just behind "setting strategy."

An even more telling discrepancy emerged in a 2007 Conference Board survey of chief executives worldwide. When asked to identify their most critical challenges from among several dozen, American executives ranked "consistent execution of strategy" considerably above "speed, flexibility, [and] adaptability to change." Their Indian counterparts reversed the ranking.[10]

In setting direction, Indian executives have understandably developed a more inductive and customer-tested approach. Given the unknowns about what customers really want to purchase and given the convulsive growth in many Indian markets—the country had fewer than 11 million mobile-phone subscribers at the end of 2002 and some 347 million by the end of 2008—executives viewed their decision-making process as a matter of recurrently testing the waters.[11] Through trial, error, and trial again, they built their product and service lines from the bottom up, focused on emerging customer demands and ever sensitive to the crosswinds moving customer preferences in one direction or another.

Flexibility and Resilience

When asked how they most differed from Western business leaders, a number of Indian executives reported being more adaptable, more flexible, and more resilient—characteristics partially explained by the prereform Indian business environment. Even today, after significant economic liberalization, India's industrial infrastructure remains abysmal. When McKinsey asked senior managers at multinational companies to rate the infrastructure of sixteen countries, they placed India in a tie for last.[12] In 2004, India devoted $2 billion to improving its roads, while China invested $30 billion.[13]

Yet the bureaucratic and structural problems that had been so vexing in the executives' early careers also instilled a personal steeliness. "Professional Indian leaders," Hindustan Unilever's Manvinder Singh Banga observed, are "quite distinct from what I see anywhere else, and they are distinct primarily because they have been trained or groomed in an extremely fluid, dynamic, and uncertain environment. The business environment in India has all those dimensions of poor infrastructure, uncertain infrastructure, and challenges from the regulatory side and with labor relations. These multiple challenges are much more than the typical consumer- or trade-challenge that you face anywhere else in the world."

As a result, Banga concluded, "Indian management is a much better-rounded management than people who have trained and evolved in more stable market places in the world." For one, Indian business leaders "have a much greater ability to cope with uncertainty, they don't get disturbed by uncertain events, they keep an even keel, and they are more balanced as they pick their pathway through." Second, "they also tend to be more creative as a result because they have to face these sorts of untoward situations almost on a daily basis, and therefore they have to really stretch into creativity across the whole business model. They are creatively thinking about the whole business model and all the levers of business."

In building an organization, Deepak Parekh of HDFC said executives must be energetic trailblazers. "Success in India is a struggle of the hurdle economy, where $5x$ energy is required to produce x," he said. "This is quite the reverse in most modern societies. The true leader is one who can counter this framework and, like an icebreaker, cut through pack ice and create a channel for others to follow. Not only will he need a machine to undertake that task, but also the inspiration, patience, and optimism to drive it and the energy to sustain it over long periods of time."

Vivek Nair, vice-chairman and managing director of Hotel Leela Venture Ltd., was reminded of the importance of personal resilience both during the aftermath of 9/11 and its devastating impact on the travel and hotel industry, and during the major rebound that followed several years later. The months after 9/11 proved extremely stressful for the hospitality industry, even in India, with suddenly empty hotel rooms necessitating drastic wage reductions and cost cutting. Not long after, though, business travel to India rebounded, with annual increases of 6 to 7 percent, and foreign tourism shot up by some 25 percent. In anticipation of the rebound, the company had invested $600 million in a set of new hotels, including one in Bangalore that has proved to be among the best-performing hotels in India. A vital capacity in weathering the storm, in Nair's view, was his ability to flexibly respond to such huge swings in demand. During the downswing, it had been essential, he said, to "inspire confidence" among the hotel's employees that "it was not the end of the world." They could not understand, he found, "how things could change so radically in a matter of just one moment." But he worked hard to reassure them, meeting with many individually and in groups. In time, the employees became more ready than would otherwise have been the case to get back on the hotel's "high-growth path"—the path he sought and the one that the company returned to several years later.

Jugaad *and Adaptation*

An appreciation for the turbulent and often frustrating barriers to doing business is essential—but so too is active surmounting of them. Creative adaptation, not weary resignation, is the way.

Vijay Mahajan, chief executive of BASIX Group, a microfinance organization, argued for many in offering his appraisal of the power of *jugaad*, an ability "to manage somehow, in spite of lack of resources." It constitutes a cornerstone of Indian enterprise, in his view, and the "spirit of jugaad has enabled the Indian businessman to survive and get by in an economy which was until the late 1990s oppressed by controls and stymied by a lack of widespread purchasing power. Adjust, of course, is the English word, but spoken in various local accents. It is used in a wide range of situations, usually with a plaintive smile. One can use it in a crowded bus, where three people are already seated on a seat for two, requesting them to 'adjust,' to accommodate a fourth person! Or it is used by businessmen when they meet government officials, seeking to 'adjust' various regulations, obviously for a consideration, to speed up the myriad permissions still required to do anything in India." Mahajan's ideas in many ways reflected the entrepreneurship that existed across business enterprises of all sizes—the ability to navigate a complex environment, find innovative ways to do business, and adapt to unfavorable business conditions.

Subhash Chandra of Zee Entertainment Enterprises said that in his experience Indian leaders seemed more adaptable than U.S. business executives. "We can bring our level of thinking down and meet with a truck driver and deal with him at his level," he said, "and at the same time we can also bring ourselves up to the level of the head of the state if required and then deal with him at that level.

"I remember when I was starting my business career, I used to run an edible oil extraction plant in my hometown. I wanted to learn how to drive a truck, and so I befriended my company truck driver, and he taught me to drive the truck, and at the same time I used to run that business even as the CEO. Later, I could go to the chief minister of the state and request him to give me an electricity connection because that was the challenge in those days due to power shortage." Now, he went on, this early experience with direct engagement had become an important asset for leading his business through market, rather than licensing, challenges.

Broad Mission and Purpose

Many Indian executives placed special stress on articulating a forward-looking vision while instilling shared values to anchor their companies. Many further emphasized the importance of aligning their vision with long-term company values, while still energizing and exciting the company's current employees. Here the difference with American executives appeared to us to be more a matter of content than kind. Both offer long-term pictures of the path ahead, but rarely did the frequent U.S. mantra of double-digit growth in earnings per share appear in our interviews. For Indian business leaders, the long-term pictures were more a matter of reaching millions of customers with new kinds of products, or helping to lift vast numbers from poverty, or giving people of limited means what had only been available to the affluent, whether air travel, mobile communication, or auto transport. While such agendas may create equivocal or even adverse reaction among Western investors, Indian business leaders used them to help create unequivocal and affirmative allegiance among company employees.

Vision and Values

Subodh Bhargava, chairman of Videsh Sanchar Nigam Ltd. (VSNL, renamed Tata Communications in 2007), told us that the maintenance of "shared values and shared vision" was critical to his own leadership. The company has made many course corrections, even strategic changes, over the past twenty-five years, he said, but the values and vision always served as the "first anchor." Bhargava emphasized the importance of his line managers "walking the talk"—living by those values and vision. Among the specific values held constant by him over the past quarter century have been personal integrity and ensuring that company decisions are apolitical, fair, and "secular." He stressed "extensive communication and absolute transparency" within the company as a way of ensuring that those values are widely embraced by his managers.

Similarly, Kiran Mazumdar-Shaw, executive chairman and managing director of Biocon Ltd., emphasized the importance of communicating clearly and truthfully to help shape organizational values: "If you are honest and up-front," she said, "people trust you and never lose that trust. I think people need to trust you to be inspired by you." B. Muthuraman, managing director of Tata Steel Ltd., emphasized "being a visionary" as a vital leadership quality. "By being visionary," he explained, "I mean somebody who is able to make people envision their future" and then "energize, enthuse, and empower them" to strive toward that goal.

Company Vision

Deepak Parekh, Executive Chairman
Housing Development Finance Corporation

Over the years, I have repeatedly been asked, "What has been HDFC's guiding principle to being the vanguard of housing finance in India?" My reply is simple: you must get in first.

Straightforward as it may appear, it requires tremendous vision to do so. One must be able to visualize the future, anticipate emerging patterns, and spot business opportunities in them. One must have the ability to create mental maps of possibilities and the relevant conditions that enable things to happen.

If I had to put it in a single sentence, I would say that a leader must have the exceptional capability of visualizing and inventing the future—an uncanny intuitiveness for what lies ahead. Jonathan Swift, author of *Gulliver's Travels*, put it so succinctly when he said that vision is the art of seeing the invisible . . .

All great organizations have a unique characteristic among their leadership teams. Not only do they have a clear vision of where they want to be in the future; they effectively convey this vision to their employees and get them to believe in it. A leader must have the ability to see in a way that compels

Automaker Mahindra's vice-chairman and managing director, Anand Mahindra, echoed that sentiment when he told us that, as a "business head in India, if you didn't have some perspective or some road map or some vision of where you thought the company [was] going, and therefore what opportunities lay ahead, you would not have been able to position yourselves [during] the last fifteen years to take advantage of those opportunities. Where I have added the most others to sit up and take notice. People want a strong vision of where they are headed. And they want to be part of it.

For a leader's vision to become a reality, his people must believe in it. To get your people sold on your vision, you must possess passion for it. Be hands-on. Get involved. Though I do not own HDFC, I have run it as if I do. All decisions of investment, lending, and dividend that I take make me feel as if I own 100 percent of my company. I do what I would have done if the company was owned by me. I have acted as an entrepreneur even though I am just a salaried employee.

Creating afresh requires leadership of an extraordinary dimension. Not only must the leader have the foresight to see the big picture before anyone else does but must also possess the ability to systematically break it down and zero in on its components.

A vision must never lie dormant. It must be consistently strengthened and nurtured by an analytical ability that assesses emerging environments and strategic alternatives and exploits opportunities as they emerge . . .

Never underestimate the importance of vision. You cannot be an effective leader if you don't have a vision—either for yourself or for the organization. It is what one sees or feels before any systematic reasoning can be structured. A vision is like a map that guides one through a tangle of bewildering complexities.

value and where I have gone and made the most difference [is] in the ability to just have an idea in my mind as to what the future should look like in terms of everything: how the organization should look, which areas it should go down," and what should be the appropriate "business model." For Housing Development Finance Corporation's Deepak Parekh, it is a matter of visualizing the future to anticipate the business opportunities ahead (see "Company Vision").

Expansive Thinking

As both a corollary of shared values and vision and a technique to realize these overarching goals, expansive thinking was placed by many of the executives at the top of their personal list. Farsighted judgment springs from many sources: experience, intuitive judgment, as well as detailed analysis of the most promising opportunities ahead. Azim Premji, executive chairman of Wipro Ltd., described broad thinking as combining "intuitive judgment and professional evaluation" with an "ability to see around corners."

For Manvinder Singh Banga, former chairman and CEO of Hindustan Unilever, India's largest consumer products company, expansive thinking is a matter of synthesizing many contextual threads: "The most important role for a leader today," he said, is being able "to make sense of all the different trends that are there in the market, so whether it is consumer trends, political trends, economic trends, technology trends—add them up and try to work out a searchlight that illuminates the path to sustainable profitable growth." Such thinking then must be conveyed throughout the organization "to get everybody on the same page so that they understand the searchlight, the pathway, and see it as clearly as you do."

Drawing on one of *Star Trek*'s catchphrases—"Dare to go where no man has gone before"—Rajesh Hukku of i-Flex Solutions, a provider of information technology services to the banking industry, defined farsighted judgment as "not just to think differently to show some difference, but think differently in terms of how you can change the lives of your customers." Broad thinking, for him, required a search for innovation and "doing things that have not been tried before."

Virtually all the leaders we interviewed stressed the importance of their own proactive roles in thinking broadly and evolving that thinking as experience dictated. Zee Entertainment chairman Subhash Chandra, for instance, emphasized the importance of transcending the immediate situation and then letting that larger picture guide his actions. When "considering some particular subject at the very, very micro level," he said, he must at the same time "create a picture of the macro situation." Conversely, he said, he must also be able to translate the macro situation back to the micro level. Chandra confessed to a tendency to get into the details of execution himself, but he also forced himself to stand back when he realized that he could "lose sight of the many issues that must be simultaneously considered" by a person in his leadership position.

Communicating Vision and Values

As important as it is to have a guiding vision and values, broadly *communicating* vision and values was seen as even more critical. On one hand, this would seem an obvious point: a leader's values and vision must be known and appreciated throughout the company to be fully realized. Yet time and again in our research and observations, we have been surprised by how little the chief executive's values and vision were appreciated or even understood by frontline employees.

Nowhere was this effort to communicate executive values and vision more important—and more challenging—than among companies that had previously enjoyed government-protected markets. Consider the uphill struggle R. S. P. Sinha, executive chairman and managing director of the government-owned Mahanagar Telephone Nigam Ltd. (MTNL), faced in 2000 when the New Delhi and Mumbai areas were thrown open to competition. His first order of business, Sinha said, was to craft a vision that could provide for sustainable advantage in a fast-moving market and then to instill it among sixty thousand employees who were accustomed to having the turf to themselves. To change this work culture and ensure the "clarity of our thinking and action and vision," Sinha spent much of his time speaking face-to-face with throngs of employees.

Or consider the unique challenges faced by Subir Raha, former chairman and managing director of Oil and Natural Gas Corporation (ONGC), when he joined the company in 2001. Publicly traded but still majority owned by the Indian government, ONGC was responsible for more than three-quarters of the country's oil and

Building Bank of Baroda

Once among the country's most respected financial institutions, Bank of Baroda was increasingly seen as a socialist relic in postreform India. The national government controlled 51 percent of its shares. Bank of Baroda paid well below what private competitors did. The bank's long-serving employees were highly resistant to change, but management couldn't use wages or stock options as motivators. The ability to fire and lay off employees was even more constrained. As the 1990s moved into the 2000s, the bank found itself eclipsed by faster, more nimble private-sector competitors.

Enter Anil K. Khandelwal, who took over as chief executive in 2005.

Khandelwal began the bank's transformation with his own version of a burning platform: meeting with bank managers and showing them financial-analyst reports recommending that investors not buy Bank of Baroda stock. Of course, the managers didn't have stock options, so this was an appeal to mission—this is a bank that should be working for the betterment of India—and also to personal pride: it's embarrassing to work in an organization of which experts think so little.

The next thing Khandelwal did was to revamp the bank's branding with a new trademark and a new spokesperson. He then ran out a pilot program in which some branches would be open twelve hours a day, from 8 a.m. to 8 p.m.—an innovation that would be radical even at most U.S. banks.

Khandelwal had a vision of how to improve Bank of Baroda's market position, but implementation relied on direct communication with staff. He called all the employees of these pilot branches to headquarters for a meeting—"from manager to messenger," as he put it—and made a sales pitch about the need to change, at the same time asking for the employees' help to do it. Because he had empowered his workers, rather than forcing change on them, they agreed to staff their branches from 8 a.m. to 8 p.m. without any overtime pay or extra compensation. The next part of the transformation, and the most important, was to have these local branches design their own marketing events to announce the new schedule, leading to an explosion of creativity—parades, pageants, you name it.

The twelve-hour banking trial was eventually rolled out nationwide, but with each local branch taking responsibility for execution. Since then, the bank has introduced "twenty-four-hour human banking" in several locations, in which regular employees, not a faraway call center, staff the branch around the clock. Since branch employees took the lead in these roll-outs as well, communication was critical. Khandelwal wrote employees letters every week, explaining the goals and the progress so far, and often met with the local branches to make the case for change.

Once the bank started to get public attention for these innovations, employee pride rose in the bank's mission. This morale boost allowed Khandelwal to convince workers to accept as necessary massive investments in new technology that would cut and restructure jobs. Along the way, he also introduced such employee-relations innovations as a direct help line to his office for those facing crucial problems in their part of the organization and a talent-hunt program to find and develop high-performing employees within Bank of Baroda. He personally directs these programs, saying that human resource issues "cannot be delegated."

Without using carrots or sticks, Khandelwal turned a stodgy, government bank into one competitive with leading private banks. He accomplished this by creating a sense of mission, communicating his vision, and persuading employees by empowering and engaging them. His job before becoming chief executive (to return to a theme of the previous chapter): head of human resources.

gas production. Though demand was up, ONGC was not. "The company was stagnating in every aspect of performance, operational [and] financial," Raha observed. The firm's results were negative, employees were demoralized, and its public image was poor.

To remedy the situation, Raha set forward a new long-term vision for the company, with a set of accompanying benchmarks for as far out as 2020. "This created a perception," he recalled, "among employees and external stakeholders that we intended to be around in the long haul and that we were not going to close out the company in three years or five years." By going public with the goals on a twenty-year time frame, he said, "people had their confidence restored!" (See also "Building Bank of Baroda.")

Transformational Leadership

The melding together of the Indian business executives' exceptional stress on improvisation, adaptability, mission, and purpose had yielded a leadership style that resembles what is sometimes captured in the concept of transformational leadership—an approach different in tenor from what is often referenced as transactional leadership.[14]

Transactional leadership is described as striking deals with subordinates, almost like a transaction, where the leader matches the individual's interests and needs to specific job-related outcomes: you want a promotion, meet these sales targets. *Transformational leadership*—or as it is sometimes popularly known, charismatic leadership—is a very different process through which the leader influences the interests and needs of subordinates, inspiring them to care about the goals of the organization: you should identify with the success of the company because its mission is important, and you should work hard because you care about that mission.

Leadership style is in part defined by the behavior of bosses toward their subordinates and the efforts made to motivate and influence those who report to the top, and we anticipated the possibility of a third style of leadership—what some might even call *nonleadership*: a more passive approach in which executives essentially leave subordinates alone and let the administrative systems manage their behavior. The most formal of the passive approaches is *management by exception*, where leaders intervene only to correct problems. Passive leadership makes sense with highly empowered employees, but it is not the only way to lead empowered subordinates.

To examine the style of Indian executives, we used the most widely used assessment of leadership in the United States, the Multifactor Leadership Questionnaire (MLQ).[15] We asked the directors of human resources at the companies whose executives we interviewed to assess the leadership style of their top bosses. (As part of the MLQ process, individual questions ask about specific leadership behavior and the responses are then gathered into more general practices.) Not surprisingly, given the picture of Indian business leadership already developed—actively engaged in building mission-driven organizations—the executives scored low on passive and avoidance practices, as seen in figure 4-3. Nor were we surprised to see that Indian business leaders ranked highest in practices that fall generally under "transformational style": inspirational motivation, idealized influence, intellectual stimulation, and individual consideration. On the transactional side, Indian leaders, like their American counterparts, are quick to use contingent reward—that is, rewards based on performance—but less prone to manage by exception: look for mistakes.

When we compared these results with those from a sample of forty-eight chief executives of U.S. *Fortune* 500 companies, however, we found that the American leaders were significantly more likely to use transactional leadership styles than were our Indian executives. Another study of fifty-six American chief executives also suggested that Indian executives create a significantly greater sense of empowerment among employees, scoring higher, for instance, on the "intellectual stimulation" category.[16]

Improvisation and adaptability, mission and purpose—together the foundation of a more transformational style—were repeatedly

FIGURE 4-3

Leadership styles of Indian business leaders

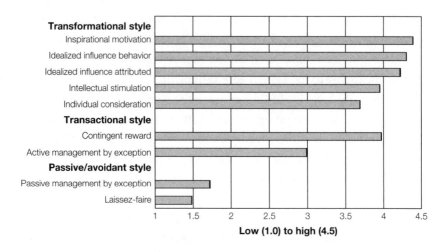

Sources: Survey of Indian Companies; and H. L. Tosi et al., "CEO Charisma, Compensation, and Firm Performance," *Leadership Quarterly* 15, no. 3 (2004): 405–420.

stressed in our interviews with the Indian business leaders. They were evident as well in the leaders' narratives of how they had built their companies in the post-1991 era of liberalization. For illustration, we turn to India's largest nonstate-owned financial institution, ICICI Bank, and the role of its long-serving transformational chief executive, Kundapur Vaman Kamath.

Leading ICICI Bank

In 1971, when K. V. Kamath began his career at the original Industrial Credit and Investment Corporation of India, the bank—created by the World Bank and the Indian government—had a relatively modest mandate: project financing for the private sector. Kamath stayed on for seventeen years before decamping for a stint with the Asian Development Bank. In 1996 he returned to a radically different ICICI as chief executive, overseeing the bank's massive transformations in postreform India. Kamath's ICICI career, in short, spans the "great divide" of the Indian economy, just as his bank is a powerful expression of the modern-day Indian business juggernaut. More to the point for our immediate purposes, the leadership principles that have evolved over Kamath's long career neatly encapsulate the themes of this chapter.

In 2000, four years into his new job, Kamath listed ICICI on the New York Stock Exchange, and it soon emerged as India's largest privately owned bank. ICICI's annual revenue of $625 million (27.2 billion rupees) in fiscal year 2002 rose to $9.1 billion (396 billion rupees) in 2008, and the company grew from 7,700 to 40,686 employees over the same period (see figure 4-4). In just seven years, the bank's employees quintupled and revenue rose more than thirteenfold. With managed assets of more than $100 billion by 2008, it became the country's largest private-sector commercial bank, investment bank,

FIGURE 4-4

ICICI annual revenue and number of employees, 2002–2008

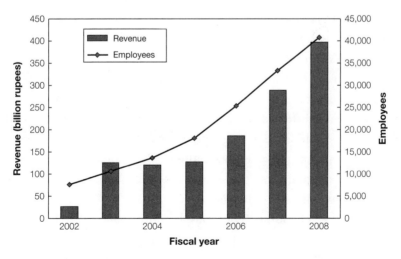

Source: Company records.

and insurance provider. ICICI ran India's biggest online trading operation and managed India's largest private equity and venture capital funds. It handled a quarter of all private remittances flowing into India, an especially significant figure since India is the world's largest recipient of remittances.[17]

In guiding this explosive growth, Kamath worked closely with the long-serving nonexecutive board chairman and former CEO Narayanan Vaghul. Together, they created a vision of transforming the institution from a development bank into a corporate and retail bank, and then into a universal bank that could provide a full array of financial services, ranging from mobile and private banking to life insurance and venture funds. Yet the implementation of these goals—and the rapid expansion that followed—was largely accomplished without bringing in experienced banking veterans who could help ICICI adjust to new business opportunities. Instead, the bank's leadership opted to combine expansive thinking about the new markets with a trial-and-error approach to finding what worked in largely untested markets.

Direct Involvement: Chanda Kochhar

One of ICICI's primary movers into the new markets had been Chanda Kochhar. Without a road map to follow, Kochhar relied heavily on direct hands-on engagement to learn how to build businesses in four distinct areas of banking. She first joined ICICI's corporate banking, then set up the bank's financing for infrastructure projects, followed by retail banking, before moving on to the firm's international banking operations. "On a personal level, it wasn't always easy," Kochhar recalled. "But as a leader, I think you need to be adaptable, so you can quickly understand and move forward in new business situations."

When Kochhar joined corporate banking, she realized that each banking division dealt separately—and relatively passively—with its corporate clients. Inventing her way forward, Kochhar created a nine-person team that was drawn from investment banking, commercial banking, securities trading, and other product areas. Her goal was to learn the principles of integrated product selling and what she termed *multifaceted leadership*. That required rapidly absorbing from others what she initially knew so little about. "I learned it is possible to quickly share knowledge and ideas with each other, rather than sitting on a pedestal, saying, 'I'm the boss, and I'm not here to learn from anybody.'"

Kochhar convened her top team every morning and evening to transform how she and her senior bankers conducted business with major clients. Rather than waiting for customers to make a specific request and then responding with a product offering, the bank identified which clients most likely needed what products, and then preemptively proposed an appropriate set of products. "Instead of sitting at our desks and waiting for clients to come and ask for products," Kochhar said, "we had to get out there and market the products to our clients."

After this success, Kochhar took a leap of faith when she joined ICICI's retail banking sector. At the time, she was running the corporate business division that was responsible for almost half of the bank's profits and assets; consumer credit was then less than 1 percent of the firm's revenue. Not surprisingly, when CEO Kamath asked her to take it over, Kochhar initially balked. "Why should I move from handling 50 percent of the bank to handling 1 percent of the bank?" she asked. In his characteristic way of foreseeing a robust opportunity even without a sure way to exploit it, Kamath responded, "Because I want you to make this business more than 50 percent of the bank."

Into the Unknown

ICICI's Kochhar-led entry into retail banking was itself uncharted territory. The "consumer-credit market was very, very new for India and for ICICI," she recalled. "I was trying to create something that was not just new for me but absolutely unknown to the organization and the country as a whole."

Fortunately, it turned out that retail banking required a skill that Kochhar had developed: a personal process of learning to lead by doing. When ICICI finally entered the retail banking industry in 2000—offering automobile, two-wheeler, and commercial vehicle loans, along with home financing and credit cards—the market was still modest, but the bank was betting it would soon explode. "Let's plan not for the small size the industry is today," Kochhar thought, but "for what the industry is going to be five years from now." Kochhar estimated that as India's annual per capita income rose above $500, substantial numbers of consumers would begin to spend and borrow, and retail banking did indeed expand as anticipated, growing by more than 50 percent per year during the mid-2000s.

To take advantage of this future market, Kochhar developed her leadership cadre from the outside. "I had to create a team of people who had worked in this industry for other banks. What I brought to that team was ICICI's strategic thinking, but when it came to domain knowledge or product nuances, I had to learn from the team. In that way, I was a kind of a leadership bridge between ICICI's way of thinking on the one hand and the domain knowledge of the team on the other hand. I had to arrive at decisions not based on past experience, but on a mix of their domain knowledge and my gut feel."

When Kochhar began her mission, the entire country had fewer than three hundred ATMs, but on the premise that success in retail banking depended on scale economies, ICICI opted to set up three thousand ATMs over the next two years (and now supports some four thousand, one of the largest networks in Indian banking). "This was a big decision," recalled Kochhar, "for which we had no past experience to tell us whether it was correct or not." It did prove correct, and within four years of entering the fray, the bank had moved from no share of a relatively small retail market to half of a substantial retail sector, making it the country's largest player in the burgeoning consumer-credit business.

Chanda Kochhar successively learned to lead within each of the bank's new areas of fast expansion. She did so through direct involvement, premised on a vision of rapidly ramping up a host of new products to transform ICICI from an industrial agency into a universal bank. Her approach entailed a combination of farsighted judgment about how that vision should translate within all of the markets, with an experimental approach to discovering what succeeded in each of them. "We need to start work with the idea that we're going to learn every day. I learn, even at my position, every single day. Whenever there's a challenge, I see an opportunity in it: you have to find a way of converting challenges into opportunities. That's the way one learns and moves forward."

A Team of Leaders

K. V. Kamath attributed his bank's trial-and-error expansion to the ready-to-learn quality among his top executives and their teams of managers. "If you look at what we have done in twelve years, and more so in the last five years, the cornerstone of whatever success we have had is people." The people whom he had in place or put in place during the late 1990s after his return from East Asia were the "talent that built the bank." Even though at the time they did "not possess any of the core skills required to build or run a commercial bank," they brought broad qualities to their jobs: intellect, entrepreneurship, resilience, adaptability, and a capacity to master what they must.

Placing significant resources in the hands of little-tested people meant, in essence, working without a safety net, but Kamath felt that he had no alternative since the country had virtually no bankers experienced in the areas he was seeking to build. "In hindsight," he admitted, "it is now clear to me that we took a huge risk."

The risks were doubled, at least, by the low-operating-cost model that rural banking in India required. Whereas a typical deposit in the West might be $10,000, a typical deposit in urban India was apt to be no more than $1,000—and in rural India only a tenth of that. That meant operating expenses had to be pared down proportionately: urban banking in India had to be conducted at one-tenth the cost of banking in the West, and rural banking at one-hundredth.

"We need to be able to conceptualize how to deliver value to this market at an extremely low cost," Kamath said. "That's where the challenge is, as well as the opportunity and the excitement."

Here, too, Kamath and his top team knew that they would have to invent their way forward if they were to successfully bank millions of unbanked villagers. A scaled-down urban branch model was still prohibitively expensive, so Kamath and his team turned to alternative, far less costly avenues for reaching the poor, ranging from nonprofit microfinance groups to local fertilizer distributors. Kamath was confident that his team could learn to profitably reach millions of poor customers through partnerships with a host of very low-cost, on-the-ground networks that already cut across rural India. "If we can do this—and we are fairly sure that we can—I think the rewards could be enormous."

In selecting people such as Chanda Kochhar for leadership roles in such a risky environment, Kamath had drawn on five criteria:

First, I look for intellect or a high level of competence. Second, I seek out entrepreneurial leaders who have the ability to pick the right people. That means looking at how the person has performed in other contexts to build teams. People who have the ability to build and manage teams are very valuable. Third, the person must have a can-do attitude. What sort of reaction do you get when you talk to him or her about a challenge? Will he go for it or is it a problem? Fourth, the right people have the ability to withstand shocks without getting flustered or losing direction. Finally, whether this is an entrepreneurial quality or not, it is an important quality that I look for in people whom we pick as leaders: the ability to focus, focus, focus without getting diverted from the core business, and to correct your course when things start going offtrack. In executing any strategy, whether you are setting up a new business unit or trying to reach profit or budget targets, things never happen quite the way your models may have predicted. That is why you need the ability to correct your course as you go along.

For all this to cohere, the company's vision and values proved the essential glue. "I think for me really the key is keeping the organizational culture right," said Kamath. When asked what he would view as his most important advice to a successor, he said, "Make sure that the DNA of the organization is what it is, or if you think that it needs to be corrected, articulate it very clearly to make sure that it happens." A central feature of the bank's cultural DNA was the defining concept of entrepreneurship. "The key challenge is to look to new horizons," offered Kamath. "Our growth so far has been based on our ability to identify opportunity horizons very early and build businesses to scale those horizons."

Witness, for example, the determination of K. V. Kamath to have his bank, ICICI, India's largest privately owned financial institution, join the ranks of international behemoths like Citigroup, Deutsche Bank, and Bank of Tokyo-Mitsubishi UFJ. "If there ever be an Ivy League of global banks," Kamath said in early 2008, "in five to ten years we have to have a few banks from China and a few from India in that league." His bank, he assured us, would count among them.[18]

A New Chief Executive

The unique Indian approach to achieving that growth was also evident in the way Kamath, who stepped down as ICICI chief executive in May 2009, went about choosing his own successor. Among the rumored possibilities was Aditya Puri, the widely respected managing director of archcompetitor HDFC Bank—a choice that would have been well in keeping with the U.S. model, where top talent tends to hopscotch among rivals (JPMorgan Chase CEO Jamie Dimon had previously worked at Citibank; the last CEO of Merrill Lynch had come up through Goldman Sachs). But as is common among India's leading enterprises, K. V. Kamath had been growing his own bench.

Kamath assigned a half-dozen high-potential managers to a series of varied and increasingly responsible jobs, and then he studied them as they prospered, and in some cases stumbled. He collected 360-degree feedback on their leadership qualities from twenty to twenty-five of each of their peers and subordinates and invited the best to take an active part in the bank's board meetings and to accompany him to the World Economic Forum in Davos, Switzerland. In the end, he and the board opted for a seasoned insider, chief financial officer Chanda Kochhar.[19]

Invented in India

In thinking about the differences between Indian business leadership and that in other major economies, we oddly found ourselves reflecting on cars: how American companies mass-produced automobiles while Toyota used lean manufacturing techniques. These distinct production models meant that businesses like General Motors and Ford Motor Company traditionally emphasized detailed divisions of labor; short-term relations with employees, suppliers, and customers; producing large numbers of standardized products with long product cycles; maintaining large inventories of parts for assemblage; and seeking to make a good, if not perfect, automobile. Toyota, by contrast, stressed teamwork, deep long-term relations with stakeholders, making customized products with short product cycles, maintaining minimal inventories and buffers, and pressing for continuous product improvement. These differences largely emerged from the distinct production challenges auto executives faced: capital was scarce in postwar Japan, so Toyota was forced to minimize its parts inventories, leading to its now-famous operating principle of seeing all buffers as waste.[20]

By the same token, many of the differences between American and Indian executives were not accidental but can be traced to the distinct circumstances confronting company leaders. Among them is an Indian market environment that has been both chaotic and replete with hidden opportunities; a licensing and regulatory regime that resisted and tested the mettle of all who sought to build private enterprise (American CEOs who complain about excessive U.S. regulation could hardly comprehend what doing business was like in

India prior to the 1991 reforms); and a traditional culture, rooted in Indian society, that places collective purpose above private gain.

Invented in Japan, Toyota's flexible manufacturing methods have been adopted by automakers around the world—from Ford to Porsche—and have proved useful in improving product quality and lowering cost internationally.[21] Similarly, though Indian business methods emerged as a logical product of the challenges their executives faced in an era of liberalization and growth, they are not necessarily limited to the Indian context. The India Way's distinct combination of vision and values, trial-and-error methods, and adaptability is likely to find application by those building and leading enterprises wherever there is a market for growth that rewards expansive thinking and personal resilience. What's more, Indian business leaders have consistently shown they share a drive to build and spread the model. Kushagra Bajaj, joint managing director of Bajaj Hindustan, the country's largest sugar and ethanol producer, said from his own experience that compared with large American companies like Wal-Mart and General Motors, Indian companies "have that fire in the belly" and we "have the desire to go and prove ourselves to the world."

Fully catching up with the West will require continued building on the India Way, said many of the executives, but also continued learning from all the world's different business ways. For Mukesh Ambani, that learning dated back some three decades to his 1979 entry into the Stanford MBA program. Despite reaching the number five spot on the 2008 *Forbes* magazine annual roster of the world's richest individuals, far outranking all American executives except Warren Buffett and Bill Gates, Ambani remained resolutely open to the best of what the West may still have to offer.[22] "Managers from India's private sector, multinational private sector, and the public sector are all learning from their counterparts from around the world," he said. "They're learning from experiences in different geographies and different sectors of the industry, and then applying them to the virgin opportunities that we have here" and abroad.

We will see whether executives elsewhere increasingly return the gaze, but we find it hard not to recommend that they do so. Of course, they should continue to draw on their own best methods—there is no reason to throw the baby out with the bathwater—but there is much to be learned from what executives in India have been inventing over the past two decades without anyone abroad quite noticing.

CHAPTER FIVE

Competitive Advantage

*Delivering the Creative Value
Proposition*

ONCE THE PRINCIPLES of people management and
executive leadership are in place and the workforce
and top team are prepared and engaged, the India Way points
toward building organizational architecture, company culture, and
fresh approaches to reaching customers into creative value propositions. Building on people management and executive leadership,
this chapter focuses on the distinctive ways in which Indian business leaders find competitive advantage and on how they succeed
through creative value propositions.

We often think of strategy formation in large U.S. corporations
as an analytical exercise, based on customer research, competitor
intelligence, industry analysis, and perceived or documented firm-
level advantage or disadvantage. The goal of a typical American

company is to find the attractive opportunities and then do what is necessary to acquire or cultivate those customers, restructuring the company if necessary to develop the products or services that customers want. Doing so requires a full-time staff devoted to finding and then targeting good opportunities.

A company's competitive strategy provides a kind of template for day-to-day business decisions but is not itself subject to short-term alteration. Carefully thought through—the raison d'être for high-end consulting firms like Bain, Booz & Co., and McKinsey—the template creates a framework for engaging in the market and guiding operational decisions. It sets forward a view on how best to compete over the next three, five, or even ten years. Indeed, competitive strategy is sometimes seen as defining the essence of what company leaders do, representing the unique value they bring to high office in return for significant compensation packages. And the unambiguous U.S. yardstick for defining successful strategy is how it translates into compelling financial results, the foundation for quarterly results and well beyond.

Being good at strategy and finance is thus a central foundation of American business leadership. Aspiring business leaders—our MBA students, for example—see strategy and finance as their ticket to the top. Over half (528 of 1,022) of the majors of the Wharton graduating MBA students in May 2008 were in strategic management or finance. After graduation, many were hoping to start at McKinsey for strategy, Goldman Sachs for finance, or their respective competitors—a career ladder that would lead to leadership roles overseeing strategy, finance, and a diverse array of other key company functions and operations, and finally to the top of the heap itself.[1]

Indian business leaders saw the situation quite differently, especially where strategy was concerned. They were not ready to farm out that role. Indeed, in response to our interview and survey queries, they reported that their most important personal priority was to remain the chief driver of their company's strategy. Such a statement sounds like a recipe for disaster. Who wants the head of a large corporation meddling in the technical details of a complex process under the direction of a professional staff? It also sounds like what one would see in smaller, start-up companies. Is this a residue, then, of a time when these business leaders, many of whom were company founders, were trying to run ever-larger and more complex corporations as if they were more intimate, entrepreneurial operations?

Perhaps that plays a minor role, but another interpretation is more consistent with what we heard from the Indian executives and other observers of Indian business. They told us that the process of creating strategy is different in these firms from what we are familiar with among American companies. Strategy in these Indian firms has an emphasis on the enduring capacities, architecture, and culture of their organizations. When these executives described their business plans to us, they generally characterized their intended strategies as based on long-term, stable competencies—required in part to respond to the intensifying competition from abroad.

Strategy in the India Way companies comes from competencies developed within the firm and is based on the operating principles we described in chapter 1: engaging the energy and commitment of employees, in part by having a social mission and purpose for the business; improvising and adapting to find ways around tough problems, illustrating the principle of *jugaad*; and coming up with creative value propositions to meet the persistent needs of long-term customers. Here we see how India Way companies turn those principles into strategies that give them a competitive advantage in the marketplace.

Assigning Priorities

Time might not be money, but its allocation tells a lot about what people value. We offered Indian business leaders a list of tasks typically considered important for top executives, and asked them to rank the tasks in relative importance based on how much time they devoted to each. The rankings by Indian business leaders are shown

TABLE 5-1

Indian business leaders' priorities

1. Chief input for business strategy
2. Keeper of organizational culture
3. Guide or teacher for employees
4. Representative of owner and investor interests
5. Representative of other stakeholders (e.g., employees and the community)
6. Civic leadership within the business community
7. Civic leadership outside the business community

in table 5-1. We also asked the top human resource executives in the same companies to answer the identical question about their chief executives' priorities. Those answers were virtually identical; the only difference was an inversion of items 3 and 4 in table 5-1.

Strategy among the Indian corporations we examined was deeply rooted within the firms, supported by a set of attributes and practices that helped drive their strategies. Building strategy meant building these capabilities and stressing alignment within the organization, ensuring that many separate practices were consistent with one another and mutually reinforcing. In this context, being the "chief input into the strategy process" did not imply that the executives were meddling in a staff function. It suggested instead that they were monitoring and maintaining the infrastructure of their organization, the firm's architecture and culture.

The difference with Western, and particularly American, priorities is substantial. Chief executives in publicly held American companies usually hold maximization of shareholder value as their most important priority. Shareholders for Indian executives were almost always well down the list—below the company's customers, below the company's employees, and below the broader Indian society. No Indian business leaders in our conversations placed shareholder value as the top company priority or advanced the view that investors were the most important stakeholder, a notable omission given that many of executives were major holders of their company shares.

TABLE 5-2

Percentage of Indian business leaders identifying leadership capacities as critical

Question: "What are the top two leadership capacities most critical to your exercise of leadership over the past five years?"

Leadership capacities	Percentage of executives
Visioning capacities: articulating, envisioning, strategic thinking, change	61
Architecture and culture capacities: organizational structure, core values	43
Individual capacities: inspirational, accountable, entrepreneurial	57
Human capital capacities: talent selection, grooming, alignment	52
External capacities: understanding competitors and markets; outside relations	22

Note: Percentages do not add up to 100 because participants listed all the capacities they thought were most significant.

What the Indian business leaders were interested in, decidedly, was creating strategy. When we asked Indian business leaders to identify the two capacities that have been most critical to their exercise of leadership over the past five years (see table 5-2), they placed their greatest stress on four internal capacities—visioning, architecture and culture, personal qualities, and human resource issues. This suggested that the leadership capacities they saw as important were connected to the development of enduring capabilities for the future.

Organizational Architecture and Culture

Strategy can only be executed in a suitable organizational architecture and cultural context. The relationship between strategy and organizational architecture has been studied in detail in the United States context. In his 1962 classic of American business history,

Strategy and Structure, Alfred D. Chandler explored how large U.S. corporations had emerged during the twentieth century. Focusing in great detail on four icons in four industries—DuPont in chemicals, General Motors in autos, Standard Oil in petroleum, and Sears, Roebuck in retail—Chandler concluded that the rise of the corporate form could be traced to inventive strategies and well-aligned corresponding structures. Leaders of the big four had adopted a clear and comprehensive business strategy and fashioned a customized organizational architecture to support it. That formulation remained much the American business hymnal for the remainder of the twentieth century and even the start of this century.[2]

Strategy drives structure, in Chandler's formulation, and the Indian business leaders we interviewed were in wholehearted agreement. But for achieving their strategy, they viewed two key components of structure—the organization's architecture and its culture—as vital foundations to be created, built, nurtured, and certainly not taken for granted. Many of these leaders spoke from long and arduous personal experience: they had been forced to create organizational architecture and culture out of whole cloth because so many of the fledgling businesses they launched or acquired initially had so little of either.

For executives working at well-established American firms, the divisions and layers and mind-sets that they inherited on joining the company had been fashioned years or even decades earlier. The health-products company Johnson & Johnson, for instance, dates to 1887. Its well-known "credo," a 303-word statement that has helped define company culture since being crafted in 1943 by founding-family descendent Robert Wood Johnson, is carved in granite at company headquarters, as Abraham Lincoln's 273-word Gettysburg Address is carved in marble on the Lincoln Memorial. And just as young Americans are sometimes called upon to memorize the Gettysburg Address—or feel impelled to do so—so new Johnson & Johnson employees master the credo.

Though Indian civilization is ancient—the Indus Valley Civilization dates back to 2600 BC—few of India's biggest companies carry a century-old lineage like Johnson & Johnson, General Electric, or J. P. Morgan. Indeed, of the dozen largest Indian companies, as measured by the *Forbes* Global 2000 Ranking for 2007, only two—the State Bank of India (1806) and Tata Steel (1907)—have ancestries that predate independence from Great Britain. The thirty-four largest Indian companies on the *Forbes* annual list have a median founding year of 1955, compared with 1888 for the thirty-four largest U.S. companies.

Especially in the technological fields, many Indian firms are so new that their founding figures are still the presiding executives, and they have had to invent their own architecture and culture along the way. That required extra work, but as we saw in earlier chapters, it also liberated Indian business leaders in many cases from the burdens of legacy structures, whether in personnel practices or in the company pyramid, though it should be noted that state-owned companies and some in the extractive sector did carry forward preexisting structures and union histories. But in less than two decades of economic liberalization, many Indian firms have had to invent their own new structures to work with their fresh ways of creating value.

Freed of the need to accommodate new conditions to old structures, companies were able to evolve organization and strategy as conditions dictated. This was especially valuable for some of India's most rapidly growing companies in newer industries: Wipro, for example, with a workforce of more than 72,000 in 2008, up from 14,000 in 2002 (greater by a multiple of 5.1); Bharti Airtel with 25,000 workers, up from 3,400 in 2002 (a multiple of 7.4); and Infosys with 94,000, up 10,700 in 2002 (a multiple of 8.8). Even some traditional manufacturers had displayed pronounced employee growth. Tata Steel employed 84,500 in 2008, nearly twice its workforce of 46,350 only six years earlier, at a time when the steel industry in most countries had been in sharp decline. In most cases, organizational architecture and company culture—far from being drags on growth (as per American giants like General Motors)—had come to be deemed *the* vehicles through which their leadership of and strategy for their fast-expanding firms could be extended and exercised.

A Committed Top Tier

Indian business leaders viewed building their top tier of managers as the single most important component of company architecture. A set of able, energetic direct reports was viewed as key, and most important of all was a commitment to the company's vision and strategy.

Executive chairman Mukesh Ambani of Reliance Industries said that building a "transformational business model" was the first step in structuring his organization, but with that in place, "aligning the leadership team to have loyalty to the vision is the next step." It was "very important," he explained, "that everybody understands the execution pieces and stays on the same page. Especially in a fast-growth economy like India, where talent has huge amounts of opportunity, it is important that we create loyalty to the cause." And then he added a thought rarely heard among western CEOs but commonly expressed within his Indian peer group: "For us, it has always been that the cause is much greater than making pure financial returns."

Once the top team was in place, business leaders emphasized the importance of pinpointing responsibilities, providing the resources to perform, and then holding team members responsible for results without micromanaging the process. For S. Ramadorai, managing director and chief executive officer of Tata Consultancy Services Ltd., for instance, empowering his staff has been vital to aggressively growing his company. A. K. Balyan, executive director of Oil and Natural Gas Corporation, reported that as a result of the "highly decentralized decision-making" pyramid that he had created, his "key executives have to function as virtual CEOs of their divisions." Fewer decisions come up to the chief executive since key executives take on their own decisions and are empowered to make them.

No Risk, No Reward

If product and service decisions were certain and risk-free, there would be no errors, but since the tumultuous Indian environment was anything but certain, Indian business leaders "have a much higher capacity to handle ambiguity in business situations," in the words of Motor Industries Company Ltd.'s (MICO) M. Lakshminarayan, and thus "are very, very flexible in handling" problems.

The executive chairman of Shree Cement, B. G. Bangur, told us he considered creativity so critical to his company's competitiveness that he had been explicitly working to ensure that his managers were comfortable with a certain error rate in their decisions. "If managers feel that failures will be a blot on their career, then most of the [innovative] projects die down because they want a very high rate of success." In "our company we are saying that innovativeness in itself is success, whether you proceed and the project succeeds or not." When a new project does not pan out, he said, "we never say it is a failure. We still say that we have learned one more way how the things will not work, and start all over again."

For Zee Entertainment's Subhash Chandra, decentralization of decision making and a tolerance for decision error had become building blocks of his company's culture. "So far we have been a very entrepreneurial group in which we did not have the corporate hierarchy or divisions or that kind of a thing," he said. Managers are encouraged to call executives for decision approval in the middle of the night, but they are also "encouraged to take decisions by themselves, without any kind" of formal authorization. That has been "the competitive advantage of our building the business so far," Chandra said. When managers make a decision "that has resulted in losses, they have never been punished or asked to leave the job." But, he added, "We do say, 'Hey, don't repeat the same mistake.'"

Pushing Decisions to the Front Lines

At some companies, tolerating errors in the name of risk taking was coupled with an architecture that pushed decisions out from under the shadow of headquarters, right into the hands of frontline employees. Nakul Anand—chief executive for the Hotels Division of ITC Ltd., one of India's largest conglomerates, with interests in food, agriculture, and tobacco—had come up through the organization and knew from personal experience how stultifying the hierarchy can appear from below. His aim as division chief, he said, "had been really to make headquarters not a control body but the 'help desk' because the biggest competitive advantage are the ideas that flow from the field."

Ajai Chowdhry, executive chairman of HCL Infosystems, India's largest personal computer maker, likewise looked to his operating units for the formulation of competitive ideas. At monthly meetings of the heads of all the HCL businesses, Chowdhry observed, "we don't discuss numbers, but we discuss breakthrough objectives." For such meetings, he said, "each and every part of the business is encouraged to come up with its own new breakthrough objectives and strategies for this year and the next three to five years." Kiran Mazumdar-Shaw, chairman and managing director of India's first biotechnology start-up, Biocon, had built risk taking into her company's culture through her own modeling—consistently pursuing biotechnology commercialization opportunities that looked exciting but also very risky.

From Risk to Speed

When uncertainty is high and risks abound, decision making can slow down due to fear of irreparable errors or career-ending blunders. To balance out that equation, several companies stressed the importance of timeliness in decision making. In the words of Anil Khandelwal, chairman and managing director of Bank of Baroda, "I think speed itself is a competitive advantage because I am competing with twenty-seven public-sector banks. Speed *should* become a competitive advantage—my capacity to do things faster, to execute faster, to come out with new products faster."

The delegation of authority, devolution of responsibility, tolerance of errors—all built into a culture of frontline risk taking and innovation—brought disadvantages too, many of the Indian executives warned. Managers in such a regime acquire a built-in permission to make decisions that might not be fully in compliance with the company center, and inept or rogue managers can make a mess of things. On balance, though, most of the Indian business leaders had concluded that the decentralization of decision-making authority had become an essential foundation for making risky decisions in India's inevitably unpredictable and fast-changing environment—a step, we should note, that is becoming the global norm in a flattened and competitive marketplace. Rather than India's business norms converging on traditional Western standards, odds are that Indian methods are already where the world is now heading.

Customer Centricity, Indian-Style

Like their Western counterparts, Indian business leaders talked of a laserlike focus on customers, but with a subtle national twist. Traditionally, market-driven business strategy relies on research to identify the best customers who offer the highest profit margins, and the goal of companies is to move in that direction. The India Way companies took a very different approach. In many firms, leaders relied instead on their company's culture to focus employee attention on customer service.

Consider, for example, the experience of Kishore Biyani, managing director of Pantaloon, India's largest retailer, with more than a thousand stores across the country. The culture at Pantaloon asked all employees to put themselves in the shoes of grassroots customers and imagine the company and the shopping experience from their perspective, not just as potential buyers but as potential *Indian* buyers.

"Our biggest competitive advantage," he said, "is our sense of Indianness in whatever we do, because we believe in India as a very different country, emerging in a different era." He sought to foster "everyone's ability to think as a customer at the caste and the community level." The practical result had been to develop retail outlets (under names like Blue Sky, aLL, and Top 10) and products that were closely tuned to the interests of various segments of Indian customers and unlike the merchandising of their international competitors. Pantaloon worked "on the Indian ethos and Indian values," he concluded, "and all our promotions are very Indian-like."

Biyani's emphasis on tailoring company culture to a specifically Indian market might seem like nothing more than an old chestnut—Who is against fostering company culture? Who does not want to meet their customers where they live?—but once again, the difference is a matter of degree, not kind, and it emerged as one of the more striking thematic differences.

Moving Sideways

The intense focus on customers carries a corollary. A company's direction is set as much by what works with customers as by a preexisting strategy for what should work. Rather than moving linearly forward, then, many of the executives reported that they move more sideways. ICICI Bank's deputy managing director, Nachiket Mor, expressed the concept well. "We are not great strategists," Mor offered bluntly. "If you were to ask me, did we know in 1996 what we were going to do in 2006, I would say we hadn't a clue. With hindsight we could always construct a story, but by foresight we hadn't a clue. And if you were to ask me where we are going to be in 2016, other than describing it in kind of general terms of asset size and capital base and all of that, I wouldn't be able to give you a more precise answer."

Indeed, ICICI's trial-and-error approach isn't the sort of strategy a traditional consulting team is likely to recommend. Rather than moving linearly toward a preordained set of objectives, the bank has sidled into adjacencies where opportunities seemed to open. For that, ICICI needed more than a grandiose business plan; it required executives who could see and then seize those possibilities. The big objectives of fast growth and full services were clear; getting there was anything but.

Strategic planning for a distant future was sure to be quickly outdated by the market's rapid progression, Mor explained. In "complex environments like India, where you know the environment changes fairly dramatically and fairly quickly," there's little benefit to "extremely long-term thinking." His time frames for building and judging company programs ranged from three to six months, not twelve to eighteen. "The animal I like to compare ourselves with is more like a crab rather than a tiger or a leopard that moves quickly towards a very prespecified destination. We move sideways because the environment is too uncertain; it evolves too rapidly." The bank did not spend much time, he said, "agonizing about core competency and what is the purpose of our business," but it moved instead to simply and quickly "seize the opportunity." The sideways movement was a product of necessity. "If you try to build a long-term plan around a certain model of the customer," he warned from experience, "it is possible it could be completely wrong."

The bank's mind-set and pay scheme reinforced this thinking through an internal rewards system "geared towards people who can quickly spot immediate opportunities and capitalize on them. There aren't a lot of rewards for people who do long-term strategic thinking. We are just much more short-term people."

Given twenty potential initiatives for ICICI, Mor would try all twenty rather than bet on what seemed the best two or three. His preference was to "fail fast" and discover through trial and error what succeeded, logic Mor put to work in building a microfinance capacity for the bank. The plan was to expand rapidly—from 20,000 clients to 4 million clients and from a million dollars lending to a billion dollars in only three years. Mor tried a host of tactics at the same time: opening branches, partnering with nonprofit organizations, even buying another bank. Since most of the clients were borrowing for the first time, he had "no idea what they would do when given the money"—whether, for example, they would want health insurance or need rainfall guarantees. In general, he observed, it was "completely unknown territory."

Not knowing precisely what the microfinance customers really needed, Mor sought to create a bank presence no more than 10 kilometers from any rural customer. Poor decisions were made, but they tended to be tactical errors. "There are clearly things that we did wrong," Mor told us, "because we focused on what we saw rather than on what we might have seen." At the same time, investors were relatively unconcerned about the sideways approach, giving the bank leeway that would be rare in the United States. Both domestic holders and international funds sought to understand how the top management team, and the CEO in particular, operated, but the lack of a specific strategy or a long-term plan did not seem a vexing concern for investors so long as they heard a company story that made sense and produced year-on-year double-digit growth. Much the same had been true of the bank's relationship with its regulators.

Unlike in American management models, product decisions may have been opportunistic, but continuity was built into enduring relationships among ICICI executives. "American companies don't really have long-term executives," Nachiket Mor told us. As a result, "relationships with their own company, and therefore with the rest of the world, seem very transactional, very much day to day." By contrast, in India, "we are going to be dealing with [the same] person for the next ten years, so no conversation is just one conversation." Consequently, in dealing with a subordinate, colleague, or superior, personal anger and harsh language are best avoided, as are any actions that can cause humiliation or a loss of face. And indeed, long-term supportive and trusting relationships among the bank's executives have proved an essential ingredient to its sideways strategy.

Innovative Structure and Strategy

Taken together, organizational architecture, company culture, and competitive strategy lie at the operational heart of the India Way. And they do so in ways and combinations that creatively respond to the market conditions and opportunities at home and abroad.

In some industries, such as information technology services, Indian firms created competitive organizations with operations based in both India and the countries of their customers. Firms such as Infosys, Wipro, and Cognizant Technology Solutions Corporation emerged as global organizations that happened to originate in India. In wireless telephone services, several Indian firms leapfrogged several generations of technology to adopt the latest mobile telephony and designed lean organizations to provide quality service at far lower costs than their counterparts in developed countries. Innovative mobile-phone firms such as Bharti Airtel and Reliance Infocom, though largely focused on the Indian market at the outset, invented new strategies that could work for companies in any geographic setting. Although Bharti Airtel was an early mover into mobile telephony, it was a later entrant, Reliance Infocomm (now Reliance Communications) that revolutionized the mobile telephony market by investing in a new network and bringing down the price of a local call to "less than what it cost to send a postcard," the exhortation of Dhirubhai Ambani to his sons Mukesh and Anil. Bharti Airtel and others had no choice but to respond, and the low-cost mobile market in India took off. Still another set of firms found ways to service the needs of the vast Indian market by capitalizing on low-cost production and catering to the specific needs of underserved domestic groups. As noted earlier, Tata Motors developed a "people's car" with very high fuel efficiency and extremely low cost to reach the subcontinent's millions of motorcycle, scooter, and bicycle riders.

To appreciate the innovative combinations of strategies and structures among the companies led by those we interviewed, we focus on three pioneering approaches: Bharti Airtel's groundbreaking reverse outsourcing of its mobile-telephone network; Cognizant's development of information technology services with an onshore quality and offshore price; and Hindustan Unilever's adoption of rural self-help groups to promote fast-moving consumer products in the countryside.

The three company studies below each illustrate how strategy comes from the principal practices of the India Way described in chapter 1: Bharti Airtel illustrates improvisation and adaptability, Cognizant demonstrates the importance of creative value propositions, and Hindustan Unilever shows the role of mission and purpose.

Bharti Airtel: Reverse Outsourcing for Scale and for Speed

If America's perception of Indian business is defined by any single image, it surely is of rows upon rows of young Indians populating customer call centers in Bangalore and elsewhere in the subcontinent under contract with American companies, including some of the great technology names such as Apple, Dell, IBM, Intel, and Microsoft.

The 2006 U.S. film *Outsourced* opened with the manager of a Seattle-based call center learning that his entire order-fulfillment department was being outsourced to India. Adding insult to injury, the newly displaced manager was asked to visit India to help the replacement operation get on its feet. Indeed, American business outsourcing to India—now well beyond call centers, to encompass architectural drawings, legal briefs, equity analysis, even medical diagnosis—has been a growing feature of cross-border business for more than a decade.

In 2004, though, Bharti Airtel turned that pattern around—via what the *Wall Street Journal* termed *reverse outsourcing*—to solve an architectural problem occasioned by its explosive growth.[3] Sunil Bharti Mittal founded Bharti Telecom Ltd. in 1996 and later renamed it Bharti Airtel. He and his company caught the wireless wave in the early part of the decade and rode it to become the country's largest telecom-service provider, with 75 million customers by late 2008—and an expected 125 million by 2010. Along the way, however, Sunil Mittal concluded that he simply could not ramp up the organization fast enough to meet its accelerating customer demand. Nor did he feel that, as a "very, very hands-on" manager, he would be able to effectively lead a far larger enterprise properly. At the same time, Mittal was facing formidable competition from archrival Reliance Infocom. His solution to surviving the multipronged challenges facing his company: concentrate on the top line, act fast to secure an early-mover advantage, and swallow the risks that always come with speed.

"One of the burning things in my story has been [to grow] the top line as fast as you can," he said. "I have always believed that bottom line will come if there is a top line." As a result, "speed and always speed has been what we have done: launch things in the marketplace, get ahead of competitors, be there, get the market share, get top line." Moreover, "given that we had very limited resources, we did not have the luxury to spend too much time on the drawing boards and fine-tuning what we were doing." If "you are caught between speed and perfection," Mittal urged his managers, often to their surprise, "always choose speed." Manoj Kohli, who became Airtel's CEO in 2007, added, "We will always be a start-up venture in our mind in terms of our hunger [and] passion to win in terms of agility."

Winning by Losing

To achieve both scale and speed, Mittal shocked the telecommunications industry in 2004 by farming out the operation of his entire phone network in a $400 million contract to Ericsson, Nokia, and Siemens. He would no longer have to acquire and maintain equipment. He would instead simply pay a lump sum to the European vendors, according to the traffic they handled and the quality they provided. He also contracted out most of Bharti Airtel's information technology services, ranging from customer billing to the company's own intranet, in a $750 million deal with IBM. So comprehensive was the outsourcing that it left virtually no IT staff on Bharti Airtel's payroll—though information technology is the very foundation of wireless telephony—and even Mittal's own desktop computer was given over to IBM management.

Mittal appreciated the risk in outsourcing his firm's core capabilities to larger and more powerful multinational companies. But he viewed the contracting firms as "the Rolls-Royces of the industry," and in any case he had signed outsourcing contracts for renewable two-year periods with exit clauses if the providers ever turned "rogue." He also concluded that the forecast growth of Bharti Airtel's subscriber base was so great that the incentives for Nokia and IBM to continue their mutually advantageous relationship with Bharti would outweigh any temptation to exploit Bharti Airtel by withholding new equipment or ratcheting up fees.

Mittal also met directly with the IBM chief executive because of the risks involved, and the IBM CEO assured Mittal that he would personally monitor the project. Our "partners are actually a very, very important part of our future," Manoj Kohli said, and "therefore being respectful of them, being transparent with our dealings" with them, "and of course having full faith in them is important." The new arrangement also required fast creation of a capacity to both oversee and collaborate with their partners, which Kohli frankly admitted they did not have at the outset.

Radical Outsourcing

Beyond doubt, Bharti Airtel's outsourcing moves defied conventional logic. Since core competencies are widely viewed as the value drivers of a firm, peripheral functions ranging from property management to employee benefits—so goes the reasoning—could, and should, be handed over to other firms for which such functions are *their* core competencies. But in outsourcing its telephone network and customer infrastructures, Mittal appeared to be placing Bharti Airtel's value drivers outside the company. "People gasped in horror," he told a reporter. "I got calls from around the world saying, 'You've gone nuts! This is the lifeline of your business, something you can't afford to lose!' "[4]

A major European CEO telephoned Mittal to warn, "You're giving your life, the very heart of your business, into the hands of outsiders. You'll regret this because nobody has ever done it and nobody will ever do it." In response, Mittal noted that, while Bharti

Airtel so far had hired only 237 people into its information technology operation, the company of the caller employed 8,000. Mittal suggested to the European executive that his 8,000 staffers would never allow him to outsource his IT function even if he wanted to do so later on. But Mittal could still do so now given his far smaller number of IT staffers, and swift outsourcing was necessitated in any case, Mittal concluded, by the imperative of scale and speed.

Managing Rampant Growth

As Sunil Mittal explained to us, a key driver in his reverse outsourcing was the constrained human resource position in which the company found itself as it was rapidly ramping up. Bharti Airtel's initial "in-house" business model had been targeting 25 million customers, but after comparing his company's operations with the few companies worldwide that were already servicing 25 million customers, Mittal doubted he could build the structure fast enough to service that large a base.

"We clearly saw that the way we were structured and the way we operated would not allow us to satisfactorily come to that point." With few employees and a still modest user base, you could "practically run the company the way you wanted," he said, but hiring the 30,000 employees he estimated to be requisite for servicing 25 million customers required a far larger and more complex structure.

Even worse, Mittal anticipated reaching 75 million to 100 million users within several additional years. In some months, Bharti Airtel was already signing up a million or more customers. Airtel could not have hired, he concluded, the more than 10,000 required employees technically trained in network and information technologies and then retain them, since other companies, like Infosys and Wipro, were also exploding in size and were often proving to be more attractive destinations for engineers than Bharti Airtel. After meeting with several large European mobile-phone companies, including Vodafone and T-Mobile, to learn how they operated, Mittal told a reporter, "I saw that these were huge companies, hugely resourced.

And it began to dawn on me: I have to be like them. But could I afford to be like them? Did we have the resources to do that? Were we the best company to attract that kind of talent? The answer, clearly, was no."[5]

Moreover, it had become a convention in the Indian telecom industry to build out 30 to 40 percent excess capacity on any new network to anticipate further short-term growth. Given its burgeoning scale, that meant that Bharti Airtel would have to spend another $300 million to $400 million over the next several years to create its extracapacity networks. Worse, Reliance Infocom, the brainchild of Anil Ambani, planned to enter the cellular market, and Mittal feared that it would choose to jump-start its services by offering extremely low rates that would have been "unthinkable" until then. Because such rock-bottom prices posed the potential of slowing or even shutting down Bharti Airtel, Mittal recalled, the possibility sent "shivers down the company's spine." Time was in short supply, too: "Given that we had about eighteen months to figure this out and compete with Reliance, we had no time to induct ten thousand people, train them, and make them think our way."

Innovating on the Value Chain

To compete on price, Bharti Airtel would have to ensure that its cost structure was held tight and would not inflate with customer growth. To compete on time, the company would also have to find some way of radically expanding in an extremely competitive labor market for telecom specialists. Thus, Mittal turned to reverse outsourcing to keep Airtel's up-front investments low, since he would not have to build more capacity than it needed at the moment, and to keep its recruitment at realistic levels, since it did not have to find the thousands of engineers who would otherwise be required. By circumventing capital spending and hiring constraints, Mittal found he could then focus the company on understanding customer preferences, regulatory barriers, and emerging markets, ranging from BlackBerry service to digital television.

FIGURE 5-1

Bharti Airtel annual revenue and number of employees, 2003–2008

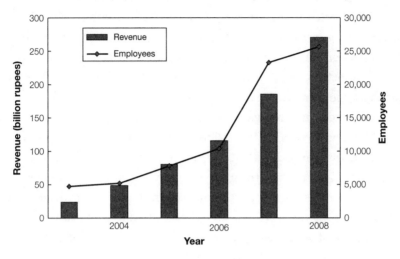

Source: Company records.

As shown in figure 5-1, the result borders on a miracle: the company slowed its own hiring without retarding its customer expansion, making it India's number one telecom provider by 2008, with more than 75 million customers, up from none a little more than a decade earlier. With revenues of $6 billion, Bharti Airtel had come to lead the pack in the Indian wireless industry, outselling its closest (and once feared) competitor, Reliance Infocom, by over 40 percent. Airtel alone accounted for more than 40 percent of the Indian wireless market share and nearly 60 percent of the market capitalization of the country's telecommunications service industry.

Improvisation and Adaptability

Bharti Airtel's massive reverse outsourcing brought another, more personal advantage, Sunil Mittal confessed. He and his brother, Rajan Mittal, also in top management, used to sit down during the company's annual budget review to decide how much to allocate to network and information technology. The "techies" already on board were "just making us look silly in those discussions because we were both incompetent to discuss those issues," Mittal said. Contracting with the outside parties eliminated the necessity of having to endure such an unhappy annual budgeting ritual. Even more important from his point of view, outsourcing meant he could still run the company in a hands-on fashion.

Unable to build an organizational structure of the usual kind that would properly service the strategy that he was bent on pursuing, Mittal transformed his strategy and organization, opting to create value and defeat rivals through company brand and customer relations rather than through his own technologies. Improvising and adapting along the way, he proved that sometimes structure is not determined by strategy, but quite the opposite, with organizational constraints resulting in a redefined strategy.

Cognizant: Creative Value Propositions for New Customer Segments

One of the more ironic claims of modern management is the solemn declaration that a company is about to become client focused or even customer centric. After all, are not companies *defined* by providing a service or product that clients and customers want and are willing to purchase? But the claim, of course, is a matter of degree and of company structure, whatever the strategy.

Consider Cognizant Technology Solutions Corporation. Initially created as a division of American parent Dun & Bradstreet (D&B) in 1994, Cognizant got on its own feet in 1998 with an initial public offering and a shot in the arm from a surge of Y2K work at the turn of the century. By 2008, this U.S.-listed and -headquartered company with a sizable Indian back-end operation supported mainframe computers and client servers at more than five hundred organizations worldwide in industries from banking and insurance to manufacturing and retail. Among its clients: Aetna, Citigroup, MCI, and RadioShack in the United States, and France Telecom, Nestlé, Nokia, and SAP in Europe.

Life, though, was not always so good. At the start of the decade, Cognizant faced a fiercely competitive global landscape. Some seven hundred Indian-based companies were providing information technology outsourcing services, many at rock-bottom prices. At the other end of the spectrum, the American "Big 5" system integrators—Accenture, BearingPoint, Capgemini Ernst & Young, Deloitte, and IBM Global Services—provided greater value-added services at higher prices. Lakshmi Narayanan, then chief operating officer of Cognizant and later chief executive, and Francisco D'Souza, a fellow executive and later also the CEO, opted to create a structure that in effect combined first-class service with rock-bottom fees. "We wanted to give the customer a Big 5 experience at an offshore price," explained D'Souza, an example of a creative value proposition that is at the heart of the India Way.[6]

Onshore Service, Offshore Cost

The first important decision Cognizant made was to steer away from acquiring new customers. The alternative strategy was to develop deeper relationships with fewer customers. To pursue that end, Cognizant converted the concept of global outsourcing into a combination of on-site service and international work. Cognizant jettisoned the conventional model of Indian IT outsourcers with headquarters in India and satellite offices near client locations in the United States and elsewhere. Instead, the company opted to be headquartered in New Jersey. Narayanan explained: "We felt that since there are a number of India-based companies who are providing these services, to differentiate ourselves we'll flip the model and be closer to the customers that we serve."

To reinforce the U.S.-centeredness, he listed the company on NASDAQ and hired many people in the United States. At the same time, he kept Cognizant an essentially Indian company, with the

FIGURE 5-2

Cognizant Technology Solutions Corporation, annual revenue and number of employees, 2000–2008

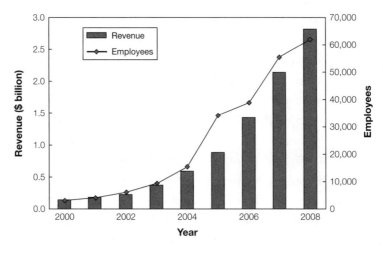

Source: Company records.

bulk of its software engineers and other employees still working on Indian pay scales. Of its 60,700 employees at the end of 2008, up from a handful in 2000, more than 70 percent were still based in India, including three-quarters of its engineers (see figure 5-2).

Compared with its Indian competitors, Cognizant's initial margins were thinner because it delivered more premium services, but over time that served to build enduring rather than spot relations with clients, relationships that in turn became a driver of sustained growth. Rapid expansion in turn became a magnet for quality talent. "When we go to market and hire talent," said Narayanan, we "emphasize that we are the fastest-growing company. 'If you come to our company, you will grow faster than anywhere else.'" The result, according to Narayanan: Cognizant was able to attract "the best and the brightest talent," and the superior talent meant superior service.

The Charlie's Angels *Dilemma*

Cognizant also devolved more power and responsibility into the hands of the managers who were geographically closest to its customers. This was required by the market, Narayanan explained, because sourcing projects was becoming more complex, requiring more sophisticated and responsive contracting managers who appreciated the industry's and clients' unique requirements. Still, most of the work was performed by employees in India, and that created a new challenge for the customer-facing on-site managers. The latter were increasingly working late into the night—India is ten and a half hours ahead of New York and thirteen and a half hours ahead of San Francisco—to resolve issues with the Indian-based bulk of their teams. "It was a little bit like *Charlie's Angels*" for the U.S.-based managers, recalled Francisco D'Souza. When "you wake up in the morning, a voice on the phone tells you what to do."[7]

To reduce the "Charlie's Angels" factor, the company created a new structure to bridge the time-geography divide, formally capturing what had already emerged informally. Cognizant instituted a "comanager" scheme in which two equally responsible managers led the sourcing team, one close to the customer and one close to the employees in India. Though separated by more than ten time zones, the comanagers were held equally to task for services results, customer satisfaction, and project revenue. The joint leadership deliberately ran against management orthodoxy positing that responsibility should be pinpointed in a single office, and Cognizant watched to make sure that the traditional tenets did not get in the way. With a new development office in Shanghai, the company even began experimenting with "three in a box" teams, with equally powerful managers at the client site, in India, and now in China as well.

At the same time, Cognizant sought to build a "global mind-set" throughout the company to support its international strategy, with new customers coming from outside India and the United States. "We changed the model," explained Narayanan. "We started expanding into Europe. One of the key things that we learned during our formative years working with D&B was to get a global mind-set," which required us "to think about people, to think about anything that we do from a global perspective and not specifically a U.S. perspective or an Indian perspective." To drive a broader perspective deep into Cognizant's makeup, the company recruited managers from many countries and assigned them to work in many other countries. In Narayanan's view, this became a key competitive advantage for the company.

Bringing the Board on Board

The company also built a culture that placed a premium on intense and enduring relations with customers. Part of that strategy involved turning away a certain number of prospective customers in favor of deepening partnerships with existing clients, and that in turn proved to be a platform for lateral expansion. "If you have delighted your customer, they will be willing to try you out in other areas, which means they will buy other service areas and other products that you produce," Narayanan told us. "Customers participating in industry seminars will say, 'We have succeeded in partnering with Cognizant, [and] I would encourage you to partner with Cognizant.'"

So strong had the culture become, that Cognizant's board of directors increasingly wanted to hear about customer satisfaction and retention rates rather than revenue growth and profit figures. The directors could see that those two parameters drove the firm's financials, and they sought to know more. As Narayanan told us, "We have a unique event every year [where] we review the strategy of the company, and the board invites certain customers to come and participate and give the board and the senior management team direct feedback. They spend some time exclusively with the board and tell us, should we continue on the strategy, [or] should we change the landscape?"

Cognizant's strategy drove its structure, but with a pioneering twist. Differentiating itself from both high-end outsourcing providers in the United States and low-end providers in India, it sought to combine high-end services with low-end costs, creating in the process an appealing value proposition. But to achieve that seemingly contradictory duality, it devised a bifurcated architecture that invested coequal authority in two managers, one outward facing and the other inward managing, and it instilled a culture that channeled energy in both directions. Together, they provided for an innovative way of creating value and "allowed us to extend the business model for the changing business environment," D'Souza concluded.[8]

Hindustan Unilever: Architectural Innovation and Creative Value Propositions

One of the unique aspects of the India Way has been the capacity of the nation's business leaders to find a competitive advantage where no one else was looking. They have often built and followed radically different structures and strategies than the Western norm, yet the practices that have flowed from those decisions have frequently proved applicable to business in other markets. Hindustan Unilever's Project Shakti, a system for selling products through rural self-help groups, is another case in point.

Out of the 4 billion people on the planet who make less than $2 a day, more than 750 million live in India, four-fifths of the populace.[9] The dominant assumption among large corporations is that the bulk of the India population has no purchasing power and thus does not represent a viable market. Although this assumption is largely incorrect, as C. K. Prahalad argues in *The Fortune at the Bottom of the Pyramid*, the problems of accessing this enormous but mostly latent customer base are still huge.[10] Nonetheless, this was the challenge Hindustan Unilever (HUL) took on with Project Shakti.

In one sense, it was only natural for the company to do so. Hindustan Unilever is well known in India for its leadership in rural marketing, and its legendary brands and products are featured regularly in case studies at Indian business schools. What's more, over the decades, HUL has not only greatly benefited from the economic expansion of India but also contributed considerably to the nation's development. HUL has consciously woven Indian policy imperatives into the company's strategies and operations, linking business interests with national interests. Doing so inevitably has caused the company to look past Western business models that use standard marketing and supply-chain practices. All that said, though, Project Shakti was a step beyond anything HUL had tried before.

Creative Value Propositions: Selling Beyond the Media's Reach

Manvinder Banga, the former chief executive of Hindustan Unilever, observed that one of the greatest challenges for selling in India is that the conventional media reaches only half the population, thus leaving more than 500 million people largely in the dark about a company's product or brand. The rural population is scattered in some 600,000 villages that are not connected to urban centers by newspapers, electronic media, rail, or even, in more than half the cases, by road. Consequently, companies that want to grow beyond urban and semiurban India to access rural customers have had to devise innovative ways to get their attention.

Enter Project Shakti, launched in 2000. (The name references strength, power, or empowerment in several Indian languages.) At the time, Hindustan Unilever was already engaged in price wars with Procter & Gamble in product markets such as fabric wash and personal care; the growth of urban markets was slowing; and the company realized that long-run survival would require opening new markets. To this end, it developed its Shakti initiative to reach fresh customers in the fast-moving consumer goods market where competition was most pitched. The concept was to draw upon women's self-help groups that had already been set up by various nongovernmental organizations and rural agencies in India. Typically comprising ten to fifteen women from a single village, these self-help groups operated as mutual thrift societies. They would combine small amounts of cash toward a common pool. Microcredit agencies such as rural development banks would then offer additional funds to finance approved microcommercial initiatives.

Hindustan Unilever built upon this infrastructure by offering entrepreneurial opportunities for group members to sell HUL products directly to fellow villagers. Shakti entrepreneurs would borrow money from their self-help groups, apply it to the purchase of HUL products, and then resell them to their neighbors. Because most of the women in the self-help groups had no prior sales or business experience, HUL hired rural-sales promoters to coach the nascent entrepreneurs. For the first several months, the Shakti villagers were rewarded with cash incentives for making a certain number of home sales calls, regardless of the amount actually sold. HUL also arranged for local banks to provide the Shakti groups with microcredit, with the proviso that the first installment toward repayment of loans did not begin immediately. The company also worked with local government departments to build acceptance of Shakti as an economic opportunity benefiting the entire community.

Broader Social Purpose and Business Growth

With Shakti, Hindustan Unilever sought to achieve its dual objectives of social impact and business growth. The self-help-group entrepreneurs worked as social influencers, increasing local awareness and changing attitudes toward usage of various products, mostly those targeted for women. At the same time, Shakti provided sustainable livelihood opportunities for the rural women. Hindustan Lever first piloted the project in fifty villages based in the state of Andhra Pradesh, and it has since extended Shakti to fourteen other states, with forty thousand new entrepreneurs as part of the program by the end of 2008. By 2010, the company planned to recruit more than a hundred thousand Shakti entrepreneurs covering five hundred thousand villages, touching the lives of more than 500 million people.

By devising a new and self-sustaining channel for reaching Indian countryside masses, Hindustan Unilever has been able to open a new market for its long-standing products. Again, a creative combination of a new structure with a fresh strategy allowed the company to achieve what conventional wisdom would have doubted. Just as with Bharti Airtel's reverse outsourcing, Hindustan Unilever's Project Shakti made the counterintuitive intuitive. And in doing so, it contributed to a mission far broader than simply its own bottom line, providing fresh livelihood to large numbers of underserved women in the countryside.

From Strategy and Structure to Competitive Advantage

The leaders of Bharti Airtel, Cognizant, and Hindustan Unilever combined innovative strategies and structures that generated creative value propositions and unique competitive advantages. In the case of Airtel, Sunil Mittal brought a vision of providing very low-cost telecommunication services to a very large population of customers. And his value proposition was that a cell-phone call should cost little more than one cent per minute—at a time when the lowest cost anywhere in the world was more than ten cents per minute.

Though Mittal's vision and value proposition were clear, he had no resources to build a structure to readily achieve them. This forced his radical rethinking of the capabilities of the firm and a transforming of the value chain. Instead of finding value in unique technologies, he would draw it from the customer interface. The resultant outsourcing of virtually all operations except marketing and customer contact proved an innovative model that yielded the lowest cost per minute for telephone service anywhere in the world. Airtel's archrival, Reliance Infocom, was also able to achieve very low-cost mobile services, and together, they pioneered a new, transformative way of doing business. This resulted in explosive growth in the use of cellular telephones, catapulting India into the second-largest market in the world, behind China, with almost 350 million subscribers.

The Cognizant strategy also represented the delivery of a vision in which clients would receive high-end services for low-end costs, and it achieved that through introduction of its comanagement organization and creation of a global mind-set. Other rising firms in information outsourcing, such as Infosys, Wipro, and Tata Consultancy, pursued similar ends, but each sought to do so through its own distinct architecture and culture. By inventing new ways for moving into high-end services at low-end costs, Cognizant and its Indian brethren were able to challenge well-established global firms such as Accenture and IBM.

Hindustan Unilever executed a strategy based on a vision of delivering products to traditionally underserved populations, those of modest or little income. Hindustan Unilever's Shakti project brought fast-moving consumer products to the rural poor through self-help village groups whose members would personally prosper from the process.

The common thread through all three companies' experience was a leadership vision that stressed enduring service to established customers and long-term gain by solving the challenges of reaching hard-to-reach customers. The companies also built organizational capabilities that went well beyond the simple exploitation of their firms' comparative advantage of low labor costs. Becoming competitive with large, seasoned firms based in advanced economies required the creation of a creative value proposition, innovation in the value chain, construction of appropriate architectural and cultural capabilities, and exploitation of distinctive aspects of the Indian environment.

Continued focus on the value proposition while building new capabilities—strategic use of technology, innovative architecture and culture, recruiting and developing talent—was not easy, and short-term results were often not quickly forthcoming. And here is where the distinctive holdings of Indian companies proved invaluable. A significant fraction of the ownership of these firms remained in the hands of the founding managers (as noted in the next chapter), and they were able to live with the trade-off of sacrificing

FIGURE 5-3

Drivers of company strategy and competitive advantage in India

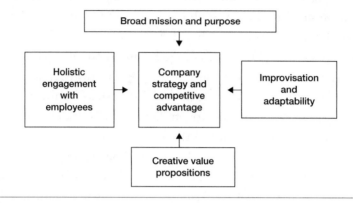

short-term profits to long-term gain more comfortably than were leaders of publicly traded firms in the West.

Figure 5-3 shows the forces and processes by which these and the other Indian executives whom we interviewed focused on building competitive advantage.

When we asked the Indian executives to identify key sources of competitive advantage in building their firms, their responses, displayed in table 5-3, pointed to the importance of three of the four major drivers of the India Way. Many of the business leaders stressed the importance of building their competitive advantage by combining several or all of these sources.

Adi Godrej, executive chairman of the Godrej Group, an industrial firm with interests ranging from precision equipment to food processing, explained that his company's growth came from a simultaneous use of several foundations of competitive advantage. His group had emphasized a value proposition in the form of branding, an innovative value chain in the use of advanced technologies, and capability building in terms of business processes that the group had, in Godrej's phrasing, "honed and developed over the years." The Godrej Group had earlier also benefited from joint

TABLE 5-3

Sources of competitive advantages reported by Indian business leaders

Question: "How have you built competitive advantage in your businesses?"

Source of advantage	Key elements	%
Holistic employee engagement	Transforming the organization; building the culture	28
	Talent development; building the top team	21
	R&D/technological innovation	19
Creative value propositions	Customer intimacy and focus	36
	Improved differentiation	24
	Outsourcing, building supplier base	23
	Efficiency seeking, cost reduction	23
	Innovative value chain	14
Broad mission and purpose	Vision, long term, transcendent	24
	Sharing corporate and groupwide resources	27

ventures with American companies such as General Electric, Procter & Gamble, and Sara Lee.

Similarly, Azim Premji, executive chairman of Wipro, reported that his company had focused on delivering high-quality processes and services. He had introduced the management method of Six Sigma, which applies detailed statistical methods to the identification and elimination of errors; but he had also emphasized acquiring and applying feedback from his customers. "Customers love us most for our humbleness," he said. "I believe, as a company, we listen carefully and are willing to learn." By combining capability building with Six Sigma and a value proposition with customer focus, Wipro under Azim Premji had become one of the country's leading technology-service firms, and a great personal and corporate success story. In 1964, at the age of twenty-one, Premji had taken over the small firm, then a vegetable oil producer, from his father. By the end of 2008, his company employed some 95,000 people in many countries.

Fresh Ideas, Long-Haul Thinking

Humility, innovation, counterintuitive thinking—none of them are guarantees of success, nor is present success a guarantee of future earnings. Circumstances change; operational steps have to be effectively executed. But when it comes to competitive advantage, large Indian companies are giving birth to fresh business ideas that combine a transcendent company vision, fresh value propositions for reaching new customers, innovative value chains for producing and distributing products and services, and a strong emphasis on building architectural and cultural capabilities for the long haul.

Like those in most national settings, Indian business leaders placed a premium on strategy. Yet they viewed strategy as a general set of enduring principles for competing, an approach to business that they deeply encoded in the architecture and culture of the company. Since so many of the executives had helped drive a meteoric growth in their firm—overseeing workforces at the time of our interviews that were sometimes larger by a factor of five or more, compared with those in the early part of the decade—they had come to view both architecture and culture as the necessary vehicles through which their leadership could be exercised and their strategy realized as their firms continued to expand.

The most important component of the architecture, the company executives said, was their top team, which they saw as an extension of their own leadership. The company culture constituted a further extension, allowing the executives to reach and align the thousands of employees on the payroll that they and their top team could no longer personally direct. Each company had developed its own unique blend of values and norms that defined its culture and its own unique way of organizing its work, but three distinctive themes in culture and organization stood out.

First, leaders emphasized a broader mission and purpose that enhanced both corporate agendas and development of the Indian market. Company leaders tended to downplay a focus on investors and shareholders, eschewing a short-term drive for quarterly results in favor of building innovative strategies and structures for longer-term growth, as evident in Hindustan Unilever's outreach to the rural countryside. Second, company executives brought substantial innovation to the value proposition, as seen in Cognizant's quality service at moderate cost. And third, the Indian business leaders emphasized holistic employee engagement with customers, a mind-set by which frontline employees would hear and provide what customers really sought, as shown by Bharti Airtel's placement of mobile phones at low prices into the hands of millions of new consumers. This is the India Way.

CHAPTER SIX

Company Governance

Fulfilling Broad Mission and Purpose

T HE GOVERNING BOARD of Western companies has traditionally been viewed as the owners' eyes and ears, ensuring that company executives take prudent risks to optimize investor value and engage in no self-serving behavior or malfeasance while doing so. But drawing on the broad sense of mission and purpose that defines the India Way, Indian directors have become more deeply engaged in guiding company directions with less of an eye or an ear on the shareholders and more of a concern for the community and the country.

The conventional American model of corporate governance is notable for its formal clarity and conceptual simplicity. Company directors are elected by the firm's stockholders—one share, one vote—to pursue and protect investor interests. Drawing on the principal-agent academic theory, directors are required to monitor the managers on behalf of the owners, but they are proscribed from managing the managers. The Business Roundtable, an association of the chief executives of America's largest firms, stipulated the behavioral path as clear as any. "The board of directors has the important role of overseeing management performance on behalf of shareholders," it declared; "directors are diligent monitors, but not managers, of business operations."[1] Directors are in the boardroom to keep executives' feet to the owners' fire, the American model asserts, and they must not become directly engaged in the company's business practices.[2]

The failures of Enron, WorldCom, Tyco, and other firms in 2001–2002 were partly attributed to the failure of their directors to even monitor their managers, let alone manage them.[3] In the wake of that evident malfunction, the U.S. government and the New York Stock Exchange sought to strengthen the monitoring function through the Sarbanes-Oxley Act of 2002 and new listing requirements in 2003. The first required that directors create an audit committee comprising independent nonexecutive directors; the second, that directors establish a compensation committee and a governance committee also composed of independent nonexecutive directors. Both initiatives tightened the definition of *independence*. The New York Stock Exchange further pushed for the creation of a "lead" independent nonexecutive director who would serve as a monitoring counterweight to the common American practices of fusing the roles of chief executive and board chair. The boards of virtually all major publicly traded American companies had by 2008, according to one annual survey, created the three stipulated committees of independent nonexecutive directors and appointed either a nonexecutive chair or an independent nonexecutive lead director.[4]

In theory, at least, these measures strengthened the monitoring hand of the board. Still, in 2009, the U.S. Securities and Exchange Commission (SEC) announced that it would investigate the governance failures at a host of financial institutions. Regardless of that outcome, the American model of independent, nonexecutive boards vigorously overseeing managers on behalf of shareholders has become not only a Wall Street convention but a global model, promoted heavily by international investors and multilateral institutions such as the World Bank and the Organization for Economic Co-operation and Development.[5]

Many countries, including India, have been swayed by that influence. The Indian counterpart to the U.S. Securities and Exchange Commission, the Securities and Exchange Board of India, commonly known as SEBI, promulgated a new set of rules in 2004 under the rubric of "Clause 49." Among the most important features was a requirement that closely reflected U.S. thinking: the number of independent nonexecutive directors should constitute at least half of the board. The implication for the oversight function was obvious: more independent nonexecutive directors would strengthen the monitoring of managers.

Riding the Tiger

As in the United States, India has had its share of monitoring failures in the wake of Clause 49, most notably in the case of Satyam Computer Services, the country's fourth-largest information technology outsourcing firm. Satyam's founder and chief executive, Ramalinga Raju, asked his board in December 2008 to approve a $1.6 billion acquisition of two other companies, and after some debate, the board unanimously supported the proposal. Institutional holders, however, revolted against the plan, dumping Satyam's stock in such a frenzy that the company lost half its market value in a single day's trading. Their complaint: the targeted companies were founded by the CEO's sons. Both firms carried the name Maytas—Satyam spelled backward—and both operated in the unrelated industries of infrastructure and real estate, building shipping ports and auto roads, not information highways. Chief executive Ramalinga Raju backed off from the acquisitions, but his reputation was fatally compromised, and several prominent nonexecutive directors resigned, their reputation for vigilance severely damaged.[6]

The story did not end there, though. Just three weeks later, Satyam's chief executive unloaded a far larger bombshell. In a January 7, 2009, letter to the Bombay Stock Exchange, Raju candidly admitted to phony accounting, inflated earnings, and a claim of more than $1.1 billion in cash, when in fact the company held just $66 million. "What started as a marginal gap between actual operating profit and the one reflected in the books of accounts continued to grow over the years," he explained, and then it "attained unmanageable proportions as the size of company operations grew." The gap between the real and the reported extended even to employment numbers: the company had publicly claimed that it employed 53,000, but the actual number evidently was some 10,000 less. In the end, said Raju, it was "like riding a tiger, not knowing how to get off without being eaten."[7]

Raju's disgrace and Satyam's fall were fittingly termed "India's Enron" by many observers. But as spectacular as the collapse was—on both the personal and the corporate fronts—it is more the exception than the rule. Malfeasance charges did not sweep across the Indian business landscape, and the obvious failure of the Satyam board to do even minimal monitoring did not emerge as the Indian norm. Moreover, as much of the developed world plunged into recession, Indian business remained relatively resilient. What some had deemed a liability—India's distinctive approach to governance—might have even proved an asset.

Ownership and Governance

Corporate governance in India differs substantially from that of the United States in the ownership structure of its firms, with many firms operating under the umbrella of business groups, and a significant number of infrastructure firms owned by the government. The roots of the distinctive way of Indian corporate governance can be traced in part to the very different ownership structures of its largest companies. Most were publicly traded, but the ownership of many remained concentrated in the promoter family's holdings.[8] While most large American firms had ownership profiles with a large number of institutional investors each holding a sliver of the firm's stock—which, taken together, constituted a substantial majority of shares—the ownership of large Indian companies generally fell into four distinct patterns.

A first group included publicly traded companies that had a majority share of their ownership in the hands of a business group, which was in turn controlled by a founding family. Among the most prominent of the business groups were those of Aditya Birla, Godrej, Anil Dhirubhai Ambani, Reliance Industries, and Tata. Most of these groups had established operating companies in disparate industries ranging from software and steel to retail and telecommunications.[9] A very few of America's more notable corporations fell in the general category of family control, often exercising authority through a separate class of stock, as at Ford Motor Company, The New York Times Company, and The Washington Post Company, but none of the American companies operated as a business group in the full Indian sense.

A second group of Indian companies consisted of stand-alone, publicly traded companies such as ICICI Bank—a model far more familiar to American investors. A third group was made up of what might become an increasingly familiar American type as global ownership spreads: publicly traded subsidiaries of multinational corporations, such as Hindustan Unilever. The fourth group, largely unfamiliar to those in Western settings until the financial crisis of 2008–2009, encompassed publicly traded but still largely government-owned companies, such as the State Bank of India, a legacy of the pre-1991 centrally planned economy.

Just as Indian companies differed in ownership structure from many American firms, so did they differ in how owners sought to exercise their rights. For the most part, the largest owners of America's premier corporations were institutional investors, whose holdings rarely exceeded 2 or 3 percent of total outstanding shares and who, in any event, had proved generally reluctant or unable to exercise their ownership rights.[10] Instead, the U.S. model was premised on an active market for corporate control that imposed an external discipline on the directors' monitoring of managers. Companies whose boards failed to fulfill their fiduciary duties found themselves subjected to unwanted takeovers in an active and independent equity market, and poor company governance was often punished by hostile acquisition or proxy battles to replace underperforming directors.[11]

Business-group companies constitute the dominant Indian form, as seen in figure 6-1, and they have often set up long-standing "shadow" boards comprising family-dominated operating committees. As one might expect, the role of the formally appointed boards of such companies was largely diminished in comparison to U.S. boards. Yet we found that whatever the ownership structure, Indian executives generally placed less weight on the board's monitoring

FIGURE 6-1

Ownership and control of 500 large Indian companies, 2006

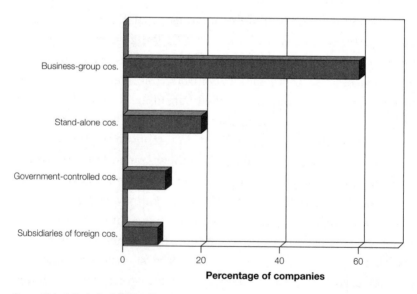

Source: Rajesh Chakrabarti, William Megginson, and Pradeep K. Yadav, "Corporate Governance in India," *Journal of Applied Corporate Finance* 20, no.1 (2008): 59–72.

function than was common in the West—at least in part because
Indian firms and their directors faced a less active market for corporate control than did their U.S. counterparts.[12] But to note that
Indian boards as a rule monitor less than American ones is not to
say that they have a less significant influence on the companies they
serve. In this as in so many other aspects of corporate life, the India
Way simply conceives of a director's role in more holistic terms.

Values-Based Governance

A first indicator of the distinct Indian governance path came when
we asked business leaders, "What are the two most distinctive
aspects of corporate governance practices in India compared to
the U.S.?" As seen in table 6-1, only a handful of the executives—
just six of the more than one hundred we interviewed—saw little
or no difference in the governance practices of the two countries.

TABLE 6-1

**Executives' perceptions of distinctive Indian corporate governance
practices compared with those prevalent in the United States**

*Question: "What are the two most distinctive aspects of corporate governance practices
in India compared to the United States?"*

Distinctive characteristics of Indian corporate governance practices	Percentage
In a state of transition	24
Product of India's regulatory regime	23
Related to family or promoter ownership	11
Lack of director independence	11
Lack of regulatory enforcement	8
Inconsistency across companies	6
Long-term focus (compared with short-term focus in the United States)	6
Importance of other stakeholders, such as employees and communities	6
Not much difference between India and the United States	6

Substantial numbers, by contrast, viewed Indian governance in a state of transition or as a distinctive product of the country's regulatory regime or ownership structure.

The transitional state of Indian governance was well captured by Rahul Bajaj, the chief executive of the Bajaj Group and chair of a committee established by the Confederation of Indian Industry in 1996 to propose governance guidelines.[13] "We are behind the U.S.," he observed, adding that Indian companies were still in the process of borrowing from abroad. At the same time, many of the companies were developing indigenous solutions to the challenges of effective governance in India, and a common theme in their solutions was an emphasis on what some have termed a *values-based governance system* in contrast to a *rules-based approach*.[14] The first is premised on a set of shared values and norms among directors, executives, and regulators on what constitutes good governance. The second is predicated on the assumption that common values and norms are not sufficient and specific rules are therefore required. American governance increasingly became more rules based in recent years, while India followed the values trail.

Compliance Versus Entrepreneurial Boards

The two approaches to governance were nicely delineated by Thomas Perkins, founder of the Silicon Valley venture capital firm Kleiner Perkins Caufield & Byers. A nonexecutive director of Hewlett-Packard from 2002 to 2006, Perkins resigned in protest over the board chair's handling of an investigation of unauthorized disclosures by board members. From that unhappy experience, Perkins drew a distinction between what he termed a *compliance board* and an *entrepreneurial board*. The former described the Hewlett-Packard board he had served on, while the latter should, in his view, characterize how boards actually operated. Directors serving on the first primarily saw their role as enforcing regulatory rules and strictly monitoring management. Directors serving on the second primarily viewed their role as a partnership with management to create new products and services.[15]

B. Muthuraman, the managing director of Tata Steel, drew a similar, sharp distinction between boards that focus on rules and those that focus on values. "The Tata Group is less rules based and more values based," he observed. "We have always believed you really cannot frame rules for corporate governance." Recognizing the inherent limitation of relying upon formal rules, he and other Tata executives and directors had thus opted for building the values-based model: "The spirit of corporate governance and the value systems" that they brought to the boardroom were far more critical for governance in the Tata Group, he said, than what he saw among American firms, where boards, in his own experience, were "less spirit based and far more procedural."

Nonexecutive directors in Indian boardrooms take up more of a strategic partnership role with company executives, akin to Perkins's role of working with management to create and market new products and services, and comparatively less of a shareholder-monitoring or rules-based role, in keeping with the American approach. Instead of functioning solely as the eyes, ears, and enforcers for absent owners, many directors had taken on the additional role of working with company executives to set the right direction for the company. Protecting shareholder value was not ignored, but Indian directors incorporated the concerns of a range of constituencies—just as Indian executives do—in reaching board decisions in partnership with management.

Socially Responsible Governance

The single most distinctive feature of corporate governance across the Indian companies we studied was this determination to balance the interests of the firm's diverse stakeholders, all the groups that have a claim on what the company does, including employees, customers, and community. What was especially striking was the emphasis on the broader community, which extended from the immediate vicinity of the business out to encompass the entire nation.

At an international forum in 2006, the chief executive of a well-known American corporation declared proudly that its headquarters happened to be in the United States, but since its manufacturing and sales were worldwide, he did not consider either his company or his leadership role as distinctly American. Few, if any, Indian executives and directors would wrap themselves in such a countryless banner. Though publicly traded and often global in operations, Indian companies were governed in ways that also pointed their decisions toward national purpose rather than eschewing it.

Consider the chairman of the Godrej Group, Adi Godrej. His group's governance, he baldly stated, was "directed towards the good of the company and not necessarily the good of one or the other of the shareholders." He added that the Securities and Exchange Board of India, the Indian equivalent of America's SEC, was properly concerned with protecting minority shareholders—those who were not part of the founding family or the primary owner—from exploitation by the dominant owners. But aside from meeting that obligation, the governing board's role was to optimize the company's success, broadly defined. "I think the most important thing in the Indian situation," he concluded, "is to ensure the corporate governance practices are directed towards the good of the company. If the corporate governance practices promote the good of the company, then all stakeholders benefit." In keeping with that sentiment, the Godrej Group had constructed schools, medical clinics, and living facilities for employees on a massive scale unknown among American companies, where directors and executives were far more likely to see employee welfare as a drag on shareholder value rather than an asset for company growth.

A Long Tradition of Social Engagement

The focus on social responsibility was particularly evident among promoter-led or family-owned businesses, some with social engagements dating back decades. Jamnalal Bajaj, the grandfather of Rahul Bajaj, chairman of the Bajaj Group, had served as a vigorous supporter of Mahatma Gandhi's movement for independence and an unswerving proponent of viewing business as devoted to a cause, not just the owner's enrichment. In the family memory of grandson Rahul Bajaj, Jamnalal Bajaj was known by Gandhi as the "merchant prince" for insisting that companies place honesty over profits and that they serve all parties to the enterprise, not just the owners.[16]

The predecessor of Tata Steel, the Tata Iron and Steel Company, had constructed an entire town in the state of Bihar, with schools, hospitals, roads, and other infrastructure around its steel-making facilities to create a fully supported living environment for its employees. As independent nonexecutive director of the Tata Group J. J. Irani put it, the firm has a responsibility to a triple bottom line that "constitutes its environmental obligation, its social responsibilities, and its financial bottom line."[17]

Even among Indian companies with little history, executives and directors pointed to the importance of serving the nation, not just the stockholders. Mallika Srinivasan, a director of Tractors and Farm Equipment Ltd., a Chennai-based manufacturer established in 1961 with annual revenue in 2008 of more than $750 million, spoke compellingly of the obligation of executives and directors to look well beyond shareholder value. Almost anywhere companies operated in India, she said, they were encircled by throngs of destitute people. Infosys, for example, maintained a first-world campuslike facility just feet from the impoverished masses of Bangalore, and the same for the surrounds of Tractors and Farm Equipment locations. Concerns about "corporate social responsibility and good governance are related to the state of development of the country," Srinivasan said. "We are seeing all these islands of prosperity surrounded by so much poverty." Social needs were stark, governmental interventions were inadequate for meeting them, and firms and their directors were thus duty-bound to step forward.

Doing Well by Doing Good

The focus on social responsibility transcended company self-interest, but executives and directors found material value in it nonetheless. The immediate costs were balanced by the promise of long-term financial advantage, a luxury that many American executives and directors had been unable to embrace, given the pressure from Wall Street for quarterly results.

Managing director B. Muthuraman of Tata Steel, for instance, saw his company's costly engagement in the community as a motivational benefit for the firm's eighty thousand employees. The Tata name, he said, had become a "very powerful brand," and it, along with the respect that the Tata Group had built in the broader community, had proved invaluable for recruiting and retaining employees at Tata Steel. Short-term a loss, but a long-term gain.

The Ambivalence of Governance

One of the prices of India's booming economy and increasing worldwide presence has been pressure to conform to global norms on multiple fronts, including corporate governance. Accordingly, SEBI moved in the direction of stronger rules for protecting shareholder rights. But the changes have not been entirely welcome. While Indian executives generally want to be viewed as world-class players, they are often reluctant to see their boards—and their businesses—become more rules oriented.

At the time of India's independence, four stock markets were already in operation, though their turnover was tiny by today's standards. Still, they had established listing and trading requirements, and subsequent legislation further strengthened shareholder protection and financial disclosure. The Companies Act of 1956, for example, held that a company's financial statements were the responsibility of the governing board, and it made directors accountable for ensuring that the company complied with contemporary accounting standards. But it was not until the reforms of 1991 that India moved toward formalization of its governance system. Driving the effort were both the need to attract foreign investment, which required even greater transparency in financial reporting, and the partial privatization of banking, which also placed a premium on reliable disclosure by borrowing firms. The rapid growth of companies in the wake of the reforms and their own burgeoning need for equity and debt added still another force for formalization.

Securities and Exchange Board of India

In 1992, at the outset of the reform movement, the government created the Securities and Exchange Board of India to oversee corporate governance and capital markets. Eight years later, in 2000, SEBI put forward a set of corporate governance guidelines that included specific requirements for board composition and the roles of the chief executive, board chair, and key committees. If the positions of the chief executive and board chair, for instance, were held by different individuals, at least 33 percent of the board must be independent nonexecutive directors; if the two roles were instead combined, at least half the board should consist of independent nonexecutive directors. The board's audit committee was to have at least three outside board members, all with financial experience and expertise. The rationale behind the reforms was straight from the rules-based view of governance. Strengthening the role of the nonexecutive independent directors would make for stronger monitoring of managers and better protection of shareholder rights.[18]

Since the strengthened governance provisions were added to the forty-ninth section of the Listing Agreement, it came to be known as Clause 49, and it specified a host of governance requirements, including disclosure of directors' fees and addition of a section on governance in the annual report. In 2002, SEBI constituted a committee chaired by Infosys's Narayana Murthy to improve Clause 49's requirements, and the revision, issued in late 2004 and implemented at the start of 2006, further tightened the definition of independent directors, strengthened the role of the audit committee, and enhanced the accountability of the chief executive and chief financial officer. Companies were required to establish risk management controls and issue a governance code of conduct, and officers were henceforward required to certify the efficacy of all internal controls, ranging from manufacturing to sales, legal, and even human resources. The parallels with the thrust of the U.S. Sarbanes-Oxley Act of 2002 were evident, including training for company directors, more specific guidelines for the financial literacy of audit committee members, and annual performance evaluations for nonexecutive directors by their peers.[19]

Sarbanes-Oxley, Like It or Not

As stringent as they were, the Clause 49 guidelines remained more lax than those found in the Sarbanes-Oxley Act, especially regarding financial disclosure and transparency. But many Indian corporations anxious to list internationally made up for the difference by adopting Sarbanes-Oxley rules despite their lengthy and expensive requirements. Some companies went all the way and listed directly on the New York Stock Exchange. Among the eleven that had done so by 2009 were several prominently mentioned in these pages: Dr. Reddy's Laboratories, HDFC Bank, ICICI Bank, Tata Motors, and Wipro. The rush to adoption, though, was not always done with a smile.

HDFC's Deepak Parekh, for one, described as a mixed blessing the heightened governance vigilance that came with full Sarbanes-Oxley compliance. "We have to follow Sarbanes-Oxley, whether we like it or not," he said. "We know it is very onerous, we know the reporting requirements are strenuous, and we have an army of people involved in that, but the worry we have is that we don't know, when we make a mistake under Sarbanes-Oxley, where we will be hauled up." HDFC did not draw more than 10 to 15 percent of its capital from the U.S. equity market, but even for that, Parekh had concluded that the burdensome listing in New York was worth the price. Others have been migrating in the same direction. "I think we are slowly moving towards the rest of the world," said Sarthak Behuria, chairman of Indian Oil Corporation. He and many other Indian companies, he said, were looking to list their companies in the U.S. as American Depository Receipts—a device that allows investors in the United States to trade in non-U.S. securities without engaging in cross-border transactions—to access the large capital markets that were simply unavailable at home.

While the Indian leaders we interviewed almost to a person described the SEBI requirements for listing companies in India as onerous, and the same for SEC requirements for listing firms in the U.S., many also conceded that the new rules might actually have facilitated the nation's economic expansion, as suggested by a research finding that good corporate governance has generally led to stronger economic growth and better performance of companies during a financial crisis.[20]

"By and large, I think the shift in the last ten years in governance has been dramatic," said ICICI's K. V. Kamath. "In a developing country context, it was thought to be impossible." But the "entire process of the way the SEBI has structured governance, the way they have heightened reporting and heightened best practices, and the way industry went ahead embracing this and how it has been popularized will all become good case studies for other countries."

Still, the diffusion of rules-based governance is far from complete. One survey of Indian companies in early 2007, for instance, reported that 57 percent had still not brought their boards into compliance with some of Clause 49's stipulations. Another study, this one in 2004–2005, found that 70 percent of a sample of 1,255 companies had complied with 80 percent or more of Clause 49's seventeen major codes.[21] As Jagdish Khattar, managing director of Maruti Suzuki, India's leading car maker, told us, "There is a lot of talk about it, but I think that we have a long way to go" to achieve full compliance.

Recruiting Independent Nonexecutive Directors

The thrust of Clause 49 has been to strengthen the oversight role of independent nonexecutive directors by increasing their numbers on the board, expanding their influence over audit and compensation, and making their role more transparent. Ideally, this should spawn boards devoted to monitoring company managers and protecting shareholder rights. The reality, though, is that Indian board members, more so than their American equivalents, tend to be recruited for almost anything other than their monitoring potential.

When it comes to monitoring management, the thrust of a rules-based approach, independence of thought, should be among the leading criteria, but as displayed in table 6-2, it ranked far down the list in our surveying, with business experience, personal reputation, and professional expertise far ahead of it. Conversely, for values-based governance, with its emphasis on entrepreneurship and collaborating with management, experience and expertise should rank high up on the list, just as they do. While the SEBI regulations pressed for strengthening the nonexecutive directors' oversight function, the Indian executives reported that when they recruited nonexecutives to their board, they used the opportunity to strengthen the directors' capacity to work in partnership with them. These attributes of directors were also closer to the entrepreneurial model referred to by Hewlett-Packard director Thomas Perkins rather than the compliance model that Perkins feared had come to pervade the American landscape.

TABLE 6-2

Executives' criteria for selecting nonexecutive directors for the governing board

Question: "What are the two most important criteria you have used in selecting nonexecutive directors?"

Criteria for selecting nonexecutive director	Percentage
Professional experience, diversity of experience	38
Reputation, credibility, track record, stature	26
Domain or functional expertise	15
Independence of thought	10
Integrity and character	5
Commitment to serving on the board	6

When asked to describe the role that nonexecutive directors play in the boardroom, the Indian executives—many of whom also served as nonexecutive directors of other firms—consistently stressed their value in providing substantive guidance on business issues and virtually never referenced their monitoring function.

"We'd Be Stupid Not to Use His Skills"

The nonexecutive component of Mahindra & Mahindra's board provides an example of how these survey results play themselves out in practice. Of the twelve directors, eight are independent, and they bring extensive background in banking and finance (Deepak Parekh, chairman of HDFC Ltd., and Narayanan Vaghul, chairman of the board of ICICI Bank Ltd.); manufacturing (Nadir Godrej, developer of the animal feed, agricultural inputs, and chemicals business of Godrej Soaps and other associated companies); technology and research (M. M. Murugappan, a member of the supervisory board of the Murugappa Group of companies, responsible for technology and research); consumer products (A. S. Ganguly, chairman of Hindustan Unilever Ltd. from 1980 to 1990 and a member of Unilever's main board from 1990 to 1997); law (R. K. Kulkarni, senior partner of Khaitan & Company, one of India's leading law firms); strategy consulting (Anupam Puri, thirty years with McKinsey & Company); and insurance (Thomas Mathew, managing director of Life Insurance Corporation of India).

None of these nonexecutive board members brought to the post special experience or expertise in monitoring management for shareholder value. What they added, instead, was broad and substantive knowledge of the business world generally and of special niches in particular. "It's not because we structured it that way," said Anand Mahindra. "It just happens to be the particular skill sets of the people we have on the board." He singled out two directors to substantiate his point: one, Anupam Puri, was an ex-director and senior partner of McKinsey who had started up McKinsey in India. "We'd be stupid if we didn't use his skills," explained Mahindra, "particularly since it cost a lot less than actually hiring him. He heads up an investment committee that we have, and that includes a fairly aggressive process that looks through a lot of the major investments or new ventures or acquisitions that we are considering in the parent company." A second director, A. Ganguly, was not only ex-chairman of Hindustan Unilever; he also had headed Unilever's worldwide R&D and still served on the board of British Airways. "A person like that brings a huge maturity and perspective," offered Mahindra, "so we've actually used him a lot, too."

Key Decisions

In our interviews, we also asked the Indian business leaders about the value that their nonexecutive directors had brought to key company decisions in the areas of acquisitions, divestitures, and strategic alliances, arguably among the most important issues that come before a board.[22] The responses, shown in table 6-3, point to the value of such directors as partners with company executives in reaching strategic decisions. The nonexecutive directors provided diverse inputs and insights, offered independent assessment

TABLE 6-3

Value of nonexecutive directors for company decisions on acquisitions, divestitures, and strategic alliance

Question: "When it comes to acquisitions, divestitures, and strategic alliances, what value have nonexecutive directors brought to the decisions?"

Value of nonexecutive directors	Percentage
Diverse inputs and insights into strategic planning and decision making	40
Independent views providing checks, balances, and restraints	21
Challenging questions and playing devil's advocate	15
Functional expertise in areas of finance, legal, tax, regulations, and mergers and acquisitions	19
Limited value	5
Monitoring shareholder value in acquisitions, divestitures, or alliances	0

of proposed actions, posed challenging questions, and contributed special expertise to strategic decisions. No one we interviewed said that their nonexecutive directors contributed much in the way of a monitor's vigilance to the company's decisions on acquisitions, divestitures, or alliances.

The Indian executives repeatedly stressed the importance of their nonexecutive directors for reaching key decisions, seeing them more as discussion partners than adjudicating monitors. Adi Godrej of the Godrej Group said that his nonexecutive board members "brought tremendous value" to his management team's decisions on transactions. Pantaloon Retail's Kishore Biyani offered much the same assessment. He had brought a number of acquisition and alliance proposals to his board, and the directors had pushed back against a substantial fraction. "The key role our board members have played in terms of decision making on these issues has been very, very major," he said. Out of ten proposals over a given period, they had on average rejected three. "Whenever there has been a discussion on a particular alliance or an acquisition, I think the outside board members have been well positioned and aware of the facts about what we are getting into. Everybody has a point of view in terms of the company's evolution—what one should and should not do—and I think they have played a key role in forcing us to think through what we are doing."

In one instance, Biyani recalled, his outside directors had rejected a proposal after they concluded that the acquisition would require too much of Pantaloon's capital. In another, the directors rejected a proposed acquisition because of the quality of the company at the top, finding that the target's governance did not meet Pantaloon's standards. The content of his board's dialogue and its decision-making criteria were focused on the business issues in the proposed acquisitions and alliances, not their potential for creating or damaging shareholder value, though the former always has implications for the latter. In the American boardroom, by contrast, immediate impact on shareholder value is typically a far more dominating concern.

Part-Time Service

Indian business leaders warned against overinterpreting the worth of the values-based decision-making partnership with the nonexecutive directors. Nonexecutive directors by definition can devote only a small fraction of their work year to the company and are thus inherently limited in the depth of what they know or the time they can take to render informed guidance. Rahul Bajaj said that for some companies, governance meant little more than "filling up the boxes, ticking them off to show that they have met all the requirements. In most Indian companies, that is the spirit of the thing, so these independent directors don't get much time to provide value even though they have the capacity to do so." After directors meet their board committee requirements, "very little time is left for strategic input" into "strategic discussions."

Still, the picture that emerged from our interviews was one of values-based governance, with a focus on guiding good strategic decisions more than appraising management performance. Nonexecutive directors were largely chosen for the professional knowledge and business experience that they would bring to the firm's strategy development and key actions. Their place in the informal networks of Indian business and society did not appear to be a primary consideration in selecting them, though the preference expressed by some of the business executives for nonexecutive directors of reputation and stature no doubt partly reflected that consideration. Nor was there evidence that the business leaders sought prominent figures primarily for their symbolic value rather than their strategic contributions to the key decisions—a practice common with outside directors in the U.S. To guide the right strategic decisions, then, the nonexecutive directors played a check-and-balance role, raising questions and providing guidance before important decisions were finalized, focusing more on the long-term development of the company than on short-term growth in shareholder value.

Convergence of East and West?

One side of a long-standing academic debate contends that governance practices of large companies worldwide are likely to converge on a set of shared practices. As large companies in major economies search for capital, goes the rationale, they will increasingly enter a worldwide equity market, where they will encounter equity investors increasingly global in scope. Regardless of their originating nation, the major players will acquire a set of shared principles and norms for good corporate governance. The other side of the debate expects only modest convergence at most. Distinct country traditions and national regulations are likely to thwart the global equity-market pressures for convergence, the argument contends, preserving much that is unique and effective in the respective national governance systems. In the end, major players such as China, India, and the United States will each sustain their own ways of governing.[23]

As seen in table 6-4, the Indian business leaders were in substantial agreement with the first side of that debate. Asked "Will your governance practices eventually converge with those of the U.S., or

TABLE 6-4

Convergence of Indian governance practices with those of the United States

Question: "Will your governance practices eventually converge with those of the United States, or will they remain distinct?"

Convergence with U.S. governance?	Percentage
Yes	51
Convergence more expected with U.K. or other national models	19
Yes, but with some modest differences	13
No	10
Movement toward a middle ground or hybrid	7

will they remain distinct?" slightly more than half concurred with the convergence forecast. Smaller fractions anticipated convergence with the governance models of the United Kingdom or other countries, and just one in ten forecast no convergence at all.

Though a majority of the business leaders anticipated convergence with the U.S. model, some forecast that the U.S. model would at the same time move toward the Indian model as well. One in five of the executives foresaw convergence around a different end point, a global best-practices model, which would include practices from the United States, India, and elsewhere. Not surprisingly, the companies that most anticipated convergence of Indian governance with U.S., U.K, or other non-Indian models were those whose revenues came heavily from international clients. Overall, however, nearly half of the executives believed that Indian corporate governance would retain some of its most compelling features, including its relative emphasis on a values-based approach, and its stress on the worth of human capital as much as stockholder capital.

B. Muthuraman of Tata Steel spoke for many: "I'm not a great admirer of the U.S. corporate governance practices at all. By framing rules, you cannot improve corporate governance. You lay down more rules, and they get broken more." By contrast, in India, in "improving your value system, you can improve the corporate governance practice." Many concurred with the call for a continued strengthening of values-based governance norms rather than an imposition of more rules.

No Guarantees

On the surface, the spectacular executive fraud at Satyam Computer Services would suggest that India's preference for a value-based board approach imperils shareholder interests. Surely, a board more attentive to rules and monitoring compliance would have heard warning bells going off. Yet a close inspection of the Satyam board reveals—as with the Enron board—a relatively strong set of independent nonexecutive directors whose composition and outward appearance would appear to meet SEBI standards for rules-based governance compliance. The board included a majority of independent, nonexecutive directors who brought strong and diverse experience to the boardroom, including expertise in venture capital, corporate governance, and public affairs. So evident was the rules-based compliance with the principles of good governance that just months before its chief executive confessed to massive fraud, the World Council for Corporate Governance presented Satyam with its Golden Peacock Award for Excellence in Corporate Governance. Similarly, the Enron board had been dominated by highly experienced and independent nonexecutive directors just before the fall, and the board had even separated its chair and chief executive roles.[24]

The moral, then, is an old one: in business as in life, there are no guarantees. If the rules-based approach helps focus attention on protecting and growing shareholder values, as ample research has demonstrated, it is no assurance against improper executive behavior if the boss's values are flawed.[25] Moreover, a laserlike focus on rules and compliance inevitably must direct attention and energy away from the other stakeholders that Indian executives and directors have generally avowed to benefit along with shareholders. Throughout Indian society and the business community in particular, corporate social responsibility is a compelling goal, and balancing diverse interests is a prescribed responsibility of company leadership.

Delivering Value

The stakeholder-informed model of governance that the Indian business leaders have embraced stands in stark contrast to the principal-agent model that has dominated so much of the American approach to governance in recent years. The latter focused executive attention exclusively on the singular objective of delivering value to shareholders. Governing boards accordingly designed compensation packages for their executives that were intended to align decisions almost entirely around the delivery of shareholder value.

The prevalence of promoter- and family-controlled companies in India and their leadership in the community is particularly important in this context. Because some of the executives at these companies are also large owners or members of owning families, they need little special incentive to look after ownership interests and are more able than their counterparts in the United States to take a long view about what is good for their company. With that longer view, it becomes possible to see more opportunities for the interests of the company and the interests of the broader society to coincide.

Short-term, mutually exclusive trade-offs between acting to advance the company and spending to benefit the community are less pronounced in the longer run, where it becomes more evident that charitable giving and community outreach can build brand value and reputational capital, both of ultimate but little immediate benefit to companies and their owners.

Governance at Infosys Technologies

To illustrate many of these themes and to see how they interplay with one another, we briefly consider the governance of Infosys Technologies. While the company clearly met international standards for rules-based governance—it listed itself in both India and the United States—it managed at the same time to build a values-based governance model, and it has worked to draw the best from both models. The Infosys board, for instance, placed a premium on both the independence and the competence of its directors. Independence provided for director monitoring of management; competence provided for director dialogue with management. Directors could thus both hold executives' feet to the fire and serve as advisers and sounding boards for executive decisions. By virtue of Infosys's American listing, the board of directors also served to bolster company credibility with investors and customers outside of India.

Infosys Technologies early adopted a rules-based approach to governance. After the Confederation of Indian Industry put forward a set of good governance rules in 1999, Infosys was one of the first companies to embrace them. As a part of a commitment to global best formal practices, Infosys decided also to comply with the Euroshareholders Corporate Governance Guidelines of 2000 and those of the U.S. Conference Board Commission on Public Trust and Private Enterprise. Infosys embraced the UN Global Compact and the governance guidelines of six countries—Australia, Canada, France, Germany, Japan, and the United Kingdom.[26] In the same spirit, it adopted the U.S. generally accepted accounting principles (GAAP) well before most other Indian companies, and in listing itself on NASDAQ, it embraced Sarbanes-Oxley as well.[27]

Infosys's governance as a result became exemplary by any set of international rules-focused standards. For instance, Crédit Lyonnais, the French financial services company, ranked Infosys as having the best corporate governance of 475 companies that resided outside North America, Western Europe, and Japan. On a 100-point overall scale gauging such issues as reporting transparency and board independence, Infosys scored 91, while the average company scored only 58.[28]

In keeping with the rules-based model, Infosys also acted to increase its own operational transparency by reporting revenues separately for its major segments, and it brought its board into compliance with SEBI's Clause 49 requirements. Eight of Infosys's fifteen directors were independent nonexecutives. The audit, compensation, investor grievance, nominations, and risk management committees were all composed of independent directors.

But Infosys has also been a practitioner of the values-based approach to governance. The directors, for instance, reflect a wide range of expertise from academe, consulting, and industry, with both domestic and international experience.[29] "The major value" of the nonexecutive directors, said chairman Narayana Murthy, has been in "asking questions that make us rethink our assumptions. That makes

Infosys Technologies
Board of Directors, 2009

EXECUTIVE DIRECTORS

N. R. Narayana Murthy, founder, chairman, and chief mentor. N. R. Narayana Murthy founded Infosys in 1981 along with six other software professionals and served as the CEO of Infosys for twenty-one years. He obtained his BE (electrical) from the University of Mysore in 1967 and MTech (electrical) from the Indian Institute of Technology, Kanpur, in 1969. Several universities in India and abroad have conferred honorary doctorate degrees on him.

Nandan M. Nilekani, founder and cochairman. Nandan Nilekani has been cochairman since 2007, and prior to that he served as CEO and managing director. In 2006, he was given the Padma Bhushan, one of the highest civilian honors awarded by the government of India. He received his bachelor's degree in electrical engineering from the Indian Institute of Technology (IIT), Bombay, in 1978.

S. Gopalakrishnan, founder, CEO, and managing director. S. Gopalakrishnan has been serving as CEO of Infosys since 2007. He is currently the chairman of the Indian Institute of Information Technology and Management (IIITM), Kerala. He holds MS (physics) and MTech (computer science) degrees from the Indian Institute of Technology, Madras.

S. D. Shibulal, founder, COO, and member of the board. S. D. Shibulal has been serving as chief operating officer since 2007. Prior to that, he served as group head of worldwide sales and customer delivery. He received a master's degree in physics from the University of Kerala and an MS in computer science from Boston University.

K. Dinesh, founder and member of the board. K. Dinesh is head of quality, information systems, and the communication design group. He completed his postgraduate degree in mathematics from Bangalore University and was awarded a doctorate in literature by the Karnataka State Open University in 2006.

T. V. Mohandas Pai, member of the board and director of human resources. T. V. Mohandas Pai joined Infosys in 1994 and has served as a member of the board since 2000. He leads efforts in the areas of human resources, education, and research. He holds a bachelor's degree in commerce from St. Joseph's College, Bangalore, and a bachelor's degree in law from Bangalore University, and is a Fellow Chartered Accountant (FCA).

Srinath Batni, member of the board. Srinath Batni joined the board in 2000 and is responsible for delivery excellence across the company. He received a bachelor's degree in mechanical engineering from the University of Mysore in 1975 and a master's degree in mechanical engineering from the Indian Institute of Science in 1979.

INDEPENDENT NONEXECUTIVE DIRECTORS

Rama Bijapurkar. Rama Bijapurkar has worked at McKinsey & Company, MARG Marketing & Research Group, Hindustan Unilever, and MODE Services. She is recognized for her expertise in market strategy and consumer issues. An alumna of the Indian Institute of Management, Ahmedabad, she is also a visiting professor at her alma mater and serves on its board of governors.

David L. Boyles. David Boyles built a career in senior leadership positions at large multinational corporations including

American Express, Bank of America, and Australia and New Zealand Banking Group (ANZ). Boyles earned an MBA degree from Washington State University and an MA and a BA in psychology from the University of Northern Colorado at Greeley.

Omkar Goswami. Omkar Goswami is the founder and chairman of CERG (Corporate and Economic Research Group) Advisory Ltd. From 1998 to 2004, he served as chief economist of the Confederation of Indian Industry. He received his master's degree in economics from the Delhi School of Economics in 1978 and earned his PhD from Oxford in 1982.

Sridar A. Iyengar. Sridar Iyengar previously was a senior partner with KPMG in the United States and U.K. and served for three years as chairman and CEO of KPMG's operations in India. He has served as an adviser to several venture and private equity funds with an interest in India. Iyengar has a Bachelor of Commerce degree from the University of Calcutta and is a fellow of the Institute of Chartered Accountants in England and Wales.

Jeffrey Sean Lehman. Jeffrey Lehman is professor of law and former president of Cornell University. He is currently a senior scholar at the Woodrow Wilson International Center for Scholars in Washington, D.C. At one point he served as a law clerk for John Paul Stevens of the U.S. Supreme Court. Lehman earned an AB in mathematics from Cornell University and Master of Public Policy (MPP) and JD degrees from the University of Michigan

Deepak M. Satwalekar, lead director. Deepak Satwalekar has been the managing director and CEO of HDFC Standard Life Insurance Company Ltd. since 2000. He has been a consultant to the World Bank, the Asian Development Bank, and the U.S. Agency for International Development. He holds a bachelor's degree in technology from IIT, Bombay, and a master's degree in business administration from The American University in Washington, D.C.

Claude Smadja. Claude Smadja is the president of Smadja & Associates, a strategic advisory firm he founded in 2001. He joined the World Economic Forum in 1987 as a director and member of the executive board. He is a graduate of the University of Lausanne, Switzerland, and serves on the International Board of Overseers of the Illinois Institute of Technology.

Marti G. Subrahmanyam. Marti Subrahmanyam is the Charles E. Merrill Professor of Finance, Economics, and International Business in the Stern School of Business at New York University. He serves as an adviser to international and government organizations, including the Securities and Exchange Board of India. He holds degrees from the Indian Institute of Technology, Madras; the Indian Institute of Management, Ahmedabad; and the Massachusetts Institute of Technology.

Source: Infosys Technologies Ltd., Members of the Board, 2009, http://www.infosys.com/about/management-profiles/default.asp.

us look at issues we may have missed and think about alternatives." At a recent board meeting, for instance, the executives and directors debated the synergistic merits of several acquisitions and alliances for the better part of three hours. The board went back and forth on the strategic issues—what were the downsides to combining different company cultures? Would management have the "bandwidth" to manage a proposed acquisition? If it were completed, would the two firms be able to cross-sell their services to each other's customers?

As the box, "Infosys Technologies Board of Directors, 2009," shows, five of seven of the executive directors are also cofounders of the company, and two are former chief executives, a practice not well received in the rules-based governance model but ideal from the values-based standpoint because they bring the personal commitments to company values that one expects in founders. Murthy reported that the board's original design and its many decisions since then have followed the same set of principles that he and his cofounders had used in creating the company to begin with, including the following:

- The softest pillow is a clear conscience.

- When in doubt, disclose.

- Don't use corporate resources for personal benefit.

- Put long-term interests ahead of short-term ones.

- A small slice of a large pie is better than a large slice of a small pie: the company's growth depends on management's sharing profits with all employees.[30]

The Distinctiveness of Indian Governance

As with human resource decisions, company leadership, and competitive strategy, so with corporate governance. India's top executives follow a path similar to, yet different from, that of their counterparts in the United States and other countries. Indeed, Dale Berra's "our similarities are different" might serve as a mantra for the entire U.S.–India business interface.

Among the more notable differences are a stronger sense of social mission, a weaker commitment to investors—especially in responding to their short-term demands—and a higher value on employees and culture. In looking upon their company's governance, these executives put values at the forefront, with a shared sense of social responsibility that calls for incorporating the interests of all the firm's stakeholders. The role of family-promoted business groups is particularly distinctive. Those who lead them combine the roles of primary owner, company leader, and prominent citizen, and their firms and their social outreach have served as models for new companies and aspiring leaders.

We can see here an important source of two principal practices of the India Way: the focus on broad mission and purpose, and the holistic engagement with employees. With a greater relative emphasis on values-based governance, Indian business leaders have been less constrained by investor insistence on steadily increasing shareholder value. Greater executive attention thus can be devoted to their company's contributions to the community and the country, not just their investor returns, and to building their workforce, not just cutting labor costs.

Encouraged by both international investors and the Securities and Exchange Board of India, many Indian firms in recent years have accepted the rules-based model so prevalent in the United States, and with good and practical cause. An early-2000s study found that development financial institutions lent more and mutual funds invested more in companies well governed by SEBI standards.[31] Yet at the same time, these firms have also embraced the values-based model that has emerged indigenously within India. As the case of Infosys Technologies shows, the two models are not mutually exclusive and indeed should be seen as compatible.

To be sure, adopting the values-based approach without the accompanying discipline of a rules-based model runs the risk of improper management exploitation of shareholders other than the founding family or the primary owner—the temptation, say, to "tunnel," or transfer cash among companies to prop up a languishing firm within a business group. As in the U.S. and other economies, Indian business can make no claim to being malfeasance-free. But the leaders interviewed for this project make a persuasive case for viewing good corporate governance as a healthy balance of rules-based and values-based principles—a model of India's own making.

CHAPTER SEVEN

Learning from the India Way

Redefining Business Leadership

THE IDEAS BEHIND the India Way are compelling. Finding novel solutions to the hard problems of long-term customers and relying on improvisation and adaptability to do so are sensible and powerful techniques for competing. The most powerful ideas in the India Way, especially for those in the broader society, come from the fact that Indian corporations have been able to succeed in the marketplace while pursuing a social mission and taking care of their employees. Social responsibility, our fifth and final area of company focus—along with people management, executive leadership, competitive strategy, and company governance, which have been the focus of our prior chapters—is an integral feature of the India Way, a direct product of its axial emphasis on broad mission and purpose.

The India Way's focus on mission and purpose with its stress on personal values, expansive thinking, and public purpose, we have found, is one element of a four-part formulation. Indian executives also place a high value on holistic engagement with their employees, seeing them as assets to be developed and celebrated. Business leaders stress improvisation and adaptability, creativity and resilience, *jugaad* and adjust. And they search for creative value propositions that speak to the needs of millions of customers with modest means. These ideas are especially timely as they represent an important alternative, indeed a challenge, to accepted ways of operating businesses.

Contrast with the U.S. Model for Leadership

The success of the India Way is important in its own right, of course, as it is crucial to the economic and social health of what will soon be the world's most populous country. It may turn out to be just as important as a model for countries elsewhere, not just those struggling to modernize but also those that are already economically developed. Can India provide an example for these countries? More pointedly, will it challenge what has been the dominant model for business in many parts of the world, that of the United States? Answering that question requires some background on the evolving practices of the U.S. model.

After World War II, when the rest of the industrial world was in tatters, American ideas about how to organize business and the economy were transferred abroad in part by the U.S. government, in part by U.S. multinationals, but also through the power of example.[1] Important lessons included the corporate model of ownership and organization, in contrast to family-owned and smaller-scale operations that were more typical especially in Europe; mass-production principles; open markets and informal oligopolies, in contrast to more formal cartels; organizational structures relying on hierarchies and complex, M-form or multidivisional models, in contrast to informal organizational forms associated with smaller, family-based businesses; and workplace organization based on collective bargaining with trade unions whose goals were explicitly practical rather than political.[2] Many, if not most, of these practices were adopted by the world's industrialized countries.

After the OPEC oil price shocks of the 1970s, the success of Japanese business coincided with the poor performance of the U.S. economy in the early 1980s to make Japan arguably the most important source of management ideas. But the U.S. model was soon to reinvent itself around a more open-market framework and stage a substantial comeback in the 1990s.

The resurgent U.S. model drew heavily on old values. Alexis de Tocqueville, the nineteenth-century French chronicler of U.S. ways, observed in *Democracy in America* that Americans "are fond of explaining almost all the actions of their lives by the principle of self-interest rightly understood," and America's culture of individual achievement has long placed a premium on being clear minded about the pursuit of one's private purpose.[3] Unbridled capitalism, American-style, held "that the common good is best served by the uninhibited pursuit of self-interest," in the words of hedge-fund manager and social critic George Soros.[4] The 1980s and '90s applications of these ideas asserted that the best way for economies to develop was to reduce the role of government—lower taxes, fewer subsidies, less regulation—and encourage private ownership and self-interest. These views were crystallized into a model for economic development and became known as the "Washington Consensus," reflecting the fact that these principles for stimulating economic growth were shared by the U.S. government and the international institutions over which it had great influence, especially the International Monetary Fund.[5]

Alan Greenspan, then chairman of the Federal Reserve Board, articulated the idea that the rest of the world was moving toward this U.S. model in his statement to Congress during the 1998 Asian financial crisis: "My sense is that one consequence of this Asian crisis is an increasing awareness in the region that market capitalism, as practiced in the West, especially in the United States, is the superior model." He went on to emphasize the importance of "greater reliance on market forces, reduced government controls, scaling back of government-directed investment, and embracing greater transparency" as being central to the U.S. approach.[6]

The U.S. business community also argued vociferously that the key to its competitiveness was the ability to restructure quickly when operations proved uncompetitive and, in turn, to be able to start up quickly in a different direction. As a practical matter, that meant having greater ability to lay off workers, close facilities, and move on. Long-term obligations to employees and efforts to protect their interests were seen as obstacles to competitiveness.[7] The apparent success of Silicon Valley and its model based on constant restructuring with job cuts and outside hiring seemed especially compelling.[8]

The central aspect of the Washington Consensus was arguably the focus on shareholders and their interest in profit maximization as the primary goal for business. An earlier generation of U.S. executives would have been perfectly comfortable with the India Way's need for executives to balance the often competing interests of "stakeholders" in the business, especially employees, the community, and shareholders. The assertion that shareholders' interests were absolutely primary was something new and became known as *financialization* because of the emphasis on financial goals and shareholder value.[9] Sociologist Ronald Dore credited this development in large part to the growing influence of an intermediating financial industry that essentially governed business by relying on free-market pricing of equity assets to reward or punish companies based on their profit performance.[10] This financial industry includes private-sector agencies that rate and evaluate companies based on the assumption of transparent financial information, as well as traders who themselves profit from the buying and selling of equities and speculation in them.

The most obvious influence of financialization was arguably the rise of financial incentives to encourage executives to operate their businesses to maximize shareholder interests in profit. In the early 1990s, less than 10 percent of total executive compensation at publicly held U.S. firms was accounted for by pay that was contingent on stock prices, but by 2003, that figure was almost 70 percent.[11] Evidence suggested that aligning the interests of executives to those of shareholders across countries led to better corporate performance, although that was perhaps not surprising given the lack of any prior systems for managing executives in many countries.[12]

Dissenting voices in the United States had long questioned the notion that profit maximization was the only goal for business, holding that the role of the executives should be more about balancing the claims of competing stakeholders and less about optimizing private wealth. But such concerns had remained those of a dissident minority and in recent years more or less disappeared. De Tocqueville's reference to America's penchant for self-interest "rightly understood"—what we often reference today as "enlightened" self-interest that includes the concerns of the broader community—had become a quaint relic of the past.

Can the India Way compete with financialization as a model for operating businesses? If not compelling enough on its own merits, the India Way benefits from the fact that the U.S. model has suffered a series of self-inflicted injuries, the most important of which is the unending (as of the time of writing) stream of corporate financial scandals that began in the mid-1990s. The common theme across all these scandals has been financial fraud in various forms driven by executives who attempted to manipulate financial results in order to improve share prices and enrich themselves. The most prominent examples were based on malfeasance on such a monumental scale that it literally brought the company down, as at Enron, WorldCom, Adelphia, and Global Crossing. But the list of companies where financial malfeasance was not quite bad enough to force the failure of the company is much longer, including Sunbeam, Waste Management, Tyco, and HealthSouth. A marker for financial irregularities is earnings restatements, in which companies revise earnings that had previously been presented as accurate, representing serious accounting errors. The General Accounting Office calculated that these restatements, once quite rare, grew by 145 percent from 1997 to 2001, with some 10 percent of all publicly traded companies restating earnings during that period.[13] Further, all the major accounting firms were involved in cases of audit failure, in which the firms were found not to have followed standard audit procedures. The fact that these scandals were so common in the United States and so much less so in other countries suggested that something about the financialization practices in the U.S. might be to blame, and the compensation systems that reward U.S. executives for improving share prices were a leading candidate.[14]

The festering financial scandals had less influence on world attitudes than the 2008–2009 financial crisis, triggered by American investment banks that had heavily incentivized their executives with stock options to optimize shareholder value but not to adequately manage enterprise risk or foresee societal damage. Poor decision making at Wall Street investment banks (Bear Stearns, Lehman Brothers, and Merrill Lynch) quickly spread to the banking sector and from there to financial institutions around the world, and led to a global recession, the worst in the United States since 1982–1983.[15] By early 2009, the extent to which much of the rest of the world blamed U.S. business practices and government policies for the 2008 financial crisis and subsequent world recession was palpable at international gatherings.[16] The crisis rekindled a simmering debate about the proper role of personal gain and shareholder value in business affairs.[17]

As a result, much of the world is ready to look past the U.S. for business models. The National Intelligence Council of the U.S. government develops probable scenarios for world events. It argues that the fastest-growing economies in the near future will likely rebuff the U.S. model.[18] Where will they turn? "State capitalism" as expressed in the Chinese model is thought to be the leading contender, where government intervenes directly and frequently in business affairs. Yet systems where government has the ability to intervene in this manner have generally not had a good track record elsewhere either in terms of economic success (exceptions include Singapore and the United Arab Emirates) or especially in

terms of liberty—a deep concern for countries with "liberal" democratic orientations.

In this context, the India Way represents an especially compelling
alternative. It preserves the logic of free markets and real entrepreneurship within the context of democratic institutions. In essence,
it preserves the heart of the capitalist model. As the same time, it
appears to avoid some of the apparent rapaciousness and excesses
of the American model that are redressed at best imperfectly via
government regulation. Companies following the India Way go well
beyond not doing harm to the social fabric to actually pursue social
improvements, in some contexts more efficiently than the government might. Consider the examples of Bharti Airtel, Tata Motors,
and Hindustan Unilever, where company leaders were determined
to build their company's capacity to provide inexpensive mobile
services, automobiles, and consumer goods to millions of traditionally underserved people of modest means.

Of course, self-interest is not far from the surface. For B. Muthuraman, managing director of Tata Steel, social responsibility includes a reputational asset. "Our history in corporate social
responsibility," he affirmed, has "enhanced the group brand." And
for some, acting responsibly in the eyes of the regulators may be a
matter of necessity. Obtaining industrial licenses and environmental clearance in the U.S. can be a straightforward, if technical,
process, while in India it can also be dependent on a reputation for
public responsibility.

But the commitment goes well beyond a private calculus. Rakesh
Mehrotra, managing director of Container Corporation of India, put
forward what is essentially an Indian version of the "stakeholder"
model of corporate governance, where business decisions strike a
balance between the interests of those who are affected by the company. Indian business leaders, Mehrotra asserts, were not driven by
"solely profit motives," as were so many of their American counterparts. Rather, they carried a self-conscious commitment to give back
to society. "The three p's of the Indian style of management," he
said, "are people, planet, and prosperity." His own company set up

a major transportation center near New Delhi, simultaneously investing in a host of social services, including schools, social centers, and health-care facilities to give nearby residents "a feeling that we are not there only to earn profits and run our business but also to care for the community at large."

Our interviews found that the country's business leaders had comfortably embraced a values-based approach to running companies centered on this concern for multiple stakeholders and their needs, not just the narrower needs of shareholders. To the obligatory role of monitoring management, Indian company directors added the role of guiding top executives, and doing so on behalf of more than one constituency. That dual-purpose service could be seen in the kinds of directors that the companies recruited to their boards, evident at Infosys and Mahindra & Mahindra, and in the ways that directors served as strategic partners, not just shareholder monitors. The multiple-constituency ideology also appeared as a driving commitment in a range of other business practices, from competitive strategy to company culture, and from talent management to personal leadership.

An important advantage of the India Way as model for business, at least for society, is in this area of governance. Keeping the activities of companies from damaging the societies in which they operate is a major challenge. Businesses that follow the financialization model and see profit maximization as their overwhelming goal always are tempted to act in ways that increase profits at the expense of the community (e.g., pollution, which can lower company costs but damage the community). To counter these incentives, governments typically impose elaborate systems of regulations and monitoring. But regulations are imperfect instruments, and both the monitoring they require and the constraints they impose on business are costly. When businesses begin with the broader interests of society as part of their goals, as happened so often among the companies we studied, they sharply diminish the need for regulation and monitoring. (See "Will the India Way Persist?")

Will the India Way Persist?

The practices behind the India Way have a long and clear intellectual lineage. Motivating through a sense of mission, for example, empowering employees, and staying close to customers have proven records. And the India Way companies are already succeeding against the best in world competition. Skeptics might argue, though, that while the India Way has succeeded so far, it is just a phase along a path of economic development. That the mission-driven approach of Indian companies and the focus on employees in particular is fostered by the values of company founders and their families, and won't last when the founders leave and professional managers take over. We know from countries with much older corporations, however, that the initial cultures of companies persist well past the departure of founders. More generally, cultures continue as long as they are perceived as being useful.

A related objection to the long-term viability of the India Way is the argument that it persists only because Indian business has been insulated from the demands of the international investment community for short-term profits. Yet Indian businesses are already subject to those pressures. Many are listed on international stock exchanges, most raise funds in international markets, and virtually all are measured and rated by international investors. Companies ultimately control how much they are willing to bend to the interests of the international financial community, and so far, the India Way directors and leaders have chosen not to pursue the interests of the investment community as their own objective. The assumption that they will eventually have to, that all businesses will eventually conform to the U.S. model, has been a hotly debated topic about which there has been no consensus.[a] But those who believe in convergence on U.S. terms have had their case considerably weakened as a result of the 2008–2009 financial crisis.

It is also possible that India's well-performing companies will simply lose steam, as many high-flying companies do in most contexts.[b] Some of the successful companies featured by Thomas Peters and Robert Waterman in *In Search of Excellence*, for instance, regressed during the ensuing decades toward middling performance.[c] While we have high-lighted the views of Indian leaders on the distinctive practices they consider most vital for explaining their growth, time will tell whether their companies can stay on top.

Yet a different question is whether Indian voters and politicians will lose patience with the India Way. Despite the extraordinary success of Indian corporations, the bulk of India's people remain mired in grinding poverty, with more than 300 million still living on less than one dollar per day. Infant mortality has stayed high, with fifty-seven deaths per one thousand live births, compared with seven in the United States. India's mushrooming middle class is increasingly es-tranged from the village life of the vast countryside, creating

a. For an example arguing for convergence, see Moses Abramovitz, "Catch-up and Convergence in the Postwar Growth Boom and After," in *Convergence of Productivity: Cross-National Studies and Historical Evidence*, eds. William J. Baumol, Richard R. Nelson, and Edward N. Wolff (Oxford: Oxford University Press, 1994). See R. Whitley, *Divergent Capitalisms: The Social Structuring and Change of Business Systems* (Oxford: Oxford University Press, 1999), for the opposing view.

b. See, for instance, Jim Collins, *How the Mighty Fall: And Why Some Companies Never Give In* (Jim Collins, 2009).

c. Thomas J. Peters and Robert H. Waterman, *In Search of Excellence: Lessons from America's Best-Run Companies* (New York: Harper & Row, 1982).

new divisions. Further, corruption in government but also in the business community has remained commonplace in India. Drawing on 2007–2008 surveys, Transparency International ranked Denmark, New Zealand, and Sweden as the world's least corrupt countries. Of 180 countries, it judged the United States as eighteenth, but it placed India at eighty-fifth.[d] While a return to the socialist past is unlikely, whether regulations and restrictions will be imposed on businesses and the economy that alter the India Way is an open question.

d. Transparency International, *2008 Corruption Perceptions Index and Methodological Note* (Berlin: Transparency International, 2008), http://www.transparency.org/policy_research/surveys_indices/cpi; World Bank, *Doing Business 2008: India* (Washington, DC: World Bank, 2008), http://www.doingbusiness.org/; World Bank, "India Country Overview 2009," http://www.worldbank.org.in/WBSITE/ EXTERNAL/COUNTRIES/SOUTHASIAEXT/INDIAEXTN/ 0,,contentMDK:20195738~menuPK:295591~pagePK:141137~piPK:141127 ~theSitePK:295584,00.html; and World Health Organization Statistical Information System (WHOSIS), http://www.who.int/whosis/en/.

Contrasting Stockholder-centric Management with Stakeholder Management

The stakeholder-based orientation of the India Way suggests the notion of compromise and mediation between goals, in particular backing off from actions that might make the most money for the business in order to pursue some other goal, such as protecting the community or helping employees. This approach would always appear to do worse in terms of financial performance than the financialization model described earlier. What could be better for profits than focusing on financial performance as the overriding goal?

Yet, as we have seen, there are many problems with the way the financialization model has played out. The notion that companies ought to operate for the benefit of shareholders does not require that companies manage toward quarterly profit targets the way many do now, for example, nor does it require that they ignore the interests of other stakeholders. It is not obvious that this approach even maximizes long-term financial outcomes for shareholders, as its short-term orientation misses both opportunities and potential landmines along the way.[19]

Even if we ignore the problems of the financialization approach, compelling reasons exist for believing that the India Way can not only compete with the U.S. model in terms of financial performance but might even beat it. One reason, described in detail in chapter 3, is that the India Way has a big advantage in motivating and engaging the efforts of employees. Exciting employees about making shareholders rich is an ongoing challenge. While it is possible to tie pay to shareholder value, it is extremely expensive to pay the average employee enough in share-based incentives to get them to focus on shareholder value. And as the financial scandals in the United States continue to illustrate, linking the pay of executives to financial performance entails substantial governance risks. It is much easier to get frontline employees animated about a social purpose, and it is easier to keep them engaged around an organization that has a sense of mission. A recent study of employee turnover in India found, for example, that the perception of a company's social responsibility is one of the main factors in retaining talent.[20]

A second factor giving the India Way an advantage in performance has to do with customers. Individuals have long memories, and doing good things for people when they have no money and are not customers for your products can redound to a company's advantage when those individuals do have money and are in the market for your products. We also know that consumers care about the values of the companies with which they do business—witness the current rush of companies touting their "green" environmental practices. At least some substantial share of customers would rather do business with companies that do good things for the community.

A third important factor that favors the India Way concerns the holistic engagement Indian companies typically have with their employees. This often translates into a concern for the employees as whole persons, not just as individuals with whom the company enters into instrumental exchange relationships. While pressure from competition in the labor market threatens to erode that mindset, concern for the human system still describes the management practices of many Indian firms. This approach can create greater identification for employees with their companies, increase their motivation to put in efforts beyond role requirements, and create a supportive, high-performance culture. While this view of employees as members of one large family is anchored in Indian culture, one of its roots ironically lies in U.S. management theories from the 1950s and 1960s and management practices during the 1960s and 1970s that emphasized the human equation. There is a notable parallel to the emphasis on quality control, which originated in the United States during the 1950s through the advocacy of W. Edwards Deming and Joseph M. Juran, that found its fullest expression not in the United States but in Japan, eventually becoming a central pillar of Japanese manufacturing management practice.

Can the India Way Translate Elsewhere?

How adaptable is the India Way model to other cultures and economies, and how much is it the product of the unique context of Indian business and life? There is no question that the Indian context is different. Consider a World Bank assessment of the ease of doing business in 181 national economies, ranging from Australia to Tajikistan. The ranking took into account the challenges in ten stages of a company's development, ranging from founding the firm and securing credit to obtaining permits, protecting investors, and enforcing contracts. In 2008, Singapore stood first, followed by New Zealand and the United States. China ranked near the middle at 83, but India fell among the lowest third, ranked at 122. On all ten criteria, Indian firms faced more challenging conditions than companies in the United States, as seen in figure 7-1.

FIGURE 7-1

Rank of the challenges of doing business in India and the U.S., 2008

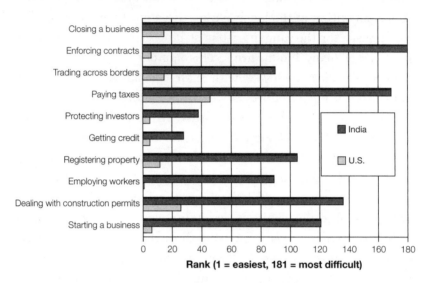

Source: World Bank, *Doing Business 2009* (Washington, DC: World Bank, 2009), http://www.doingbusiness.org/.

The relative competitiveness of the Indian and American economies also displayed the same wide disparities. The World Economic Forum annually assesses country competitiveness, defined as the presence of institutions, policies, and related factors that determine a nation's productivity. The forum took twelve factors into account, and, as seen in figure 7-2, it ranked India far below the United States on all twelve. Overall, the United States placed first, followed by Switzerland and Denmark, while India finished fiftieth among 134 nations.

Moreover, the relative competitiveness of the Indian economy on these dimensions had shown no marked improvement over the past decade, at least as gauged by the World Economic Forum. For the ten years from 1999 to 2008, the Indian economy bounced around in the competitiveness ranking, from 43 to 57. When business leaders were surveyed in 2008 as part of the forum's analysis, Indian

FIGURE 7-2

Rank of country competitiveness for India and the U.S., 2008

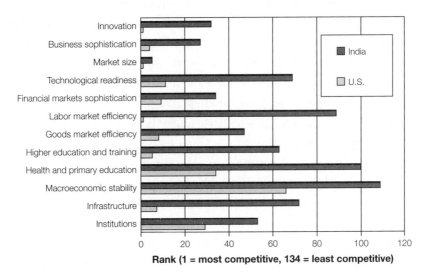

Rank (1 = most competitive, 134 = least competitive)

Source: Michael E. Porter and Klaus Schwab, *The Global Competitiveness Report 2008–2009* (Geneva, Switzerland: World Economic Forum, 2008).

executives said that the most problematic factors for doing business in their country were inadequate supply of infrastructure, inefficient government bureaucracy, and corruption.[21] India Way companies take on more community responsibilities perhaps because they need to in order to get business done. They have to spend more time and resources training employees, for example, because the schools and private training institutions are not up to the job. They work to improve the infrastructure of their communities because it is difficult to get business done in them otherwise. Whether the investments in employees and in the communities would be as useful in countries where the infrastructure is better is an open question.

All countries face challenges in the public realm, of course, and it is hard to argue with the idea that societies are better off if the business community is actively engaged in helping address those challenges. In prereform years, business leaders were "shunned and treated with disdain," recalled Emcure Pharmaceuticals' Humayun Dhanrajgir. In the wake of the 1991 reforms, Indian companies came to play a more prominent role in addressing India's enormous social ills. Many in India's government came to recognize not just the private sector's ability to generate surplus but its strongly felt obligation to help alleviate India's deep-rooted social ills. Now, business leaders were warmly welcomed into the corridors of power, serving on a host of advisory bodies and consultative boards. Instead of treating companies as little more than license supplicants, government officials came to see them as policy allies, turning to them for help in addressing the problems of infrastructure, poverty, and beyond. Witness how Prime Minister Manmohan Singh asked Anil Ambani to remain in the country to help calm the nation in the wake of the 2008 terrorist attack on Mumbai. A U.S. analogy might be found in the frequently misinterpreted comment by General Motors' chief executive Charles Wilson on how he focused his company on the war effort during World War II: "For years I thought what was good for the country was good for General Motors and vice versa." But more recent parallels do not come to mind.[22]

In fact, Indian business leaders did not wait for government to come asking for assistance. Indian executives openly thrust themselves into public dialogue over societal goals and the future of the Indian economy. Mukesh Ambani, for instance, used a business-law conference in 2009 to urge the audience to focus not on business or legal matters but on the fact that at a time when the world's population was aging, India's was actually becoming younger, with more than 400 million people below the age of nineteen. If properly trained and employed, he said, India's young could become a source-country, not just a company, advantage.[23]

Bill Gates recently called for a new approach to business, a new form of capitalism where business aims to solve social problems and not just make money, an approach that sounds remarkably like the India Way. At least so far, there have been few takers in the United States. Few business leaders stepped forward to help guide America through the economic crisis of 2008–2009, standing in sharp contrast, for example, to the role, albeit a controversial one, played by banker J. Pierpont Morgan in reversing a financial crisis a century earlier.[24]

But the India Way is more than simply social responsibility. It is an approach to business strategy, to the pursuit of competitive advantage. Social responsibility fits into that approach, but it is only part of the model. And as we described in chapter 2, while the India Way is not a direct transference of Indian values and norms, it is rooted in a legal, cultural, and economic context. How much of the India Way can translate to other contexts? More to the point, if you are a business leader in another society, where the infrastructure and values are different, what aspects of the India Way can be applied to your operations?

The India Way As a Guide for Individual Leaders

The question about what translates is most pressing for leaders of publicly held companies in the United States—the big enterprises— as they operate in a business environment where the pressure to manage in ways that maximize shareholder value is intense. They cannot be expected to drop the focus on shareholder value and operate like Indian companies. What we argue, though, is that even publicly held U.S. companies need to push back against at least the extreme versions of the shareholder-value approach, the idea that the company ought to be managed in order to produce high and predictable profit levels every quarter. Instead, they need to create at least enough space from the short-term pressures of quarterly profits to be able to operate and execute business strategy.

The problem with the short-term approach to maximizing quarterly profits is that it ends up having everything about the business operate backward: rather than setting out a strategy for competing, making investments to execute it, and then earning a return, this extreme version starts with a target rate of return and then adjusts everything about the way the business runs to achieve that return each quarter. Investments, programs, even strategies end up changing quarter-by-quarter in order to hit the target. This approach makes it almost impossible for a company to sustain any serious business strategies as the company itself has to constantly adjust to accommodate the variations and uncertainties that come from the markets.

Being able to sustain any kind of competitive strategy requires taking a longer-term perspective, and here again we find an advantage for the India Way. The most fundamental attribute of the India Way is that it offers a distinctive model of business strategy, a way to compete and succeed in the marketplace, and a different way of thinking about strategy than we see in most U.S. businesses. As we described in detail in chapter 5, leading Indian companies look for the source of competitive advantage internally, developing competencies that make them capable of solving the hard challenges presented by their customers. U.S. companies tend to be focused more outside the firm, looking for value in mergers and acquisitions, chasing new customers, or exploring new markets. Researchers in the field of business strategy talk about the distinction between spending resources on exploration versus exploitation, on seeking new opportunities versus pursuing them in depth.[25] India Way firms focus on the latter, while their U.S. counterparts concentrate on the former.

There are reasons for thinking that exploitation has become more difficult as the economy becomes more global. It is more difficult, for example, to find opportunities where competitors are weak (the classic exploitation strategy) once markets are open to global players. It is also more difficult to move operations around in search of cheaper labor given that so many competitors have already done that, bidding up local labor costs. Because of this, researchers who study strategy have come to see the sources of competitiveness as more often being inside the company, as with the India Way companies, with competencies that allow them to do things that their competitors cannot.

In focusing on their internal competencies—on their employees and their skills—Indian executives can do things their competitors

cannot. They can direct strategy at the core needs of long-term customers and execute strategy through persistence and adaptability.
They can see their task as knitting these components together, focusing on aspects like articulating a social mission and building
organizational culture as part of the glue that makes an internally
focused strategy possible.

What does all this mean for business leaders? How can they
adapt the India Way approach to business strategy?

The first point to keep in mind is that company leaders have enormous power over what organizations do, perhaps most importantly by
directing the attention and energy of their organization. Given that,
the place to begin adapting the India Way is for leaders to pay attention to the process of creating strategy, to focus the energy of the
business on that task. A simple way to do so is for the leaders to ask
this question: what are we better at than our competitors? In businesses that do not have an internal focus on strategy, this is a hard
question to answer, and it provokes much soul searching when managers are quizzed by the chief executive. Succeeding with the India
Way approach begins by developing a good answer to that question,
finding something that your business is better at than its competitors. Then the task of leaders is to keep the focus on that competency: communicating the idea that we are good at this task, and it
should be the focus of the way we compete with customers. When the
India Way leaders reported that setting strategy was their number
one priority, they meant this process of getting the business focused
on the competencies that drive its competitive advantage and keeping the organization from wasting time and effort on other priorities.

The focus on internal competencies may seem to raise another
question: what creates those competencies? But the answer to that
is always the same: it is through people, through hiring the right
ones, developing talent internally, and especially engaging the energy of employees with a sense of mission, with empowerment, and
with an architecture and a culture that reinforce these outcomes.
Certainly, as we found in chapters 3 and 4, that is true of many large
Indian companies.

This takes us to a very practical and tangible list of actions that leaders who want to borrow from the India Way should take. These actions help build the capabilities that can drive an internal approach to strategy. An important attribute of these practices is that it is hard to see a downside to them. They are likely to have a positive impact even if pursued separately.

- *Establish the sense of mission.* The chief executive and the top leadership team are the only ones who can establish a social purpose for businesses: what are the positive effects our business has on the broader community? Not all businesses can come up with an answer to that question, but merely asking it again focuses the attention of the organization. It is easier to engage employees around social mission than around the goal of making a shareholder rich. Some businesses have an easier time creating a sense of mission. Pharmaceutical companies like Amgen and Johnson & Johnson, for example, routinely describe their purpose as saving lives and use that purpose in their recruiting. Even those whose business operations are not focused on a social purpose can create something similar, even if done as an ancillary activity. Home Depot, for example, was widely praised for its support of U.S. Olympic teams and of individual athletes. The company reported positive effects on employee morale as well as on customer reactions.

- *Engage employees.* This idea begins with recognizing that the motivation and commitment of employees is not something that should be taken for granted. It has to be secured. Ordering employees to do something will certainly get them to do it, but getting their full effort and energy is another matter. The India Way leaders take employee engagement seriously, and their effort begins with communication: explaining the challenge and the need for the solution. As we saw with the example of Bank of Baroda, this process can often be one of persuasion, with the leaders meeting with employees to listen to concerns and answer questions. The last step in the process of engagement is to truly empower employees: letting them come up with solutions and—this is the hard part—trusting those solutions enough to try them out even if the leaders don't agree.

- *Manage the culture.* Organizational culture is the implicit norms and values that tell people how to behave. Culture is revealed by looking at how things actually get done. In most companies, it is created unconsciously. The leaders may talk about wanting to change the culture, but they do nothing about it. India Way leaders, in contrast, make it a top priority. They focus attention on having a culture that reinforces the behaviors they want in the organization. Perhaps the most powerful way employees learn about culture is to watch what the leaders do. That is why so many of the India Way leaders said that a priority for them is to act as a role model for employees. No doubt most chief executives think that they are models in terms of the amount of work they do. But are they also role models in terms of the level of perks they enjoy, how much they are paid, and how they deal with others in the organization? Recall the model of Vineet Nayar of HCL, who posted his own 360-degree feedback evaluation on the company's Web site for all to see. Would other executives be equally willing to do that?

- *Focus on alignment.* To get the most out of these practices, it is important to think about how they fit together: are the culture and the mission of the organization aligned, and most important, are we managing these aspects in ways that reinforce our competencies as a business? It is possible to have a wonderful strategy, a profound mission, and still have a failing organization because these attributes are not supporting the strategy of the business. The chief executive and the leadership team are in the unique position of being able to see whether the individual practices of the organization align and drive the competencies the organization needs in order to pursue its approach to business, and, if those practices do not align, to fix them.

These practices are not that *novel*. But when we look at contemporary businesses elsewhere, especially in the United States, we see quite different patterns. American chief executives focus much of their attention outside the operation—dealing with investors and regulators, looking for opportunities for mergers and acquisitions and for new businesses, often delegating strategy to a staff function. U.S. companies rarely have a sense of social mission at their core, and their leaders do not see managing culture and engaging employees as personal responsibilities. The era of charismatic CEOs with personal brands and high profiles in the outside community stands in stark contrast to the India Way leaders, who expect to be role models in their behavior for individual employees. These differences help explain why India Way companies focus on long-term customers because those relationships are at the heart of the organization, why they see themselves as extended families with mutual obligations, and why they bang away at hard, persistent challenges until they crack them. They also explain why U.S. companies see their competitiveness as centering on the opposite of persistence, the ability to change in response to new opportunities with a "free agent" workforce and a leadership team focused on the outside environment.

In Closing

The experience of Indian business—and the roaring success of the Indian economy—points the world toward a different enterprise model. Rather than wholeheartedly embracing American-style "unbridled capitalism," the India Way seems to have settled voluntarily on a more bridled version. The nation's leading business figures, we found, were pursuing strategies not strictly tethered to the disciplined pursuit of private profits. Threaded through their accounts was an accent on the long-term benefits not just for their company but also for the country. Asked what they would want to constitute their single most important legacy when they stepped down from their company's leadership, more often than not these leaders mentioned societal benefits. Meanwhile, the distinctive features of the Western model—the riveting focus on shareholder value to the exclusion of other values, the reliance on financial incentives to entice executives to pursue that goal, and the overall belief that the pursuit of self-interest in this manner will ultimately benefit society, eliminating any need for public oversight—have all come to be questioned by the most mainstream of voices, especially as economies eroded around the globe during the 2008–2009 recession.

We have identified key components that make up the India Way, but arguably its critical aspect is the fact that the separate components are integrated into a coherent model. The tight fit between the way executives lead their employees and the way they pursue business strategy allows them to identify a social purpose and match it to business needs. The ability to perform this integration stems from the leaders, who act as the equivalent of choreographers or conductors, knitting these components together through their ability to articulate missions, communicate them to employees, manage organizational architecture and culture, and more generally set priorities. In this way, the whole of the India Way becomes greater than the sum of its individual practices. Focusing on these challenges inside the organization may be the greatest point of difference as contrasted with Western business leaders.

The most important lesson from the India Way might therefore be the light it shines on the American way, at the moment arguably the dominant model for business. The India Way demonstrates the power of collective calling over private purpose, of transcendent value over shareholder value. These ideas are hardly unknown in the United States and indeed were common a generation ago. In the wake of the greatest collapse of American business confidence in more than seventy-five years, the time may be ripe for U.S. company leaders to move back to the future.

Growth of the India Way

THE GROWTH RATE OF THE Indian economy has far outstripped that of the United States in recent years. The American GDP in 2008 stood at 1.64 times its size in 1990, while the Indian GDP had increased over that same eighteen-year period by a factor of 3.02 (see figure A-1). The disparity in growth rates is likely to increase even further. At the writing of this book, the U.S. economy was in the grip of the worst recession since the Great Depression, with negative GDP growth forecast for much of 2009. Though India's growth was expected to slow as well, forecasts still anticipated Indian GDP expansion in 2009 of better than 5 percent.[1]

While the Indian economy has been growing at a considerably higher rate than that of the United States, foreign investment, both coming into and going out of India, has been surging even more rapidly. As seen in figure A-2, annual foreign direct investment—the placement of capital in an enterprise based in India—rose from $100 million in 1990 to $21.8 billion in 2007. At the same time, annual Indian direct investment abroad rose from $2.5 million in 1990 to $13 billion in 2007.

FIGURE A-1

Gross domestic product in constant domestic currency, U.S. and India, 1990–2008

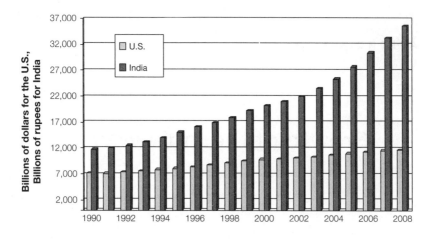

Source: International Monetary Fund, World Economic Outlook Database, April 2009.

FIGURE A-2

Indian foreign direct investment inflows and outflows, 1990–2007

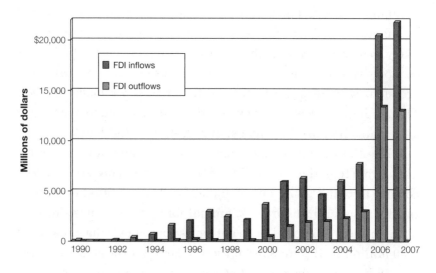

Source: Euromonitor International, Global Market Information Database, August 2009.

Mergers and acquisitions by foreign companies in India—and by Indian companies abroad—displayed comparable growth, as shown in figure A-3. In 1990, Indian companies deployed $2 million in merging with or acquiring companies abroad, but by 2008 that number had reached $12.3 billion. In 1991, foreign companies had spent less than $1 million in merging with or acquiring Indian enterprises, but by 2008 that number had grown to $6.4 billion.

Other trend lines displayed much the same upward slope. As shown in figure A-4, private equity investing in India rose from under $1 billion annually in the early part of the 2000s to $14 billion in 2007. Inflation was under control, and the surging real growth was pulling tens of millions out of poverty, as seen in figure A-5. While the Indian population has more than doubled since the 1960s, the GDP has risen eightfold over the same period. GDP per capita, adjusted with year 2000 U.S. dollars, rose from $181 in 1960 to $686 in 2007, as displayed in figure A-6.

FIGURE A-3

Indian transnational mergers and acquisitions, 1990–2008

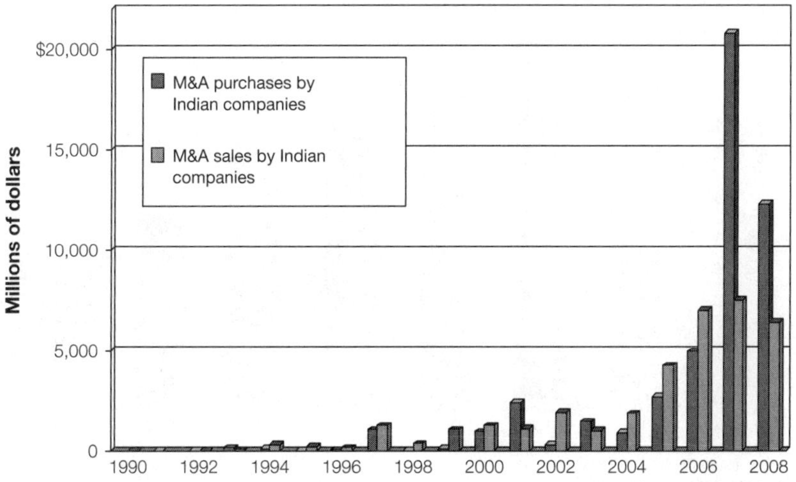

Source: Euromonitor International, Global Market Information Database, August 2009.

FIGURE A-4

Private equity investment in India, 2000–2007

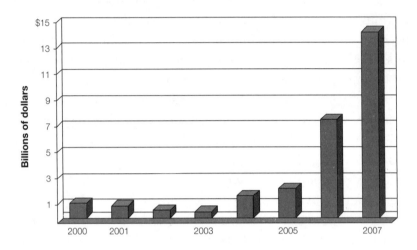

Source: India Venture Capital Association, 2008.

FIGURE A-5

Poverty rate in India, 1974–2007

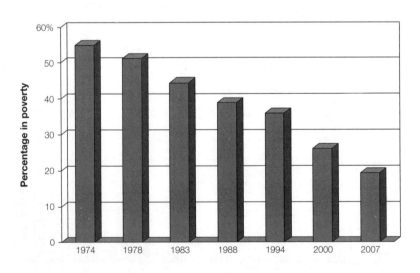

Source: Central Statistical Organization, Government of India, 2009.

FIGURE A-6

GDP per capita in India, 1960–2008

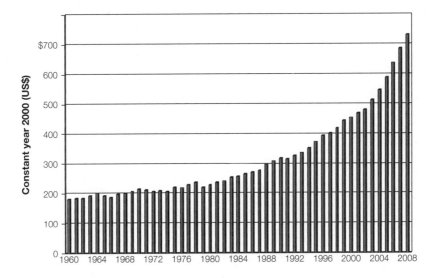

Source: *World Development Indicators*, WDI Online, 2009, http://www.worldbank.org/.

Indian Business Leader Interviews and Survey

WE INTERVIEWED A HOST OF Indian executives in 2007–2009, taking notes and digitally recording the dialogue. The business leaders were associated with ninety-eight companies, and their firms belonged to a wide range of industries, as seen in table B-1. Twenty-four of the companies were part of a conglomerate, twelve were in banking, ten in information technology, and nine from pharmaceuticals and biotechnology. Also included were firms from oil and gas, automobiles and auto parts, fast-moving consumer goods and retail, specialty chemicals, beverages and foods, and a host of other sectors. India is a nation of *business groups*—sets of legally separate firms with significant fractional ownership held by a family or other companies in the group, and with shared directors, a common identity, and an ability to coordinate actions. Twenty-six of the firms we studied belonged to one or another of these groups, including Bajaj, Bharti, Godrej, RPG,

TABLE B-1

Companies of Indian business leaders interviewed

Industry	Category	Percentage
	Banking and finance	12.5
	Information technology	11.5
	Pharmaceuticals and biotechnology	11.5
	Chemicals	6.3
	Oil and gas	6.3
	Automobiles and auto parts	5.2
	Retail and fast-moving consumer goods	5.2
	Highly diversified	5.2
	Industrial equipment	4.2
	Steel	4.2
	Beverages and foods	3.1
	Commercial vehicles and trucks	3.1
	Telecommunications	3.1
	Airlines	2.1
	Cement	2.1
	Consumer electronics	2.1
	Electric utilities	2.1
	Heavy construction	2.1
	Shipping and transportation services	2.1
	Agricultural machinery	1.0
	Broadcasting and entertainment	1.0
	Glass	1.0
	Health care	1.0
	Hotels	1.0
	Mining	1.0
Listed on public stock exchange	Yes	91.7
	No	8.3
Main exchange	Bombay Stock Exchange	87.5
	Other	5.1
	None	7.3
State-owned enterprise (>50%)	Yes	18.8
	No	81.2
Multinational	Yes	82.3
	No	17.7

TABLE B-1 *(continued)*

Family groups	Ambani (Reliance Industries)
	Bajaj
	Bharti
	Birla (Aditya)
	Birla (C. K.)
	Dhoot
	Godrej
	Goenka (RPG Group)
	Jindal (O. P. Jindal plus JSW Group)
	Khorakiwala
	Mahindra
	Murugappa
	Piramal
	Premji
	Rao
	Tata

Jindal, Mahindra & Mahindra, Murugappa, Reliance Industries, and Tata. Ninety-one of the firms were listed on a stock exchange, with eighty-six on an Indian exchange and the others on Amsterdam, New York, Paris, and Swiss exchanges. Eighty of the companies were private sector, eighteen others largely state owned. Seventeen were subsidiaries of an international parent, such as Hindustan Unilever, a publicly listed Indian firm that is also a subsidiary of the Anglo-Dutch Unilever.

For the interviews, we targeted one top executive per company, but in several cases we had the opportunity to interview two—the chief executive and the nonexecutive chair—or even more. Of the 105 individuals interviewed, 102 were active executives at the time of the interview. Forty-two were *promoters,* a uniquely Indian term for those who are both primary owners and top executives. The executives' titles were an Anglo-American mix, with 71 managing or executive directors, 51 chairmen, 9 chief executives, 9 vice-chairmen, and 4 presidents or chief executives of divisions, as seen in table B-2.

TABLE B-2

Characteristics of Indian business leaders interviewed

Age in years	Category	Percentage
	30–39	2.9
	40–49	17.1
	50–59	51.4
	60–69	21.9
	70–79	2.9
	No age given	3.8
Gender	Male	96.2
	Female	3.8
Educational level	No degree	2.0
	Bachelor's degree	92
	Master's and professional	82
	Honorary doctorate	6.0
	Doctorate	5.0
Area of study	Arts and sciences	30
	Business	74
	Engineering	37
	Law	9.0
	Medicine	2.0
	Military	1.0
	Social work	3.0
	Veterinary medicine	1.0
	None	2.0
Titles	Promoter or promoter group	40
	Founder or cofounder	10
	Chairman	49
	Vice chairman	9.0
	Managing/executive director	68
	Chief executive officer	9.0
	Chief financial officer	2.0
	President or division head	4.0
Executive status	Executive	97.1
	Nonexecutive	2.9

TABLE B-3

Educational institutions of interviewed Indian business leaders

Indian schools		U.S. schools		Other schools	
BITS, Pilani	3	Cornell University	1	Asian Institute of Management	1
Kolkata University (Calcutta)	2	Duke University	1	CEDEP/INSEAD	1
IIM, Ahmedabad	9	Harvard University	8	ICA of India, England, and Wales	1
IIM, Bangalore	2	Illinois Institute of Technology	1	London Business School	1
IIM, Kolkata (Calcutta)	2	Massachusetts Institute of Technology	4	Melbourne University	1
IIT, Delhi	5	New York University	1	Norwegian Shipping Academy	1
IIT, Kanpur	2	Northwestern University	1	Royal College of Surgeons	1
IIT, Kharagpur	2	Purdue University	2	Technische Hochschule für Chemie	1
IIT, Madras	2	Rutgers University	1	University of Aston	1
IIT, Mumbai (Bombay)	2	Stanford University	2	University of Leeds	1
St. Stephen's College, Delhi	2	University of Michigan	2		
University of Delhi	4	University of Texas	1		
University of Mumbai (Bombay)	3	Wharton School, University of Pennsylvania	3		
University of Roorkee	2				
Total	**42**		**28**		**10**

Note: BITS = Birla Institute of Technology and Science; IIM = Indian Institute of Management; IIT = Indian Institute of Technology.

The educational institutions attended by the business leaders we studied were global and diverse: of the 105 executives, 9 had attended the Indian Institute of Management at Ahmedabad, 8 had been at Harvard University, 5 at the Indian Institute of Technology at Delhi, 4 each at the University of Delhi and Massachusetts Institute of Technology, and 3 each at the University of Mumbai (Bombay) and the Wharton School of the University of Pennsylvania. Overall, as shown in table B-3, 42 of the executives had attended an Indian school, 28 an American school, and 10 elsewhere abroad.

By way of a benchmark, consider a study of 128 premier American business leaders presiding over their firms in a recent period. When our Indian business leaders are compared with them, they are both similar and different: the Indians and the Americans have comparable levels of undergraduate education, but significantly higher proportions of the Indian executives hold advanced degrees, were educated abroad, and had founded their firm or were members of a founding family. Some 90 percent of the American business leaders had completed a college degree, on a par with the 92 percent among the Indian business leaders. Of the American business leaders, 45 percent held a master's or other professional degree, while 82 percent of the Indian business leaders were so educated. A quarter of the Americans had established their company or were founding-family members; half the Indians were founders or members of a promoter—usually family—group. Among the American business leaders with MBA degrees, 90 percent earned them at one of seventeen top-ranked American institutions; among the Indian business leaders with master's and professional degrees, the dispersion among institutions was far greater. Most of the American business leaders held degrees from U.S. institutions, while a third of the Indian business leaders had been educated abroad, primarily in U.S. schools.[1]

All of those we interviewed are identified in table B-4 with their titles and companies at the time of the interview, and a biographical sketch follows. In addition, we asked the senior executive for human resources at each of these companies to complete a lengthy online set of questions about their company.[2]

TABLE B-4

Interviewed Indian business leaders

Indian executive	Title	Company	Survey
Anu Aga	Nonexecutive director, promoter-director	Thermax Ltd.	Yes
M. A. Alagappan	Executive chairman of the Murugappa Group	Tube Investments of India Ltd. (Murugappa Group)	
Mukesh D. Ambani	Executive chairman and managing director	Reliance Industries Ltd.	
Nakul Anand	Divisional chief executive	Hotels Division, ITC Ltd.	Yes
Dr. Shailesh Ayyangar	Managing director, whole-time director	Aventis Pharma Ltd.	
P. Rama Babu	Managing director	E.I.D. Parry (India) Ltd.	
Kushagra Bajaj	Joint managing director	Bajaj Hindustan Ltd. (Bajaj Group)	
Rahul Bajaj	Executive chairman, promoter-director	Bajaj Auto Ltd. (Bajaj Group)	Yes
Shishir Bajaj	Executive chairman and managing director, promoter-director	Bajaj Hindustan Ltd. (Bajaj Group)	
Arun Balakrishnan	Chairman and managing director	Hindustan Petroleum Corporation Ltd.	
A. K. Balyan	Executive director	Oil and Natural Gas Corporation Ltd. (ONGC)	Yes
Proshanto Banerjee	Former chairman and managing director	Gas Authority of India Ltd. (GAIL)	
Sumantra Banerjee	Managing director and wholetime director	CESC Ltd.	Yes
Manvinder Singh Banga	President, food, home, and personal care (former chairman and chief executive, Hindustan Unilever)	Unilever	
B. G. Bangur	Executive chairman, promoter-director	Shree Cement Ltd.	Yes
Sarthak Behuria	Executive chairman	Indian Oil Corporation Ltd.	
Subodh Bhargava	Chairman	Videsh Sanchar Nigam Ltd. (VSNL, Tata Group)	Yes
Hari S. and Shyam S. Bhartia	Executive cochairman and managing director, promoter-director	Jubliant Organosys Ltd.	Yes
O. P. Bhatt	Executive chairman	State Bank of India Ltd.	Yes
Sanjeev Bikhchandani	Managing director, chief executive officer, and promoter-director	Info Edge (India) Ltd.	Yes

(Continued)

TABLE B-4 (*continued*)

Indian executive	Title	Company	Survey
Kumar Mangalam Birla	Chairman	Aditya Birla Group	Yes
Kishore Biyani	Managing director, promoter-director	Pantaloon Retail (India) Ltd.	Yes
Subir Bose	Managing director, wholetime director	Berger Paints India Ltd.	Yes
Subhash Chandra	Chairman, promoter-director	Zee Entertainment Enterprises Ltd. (Essel Group)	Yes
Ashwin C. Choksi	Executive chairman, managing director, and promoter-director	Asian Paints Ltd.	
Ajai Chowdhry	Executive chairman, promoter-director	HCL Infosystems Ltd.	Yes
P. Dasgupta	Managing director and chief executive officer	Petronet LNG Ltd.	Yes
Saroj K. Datta	Executive director	Jet Airways (India) Ltd.	Yes
Y. M. Deosthalee	Wholetime director and chief financial officer	Larsen & Toubro Ltd.	Yes
P. N. Dhoot	Wholetime director, promoter-director	Videocon Industries Ltd. (Videocon Group)	
S. B. Ganguly	Executive chairman	Exide Industries Ltd.	
Adi B. Godrej	Executive chairman, managing director, promoter-director	Godrej Consumer Products Ltd. (Godrej Group)	Yes
Sanjiv Goenka	Board member of RPG Enterprises and vice-chairman of the RPG Group	RPG Enterprises Ltd. (RPG Group)	Yes
R. Gopalakrishnan	Executive director	Tata Sons Ltd.	
G. R. Gopinath	Managing director, promoter-director	Deccan Aviation Ltd. ("Air Deccan")	Yes
Dipak B. Gupta	Executive director and wholetime director	Kotak Mahindra Bank Ltd.	Yes
S. Hajara	Executive chairman, managing director, and wholetime director	Shipping Corporation of India Ltd.	
Kewal Handa	Managing director, wholetime director	Pfizer Ltd. (India)	Yes
Rajesh Hukku	Executive chairman and managing director	i-Flex Solutions Ltd.	
Naveen Jindal	Executive vice-chairman, managing director, and promoter-director	Jindal Steel & Power Ltd. (Jindal Group)	Yes

TABLE B-4 (*continued*)

Sajjan Jindal	Vice-chairman, managing director, and promoter-director	JSW Steel Ltd. (Jindal Group)	
Praveen P. Kadle	Executive director–finance, wholetime director	Tata Motors Ltd. (Tata Group)	
K. V. Kamath	Managing director and CEO	ICICI Bank Ltd.	Yes
Rana Kapoor	Managing director and CEO	Yes Bank Ltd.	
Anil K. Khandelwal	Chairman and managing director	Bank of Baroda	Yes
Jagdish Khattar	Managing director	Maruti Suzuki India Ltd.	Yes
Habil F. Khorakiwala	Executive chairman, managing director, and promoter-director	Wockhardt Ltd.	
Chanda Kochhar	Joint managing director and chief financial officer	ICICI Bank Ltd.	Yes
Manoj Kohli	CEO and joint managing director	Bharti Airtel Ltd. (Bharti Group)	Yes
Naveen Kshatriya	Managing director, whole-time director	Castrol India Ltd.	
M. Lakshminarayan	Joint managing director, promoter-director	Motor Industries Company Ltd. (MICO, Bosch Group)	Yes
Anand Mahindra	Vice-chairman and managing director	Mahindra & Mahindra Ltd.	Yes
Harsh Mariwala	Executive chairman, managing director, promoter-director	Marico Ltd.	
Kiran Mazumdar-Shaw	Executive chairman, managing director, promoter-director	Biocon Ltd.	Yes
Rakesh Mehrotra	Managing director	Container Corporation of India Ltd. (CONCOR)	Yes
Sunil Bharti Mittal	Chairman and managing director	Bharti Airtel Ltd. (Bharti Group)	
Nachiket Mor	Former deputy managing director	ICICI Bank Ltd.	Yes
P. K. Mukherjee	Managing director, promoter-director	Sesa Goa Ltd. (Sesa Group)	Yes
N. R. Narayana Murthy	Joint chairman and chief mentor	Infosys Technologies Ltd.	Yes
B. Muthuraman	Managing director, whole-time director	Tata Steel Ltd. (Tata Group)	Yes

(*Continued*)

TABLE B-4 (*continued*)

Indian executive	Title	Company	Survey
M. V. Nair	Chairman and managing director	Union Bank of India Ltd.	
Vivek Nair	Vice-chairman, managing director, promoter-director	Hotel Leela Venture Ltd.	Yes
Lakshmi Narayanan	Vice-chairman	Cognizant Technology Solutions (U.S.)	
V. R. S. Natarajan	Executive chairman and managing director	Bharat Earth Movers Ltd. (BEML)	
Anand Nayak	Head of human resource development	ITC Ltd.	Yes
Vineet Nayar	CEO and wholetime director	HCL Technologies Ltd.	
H. V. Neotia	Former managing director, redesignated as additional director	Ambuja Cement Eastern Ltd.	Yes
T. V. Mohandas Pai	Member of the board, director of HR, education and research, and administration	Infosys Technologies Ltd.	
Deepak S. Parekh	Executive chairman, wholetime director	Housing Development Finance Corporation Ltd. (HDFC)	
Allen Pereira	Executive director, whole-time director	Oriental Bank of Commerce Ltd.	
Ajay G. Piramal	Executive chairman, promoter-director	Nicholas Piramal India Ltd. (Piramal Enterprises Group)	Yes
Satish Pradhan	Executive vice president, group human resources	Tata Sons Ltd. (Tata Group)	
G. V. Prasad	Vice-chairman and chief executive	Dr. Reddy's Laboratories Ltd.	Yes
Azim H. Premji	Executive chairman, managing director, promoter-director	Wipro Ltd.	Yes
Aditya Puri	Managing director, wholetime director	HDFC Bank Ltd.	Yes
Madhabi Puri-Buch	Executive director	ICICI Bank Ltd.	Yes
Subir Raha	Former chairman and managing director	Oil and Natural Gas Corporation Ltd. (ONGC)	
B. Ramalinga Raju	Executive chairman, promoter-director	Satyam Computer Services Ltd.	
Arun Bharat Ram	Executive chairman, promoter-director	SRF Ltd.	Yes

TABLE B-4 (*continued*)

K. Ramachandran	Vice-chairman and managing director; CEO for India	Philips Electronics India Ltd.	Yes
S. Ramadorai	Chief executive officer and managing director	Tata Consultancy Services Ltd. (Tata Group)	Yes
K. Ramakrishnan	Chairman and managing director	Andhra Bank	
C. K. Ranganathan	Chairman and managing director	CavinKare Pvt. Ltd.	Yes
G. M. Rao	Founder, chairman and managing director	GMR Group	Yes
M. B. N. Rao	Chairman and managing director	Canara Bank	
Prathap C. Reddy	Executive chairman	Apollo Hospitals Enterprise Ltd.	
P. V. Ramaprasad Reddy	Chairman	Aurobindo Pharma Ltd.	Yes
Mukesh Rohatgi	Executive chairman and managing director	Engineers India Ltd. (EIL)	Yes
S. K. Roongta	Chairman and wholetime director	Steel Authority of India Ltd. (SAIL)	
Raman Roy	Chairman and managing director	Quatrro BPO Solutions Pvt. Ltd.	Yes
B. Sambamurthy	Executive chairman and managing director	Corporation Bank	
T. Sankaralingam	Chairman and managing director	NTPC Ltd. (formerly National Thermal Power Corporation Ltd.)	Yes
B. Santhanam	Chairman and managing director	Saint-Gobain Glass India Ltd.	Yes
Ravi Santhanam	Managing director, executive director	Hindustan Motors Ltd. (Birla Group)	Yes
Kamal K. Sharma	Managing director	Lupin Ltd.	
Percy Siganporia	Managing director, wholetime director	Tata Tea Ltd. (Tata Group)	
Analjit Singh	Cofounder, executive chairman, promoter-director	Max India Ltd.	Yes
Malvinder Mohan Singh	Managing director and chief executive director, promoter-director	Ranbaxy Laboratories Ltd.	Yes
Ashok Sinha	Chairman and managing director	Bharat Petroleum Corporation Ltd. (BPCL)	Yes

(*Continued*)

TABLE B-4 (*continued*)

Indian executive	Title	Company	Survey
P. M. Sinha	Former chairman	PepsiCo India Holdings	
R. S. P. Sinha	Executive chairman and managing director	Mahanagar Telephone Nigam Ltd. (MTNL)	Yes
Ashok Soni	Managing director	Voltas Ltd. (Tata Group)	Yes
Ashok Soota	Chairman and managing director	MindTree Consulting Ltd.	Yes
Mallika Srinivasan	Director	Tractors and Farm Equipment Ltd. (TAFE)	
Ravi Uppal	Chairman of ABB Ltd. (India); and for the parent company, ABB Ltd., president of global markets and ABB Group executive committee	ABB Ltd. and ABB Ltd. (India)	Yes

Supplemental Interviews

We also interviewed an additional set of individuals who are well familiar with Indian business leaders (see table B-5).

Biographical Sketches

Biographical sketches of those interviewed in the primary and supplementary groups follow:

Anu Aga became executive chairperson of the Thermax Ltd. in 1996 and two years later became nonexecutive chairperson. She retired as chairperson in 2004. Aga has been active in the Confederation of Indian Industry (CII) and served as the chairperson of CII's western region. She now works closely with the philanthropic Thermax Social Initiative Foundation. Aga holds a postgraduate degree in medical and psychiatric social work.

Rakesh Aggarwal is director of Sony Entertainment Television Pvt. Ltd. and director of World Media Group Pvt. Ltd., both based in Singapore. He is also a board member of the Nanyang Business

TABLE B-5

Supplemental interviews

Individual	Title	Organization
Rakesh Aggarwal	Director	Sony Entertainment Television
Sushanta Banerjee	Founder and principal	Samuday Psycon
Neeraj Bharadwaj	Managing director	Apax Partners
Amit Chandra	Managing director	Bain Capital, Mumbai
Atanu Dey	Chief economist	Netcore Solutions
Humayun Dhanrajgir	Chairman	Emcure Pharmaceuticals
Akhil Gupta	Senior managing director	Blackstone Group
Rajesh Jain	Founder and managing director	Netcore Solutions
Vijay Mahajan	Chief executive and managing director	BASIX
Rajat Nag	Managing director general	Asian Development Bank
Raaj Sah	Professor, Harris School of Public Policy Studies and the College	University of Chicago
Sanjeev Sanyal	Director of global markets research	Deutsche Bank
Partha Sarkar	Board member	Escorts Finance
Anil Sharma	Vice president, human resources	ITC Hotels Division

School advisory board. A career banker, he worked for fifteen years for Citibank in India, Thailand, Sri Lanka, and Singapore, and for seven years with Union Bank of Switzerland, Singapore, as chairman of the East Asia Credit Committee.

M. A. Alagappan is the executive chairman of the Murugappa Group's corporate board. He is also a committee member of the Federation of Indian Chambers of Commerce and Industry (FICCI) and the Southern India Chambers of Commerce and Industry (SICCI). He served as honorary consul of Hungary in India for the southern region. Alagappan did his graduate work in management at the University of Aston, UK.

Mukesh D. Ambani has been with Reliance Industries Ltd. (RIL), India's largest business house, since 1981. He now serves as RIL's chairman and managing director. In addition to his business activities, he is a member of the prime minister's Advisory Council on Trade and Industry and the Council of Scientific and Industrial Research (CSIR), India. He pursued an MBA from Stanford, and serves on the advisory board of Stanford's Graduate School of Business.

Nakul Anand joined the Hotels Division of ITC Ltd. as a management trainee in 1978. Since then he has held various positions in ITC Welcomgroup's hotels, including that of general manager of the flagship hotel, ITC Hotel Maurya Sheraton and Towers. He is currently the divisional chief executive of the Hotels Division of ITC Ltd. He has won a number of awards for excellence, including General Manager of the Year.

Shailesh Ayyangar became managing director of Aventis Pharma Ltd. in 2005. He held senior sales and marketing positions in SmithKline Beecham Pharmaceuticals and GlaxoSmithKline (GSK) in both India and Great Britain. He was also on the board of SmithKline Beecham Pharmaceuticals before its merger with Glaxo Wellcome. A graduate in veterinary science, Dr. Ayyangar holds a postgraduate degree in business management from the Indian Institute of Management (IIM), Ahmedabad, Gujarat.

P. Rama Babu joined E.I.D. Parry (India) Ltd. in 1983 and served as managing director from 2004 to 2008. He played a key role in the turnaround of E.I.D. and in its expansion and acquisitions, and he oversaw operations relating to the Sugar and Chemical Divisions of E.I.D. He serves as director of E-Commodities Ltd. and Trichy Distilleries and Chemicals Ltd. Babu holds a master's degree in social work and labor welfare.

Kushagra Bajaj has served as chief executive of Bajaj Hindustan Ltd. (BHL), a major Indian producer of sugar and ethanol, since 2001 and was appointed as joint managing director in 2007. He is responsible for overall operations of BHL and its subsidiary companies. He has a BS in economics, political philosophy, and finance from Carnegie Mellon University and earned his MS in marketing from Northwestern University.

Rahul Bajaj serves as executive chairman of the Bajaj Group of companies, including Bajaj Auto Ltd., India's premier two- and three-wheeler company. He was twice the president of the Confederation of Indian Industry (1979–1980, 1999–2000). He is also on the executive board of the Indian School of Business and is a member of the Prince of Wales International Business Leaders Forum. He graduated from Harvard Business School.

Shishir Bajaj has been managing director of Bajaj Hindustan Ltd. since 1988 and serves as its chairman. He has also served as president of the Indian Sugar Mills Association and as chairman of Indian Sugar and General Industry Export Import Corporation Ltd. He is a member of the western regional council of CII and the managing committee of Bombay Chambers of Commerce and Industry. He received his MBA from New York University.

Arun Balakrishnan became chairman and managing director of Hindustan Petroleum Corporation Ltd. (HPCL) in 2007. Prior to this assignment, he was HPCL's director of human resources. The Institution of Engineers (India) has recognized him for "his outstanding contribution to the profession of chemical engineering." Balakrishnan has a chemical engineering degree from the Government College of Engineering, Trichur-Kerala, and an MBA from the Indian Institute of Management, Bangalore.

A. K. Balyan has been director, human resources, of Oil and Natural Gas Corporation Ltd. since 2003. Balyan has thirty years of experience and had held several field and staff assignments in various disciplines, including analytical geo-chemistry lab, mud engineering, planning, and monitoring of exploration activities. Balyan holds a doctorate degree in chemistry from Technische Hochschule für Chemie, Merseburg, Germany, and is an alumnus of IIT, Delhi.

Proshanto Banerjee is the former chairman and managing director of Gas Authority of India Ltd. (GAIL), the largest natural gas transmission and marketing company in India. Prior to joining GAIL, he was the executive director (marketing) of Indian Oil Corporation. A chemical engineering graduate from the Institute of

Technology, Varanasi, Banerjee did his master's in marketing management from the Jamnalal Bajaj Institute of Management Studies, Mumbai.

Sumantra Banerjee has been managing director of CESC Ltd., an electrical services company, since 1993. He also serves as chief executive and president of RPG Power and Retail Groups. He has over thirty-two years of experience in India and abroad in manufacturing, engineering, finance, marketing, and general management functions. He received both his MS and MBA degrees in the United States.

Sushanta Banerjee is founder and principal consultant of Samuday Psycon and board member of Sumedhas, Academy for Human Context, both based in New Delhi. He has been at the forefront of developing the applied behavioral sciences field in India and has consulted with over a hundred organizations from the corporate sector, banks, and elite educational and religious institutions. He has also taught at IIM, Ahmedabad, as visiting faculty since 1973.

Manvinder Singh (Vindi) Banga was appointed president of the Home, Personal Care, and Food Division of Unilever in 2008. He is actively involved on the boards and managing committees of many organizations, including the Confederation of Indian Industry, the Indian Institute of Management, Ahmedabad, and the Indian School of Business, Hyderabad. He completed his postgraduate degree in management from the Indian Institute of Management.

B. G. Bangur serves as executive chairman of Shree Cement Ltd. and has over fifty-two years' experience in the cement industry. He is also the director of The Didwana Industrial Corporation, NBI Industrial Finance Company, Khemka Properties, and Digvijay Finlease. In addition, he is actively involved with various philanthropic and charitable organizations. He holds a BCom (honors) from Calcutta University.

Sarthak Behuria is the chairman of Indian Oil Corporation Ltd. He is also the part-time chairman of IBP Co., Bongaigaon Refinery and Petrochemicals, Indian Oil Tanking, and Lanka-IOC. He has more than three decades of experience in the field of oil refining and marketing. Behuria is an alumnus of St. Stephen's College, Delhi, and the Indian Institute of Management (IIM), Ahmedabad.

Neeraj Bharadwaj is managing director and country head of Apax Partners (India), a private equity firm. Bharadwaj joined Apax in 1999 and has led deals like JAMDAT Mobile, WiderThan, and NXP. He was previously with McKinsey & Company, Goldman Sachs, and Morgan Stanley. He holds a BS in economics from the Wharton School of the University of Pennsylvania, and an MBA from Harvard Business School.

Subodh Bhargava is chairman of Tata Communications and chairman emeritus of the Eicher Group. He has served as president of the CII as well as the Association of Indian Automobile Manufacturers; he has also been vice president of the Tractor Manufacturers Association. Bhargava has been closely associated with technical and management education in India. He holds a degree in mechanical engineering from the University of Roorkee.

Hari S. Bhartia is cochairman and managing director of Jubilant Organosys Ltd., which specializes in pharmaceutical drug discovery and development. He has been a member in several educational and science and technology programs of the government of India. Bhartia is also a member of the Communication Working Group of the Global Roundtable on Climate Change, Columbia University. He is a chemical engineering graduate of the Indian Institute of Technology, Delhi.

Shyam S. Bhartia is chairman and managing director of Jubilant Organosys Ltd. Bhartia has also served as director on the board of Air India, and on the boards of governors of Indian Institute of Management, Ahmedabad, and Indian Institute of Technology, Mumbai. Currently, he is a member of the executive committee of FICCI. He received his ICWA degree from the Institute of Cost and Works Accountants of India (ICWAI).

O. P. Bhatt became chairman of the board of State Bank of India Ltd. in 2006. Prior to this appointment, he was managing director of the State Bank of Travancore. He has also been chief general manager of the North Eastern Circle of the bank and general manager (retail) at Lucknow. He has had foreign assignments in both London and Washington. Bhatt has an MA in English literature.

Sanjeev Bikhchandani is managing director and CEO of InfoEdge (India) Ltd., an Indian provider of online recruitment, matrimonial, and real estate classifieds. He has been visiting faculty and guest lecturer at IIM, Ahmedabad; Institute of Management Technology (IMT), Ghaziabad; Times School of Marketing; and Delhi School of Communication. He received his BA degree (honors) in economics from St. Stephen's College, Delhi University, and his PGDM from the Indian Institute of Management, Ahmedabad.

Kumar Mangalam Birla is the chairman of the Aditya Birla Group, a leading Indian and international business group with assets in excess of US$28 billion. A graduate of the London Business School, Birla has served on numerous regulatory and professional boards, including the central board of directors of the Reserve Bank of India and the national council of the Confederation of Indian Industry.

Kishore Biyani is the managing director of Pantaloon Retail (India) Ltd., a leading India retailer, and CEO of Future Group. He was given the Ernst & Young Entrepreneur of the Year 2006 award in the services sector and the Lakshmipat Singhania–IIM Lucknow Young Business Leader Award by Prime Minister Manmohan Singh in 2006. He holds a bachelor's degree in commerce and a postgraduate degree in marketing.

Subir Bose serves as managing director of Berger Paints India Ltd., a major Indian manufacturer of paints and varnishes. He also serves on the boards of BNB Coatings India Ltd. and DIC India Ltd. Bose has a BTech from the Indian Institute of Technology and a postgraduate degree in management from the Indian Institute of Management, Ahmedabad.

Amit Chandra has been managing director of Bain Capital, Mumbai, since early 2008. Chandra spent most of his professional career at DSP Merrill Lynch, India's leading investment bank, retiring from there in 2007 as its board member and managing director. Chandra was named a Young Global Leader by the World Economic Forum in 2007. He is a trustee/board member of The Akanksha Foundation, GiveIndia, and Credibility Alliance.

Subhash Chandra is chairman of Zee Entertainment Enterprises Ltd. and chairman and promoter of the Essel Group of companies. The Confederation of Indian Industry chose Chandra as the chairman of the CII media committee for two successive years. In 2004, the trade group FICCI named him Global Indian Entertainment Personality of the Year. He is also a trustee for the Global Vippassana Foundation.

Ashwin Choksi is executive chairman and managing director of Asian Paints Ltd. He became chairman of the company in 1998. Asian Paints, which currently operates in twenty-two countries across the world, is India's largest paint company and ranks among the top ten decorative coatings companies in the world. *Forbes Global* magazine ranked Asian Paints among the "200 Best Small Companies in the World" for 2002 and 2003.

Ajai Chowdhry is the executive chairman of HCL Infosystems Ltd., a firm specializing in IT hardware. He was also part of the IT task force set up by the prime minister of India to give shape to India's IT strategy. Chowdhry has a bachelor's degree in electronics and communication engineering and attended the Executive Program at the School of Business Administration at the University of Michigan.

P. Dasgupta is the managing director and CEO of Petronet LNG Ltd., a company formed by the government of India to import, store, and transport liquefied natural gas. Prior to joining the company in 2003, he worked as chief financial officer for Essar Telecom-Essar Teleholdings Ltd. Dasgupta completed his bachelor's degree in commerce from Ravi Shankar University, Raipur, in 1967.

Saroj K. Datta is the executive director of Jet Airways (India) Ltd., a company he has worked for since its inception in 1993. Datta has over forty years of experience in civil aviation in India and abroad, including prior positions with Air India and Kuwait Airways. He completed his education at St. Stephen's College, Delhi, with a postgraduate degree in economics.

Y. M. Deosthalee is chief financial officer and director for Larsen & Toubro Ltd., India's largest engineering and construction conglomerate. Deosthalee joined the company in 1974 and was elevated to general manager (finance) in 1990, later becoming its CFO. In 1995, he was appointed to the board. Larsen & Toubro, which has offices in the United States, Europe, the Middle East, and Japan, made the *Forbes* Global 2000 list in 2006.

Atanu Dey is chief economist of Netcore Solutions Pvt. Ltd., a software company. Previously, he was product manager at Hewlett-Packard. From 2001 to 2002, he was Reuters Digital Vision Fellow at Stanford University. Dey has a bachelor's degree in mechanical engineering from Nagpur University. He also did postgraduate work in computer science at Rutgers University and IIT, Kanpur, and has a PhD in economics from the University of California, Berkeley.

Humayun Dhanrajgir is chairman of Emcure Pharmaceuticals Ltd. Previously, he was vice chairman and managing director of Glaxo India Ltd. and former president of the Organization of Pharmaceutical Producers of India (OPPI). Dhanrajgir joined Emcure's board in 2000. Dhanrajgir is a graduate in chemical engineering from Loughborough University, a U.K. Member–Institution of Chemical Engineers, a U.K. Chartered Engineer, and a graduate of Harvard's Advanced Management Program.

Pradipkumar N. Dhoot is a director for Videocon Industries Ltd., a manufacturer of consumer electronics and appliances. He is an industrialist with diversified business experience spanning more than three decades and is one of the core promoters of the Videocon Group. In 2005, India's Consumer Electronics and TV Manufacturers Association (CETMA) conferred on him the Man of Electronics 2005 award.

S. B. Ganguly served as executive chairman and chief executive officer of Exide Industries Ltd., a manufacturer of electric batteries, until 2007. He now serves as chairman emeritus of the board he first joined in 1991. Ganguly, a qualified chemical engineer, joined the company in 1986, and prior to that he was director of research and technical for Dunlop India Ltd.

Adi B. Godrej is executive chairman and managing director of Godrej Consumer Products Ltd. and chairman of the Godrej Group. Godrej is a former member of the dean's advisory council of MIT Sloan School of Management and serves on the Wharton Asian executive board. He is also a member of the national council of the CII and the governing board of the Indian School of Business.

Sanjiv Goenka is a board member of RPG Enterprises and vice chairman of the RPG Group, whose businesses include power, tires, entertainment, organized transmission engineering, retailing, and IT. His current positions include chairman of the board of governors, IIT, Kharagpur; and member of the board of governors, International Management Institute, New Delhi. He has also served as honorary consul of Canada in India.

R. Gopalakrishnan is executive director of Tata Sons Ltd. (Tata Group). He began his business career in 1967, working as a management trainee for Hindustan Unilever, and eventually became its vice chairman. After thirty-one years of working for various Unilever companies, he joined Tata Sons in 1998. Gopalakrishnan is a graduate in physics from Calcutta University and in engineering from IIT, Kharagpur.

G. R. Gopinath is the managing director of Deccan Aviation Ltd. (Air Deccan, now Kingfisher Red), a no-frills, low-cost airline service in India. He is also a pioneer in the field of organic farming and sericulture. In 2007, the French government gave him the Chevalier de la Légion d'Honneur award for his contributions toward Indo-French cooperation in aviation. Gopinath is an ex–army officer who graduated from India's National Defense Academy.

Akhil Gupta is a senior managing director of The Blackstone Group and chairman of Blackstone India based in Mumbai; previously he served as CEO, Corporate Development, for Reliance Industries Ltd. and Reliance Infocomm Ltd. He began his career at Hindustan Unilever, India's multinational corporation, worked with Strategic Planning Associates and ICF in Washington, DC, and then served as an officer with several American retail/manufacturing firms. He received his

BTech degree in chemical engineering from the Indian Institute of Technology, Delhi, and an MBA from Stanford University.

Dipak Gupta is executive director of Kotak Mahindra Bank Ltd. and has over eighteen years of experience in the financial services sector, fourteen years of which have been with the Kotak Group. Prior to joining the Kotak Group, he was with A.F. Ferguson and Company for approximately six years. Gupta has a BE (electronics) degree and a PGDM from the Indian Institute of Management, Ahmedabad.

S. Hajara is executive chairman and managing director of Shipping Corporation of India Ltd., the largest shipping company in the country. He is a member of the CII national council and has served as a delegate to many international conferences on shipping and maritime matters. Hajara has a PGDM from IIM, Kolkata, and an LLB degree from Kolkata University.

Kewal Handa is managing director of Pfizer Ltd. (India). He is also a visiting faculty member at the Narsee Monjee Institute of Management Studies and an international trainer of the Indian Junior Chamber. Handa is a member of the Institute of Cost and Works Accountants of India and the Institute of Company Secretaries of India. He holds a master's degree in commerce from Sydenham College, Mumbai.

Rajesh Hukku is the executive chairman and managing director of i-Flex Solutions Ltd., a global banking software company with customers in more than 120 countries. Prior to leading i-Flex, he worked for Tata Consultancy Services and headed Citicorp Overseas Software. Hukku received a bachelor's degree (honors) in electrical and electronics engineering from the Birla Institute of Technology and Science in Pilani, Rajasthan.

Rajesh Jain is founder and managing director of Netcore Solutions Pvt. Ltd., a software solutions company. He is best known for his launch of the Indian Web portal India World in 1995. India World was acquired by Satyam Infoway (Sify) in November 1999 for $115 million in one of Asia's largest Internet deals. Jain has an MS from Columbia University and a BTech from IIT, Mumbai.

Naveen Jindal is executive vice chairman and managing director of Jindal Steel & Power Ltd. In addition to his executive duties, he is also a member of Parliament from the Kurukshetra constituency. Jindal led a successful campaign resulting in the India Supreme Court's historic judgment in 2004 affirming Indians' right to fly the national flag freely. He holds an MBA from the University of Texas.

Sajjan Jindal is the vice chairman and director of JSW Steel Ltd. and director of JSW Energy Ltd. He has over twenty years' experience in the steel industry and developed several new kinds of steel. Additionally, he is on the board of governors of the Indian Institute of Management, Indore, and is a member of the TTD Development advisory council and the Bombay chapter of the Young Presidents' Organization.

Praveen Kadle is the executive director, finance, for Tata Motors Ltd. (Tata Group). Prior to joining Tata Motors, Kadle was chief financial officer of Tata-IBM Ltd. He is also a member of the Institute of Chartered Accountants of India, the Institute of Cost and Works Accountants of India, and the Institute of Company Secretaries of India. Kadle is an honors graduate in commerce and accountancy from Mumbai University.

K. V. Kamath, former chief executive of India's second-largest banking and financial services conglomerate, ICICI, joined the company in 1971, moved to the Asian Development Bank in 1988, and returned to ICICI in 1996 as managing director and CEO. He became the nonexecutive chairman of ICICI Bank effective May 1, 2009. He served as president of the Confederation of Indian Industry, the nation's leading business association, from 2008 to 2009.

Rana Kapoor is founder, managing director, and CEO of Yes Bank Ltd. Kapoor is a member of the CII national council, FICCI's national executive committee, and the government of India's Board of Trade. Ernest & Young named him Start-up Entrepreneur of the Year 2005. He holds an MBA degree from Rutgers University in New Jersey (1980), and a bachelor's degree in economics (honors) from the University of Delhi (1977).

Anil Khandelwal serves the Bank of Baroda as its chairman and managing director. With over thirty-five years of banking experience, he has also been a member on several government committees, the Reserve Bank of India, and the Indian Banks' Association. Khandelwal holds a bachelor's degree in chemical engineering, a master's degree in business administration, a doctorate degree in management, and a postgraduate degree in law.

Jagdish Khattar served as the managing director of Maruti Suzuki India Ltd., a major automobile manufacturer in South Asia. Prior to this experience, Khattar, an officer of the Indian Administrative Services, held many government positions overseeing numerous Indian industries, including tea, steel, cement, and road transportation. Khattar completed his bachelor in arts (honors) degree from St. Stephen's College, University of Delhi, and his LLB from Delhi University.

Habil Khorakiwala is chairman of the Wockhardt Group. He is the president of FICCI and a member of the National Manufacturing Competitiveness Council, established by Prime Minister Manmohan Singh. He is the former president of the Indian Pharmaceutical Alliance (IPA), the leading association of research-based Indian pharmaceutical companies. He holds a master's degree in pharmaceutical science from Purdue University and is an alumnus of Harvard Business School.

Chanda Kochhar became the CEO and managing director of ICICI Bank, India's second-largest bank and financial services firm, in May 2009. Prior to that, she was the CFO and joint managing director of ICICI Bank. From 2007 to 2009, she headed the Corporate Center, responsible for ensuring strategic consistency across ICICI's business activities. Kochhar has consistently figured in *Fortune*'s list of "Most Powerful Women in Business" since 2005.

Manoj Kohli is CEO and joint managing director of Bharti Airtel Ltd., a cellular service provider. Previously, Kohli held multiple roles as president and CEO, head of mobile services at Bharti Airtel. Kohli holds degrees in commerce and law and an MBA from Delhi University. He also attended the Executive Business Program at the Michigan Business School and the Advanced Management Program at Wharton.

Naveen Kshatriya is managing director of Castrol India Ltd., which provides oil lubricants for cars, motorcycles, and commercial vehicles. He started his career with Hindustan Lever and eventually joined the board of Castrol India as director, Consumer Division, in 1998. In early 2000 he was assigned to Hong Kong as regional marketing director, Castrol (Consumer) Asia Pacific. Kshatriya graduated in mechanical engineering from IIT, Kharagpur, in 1971.

M. Lakshminarayan is joint managing director (JMD) of Motor Industries Company Ltd. (MICO), a flagship of the Bosch Group in India. After working for Tata Motors at the Pune plant for over sixteen years, he joined MICO in 1987. In 2000 he became a MICO board member and was designated the JMD in charge of manufacturing. Lakshminarayan holds a master's degree in technology from the Indian Institute of Technology, Mumbai.

Vijay Mahajan is BASIX Group CEO and managing director of BSFL. He is a member of the Committee on Financial Inclusion, the Microfinance Equity and Development Fund, and is also on the board of Consultative Group to Assist the Poor (CGAP). He was selected as Outstanding Social Entrepreneur at the World Economic Forum, 2003. Mahajan was educated at IIT, Delhi; IIM, Ahmedabad; and the Woodrow Wilson School of Public and International Affairs at Princeton.

Anand Mahindra is vice chairman and managing director of Mahindra & Mahindra Ltd., an international operation specializing in automobiles and farm equipment. He is a past president of the Confederation of Indian Industry and the Automotive Research Association of India. Mahindra is an alumnus of both Harvard College (1977) and Harvard Business School (1981), and is currently on Harvard Business School's Asia Pacific board.

Harsh Mariwala is executive chairman and managing director of Marico Ltd., a business specializing in hair care, skin care, and healthy foods. Mariwala is also vice president of FICCI. Under Mariwala's leadership, Marico has been rated as one of "India's Most

Innovative Companies" (Business Today–Monitor Group Innovation Study, 2008). Marico was selected as one of eight Indian companies in S&P's Global Challengers list (2007).

Kiran Mazumdar-Shaw is executive chairman and managing director of Biocon Ltd., a global biotechnology firm based in Bangalore, India. She presently serves on the advisory council of the government's Department of Biotech, which is responsible for charting a progressive growth path for Indian biotechnology. She has been presented with the Padma Shri and Padma Bhushan awards by the president of India for her pioneering efforts in industrial biotechnology.

Rakesh Mehrotra is the managing director of Container Corporation of India Ltd. (CONCOR), an Indian government enterprise operating inland transport services, clearance, and cargo-handling facilities throughout India. Prior to being managing director, he was director (projects) for CONCOR. Mehrotra also serves on the boards of Fresh and Healthy Enterprises Ltd., a subsidiary, and Gateway Terminals India Pvt. Ltd., a joint venture.

Sunil Bharti Mittal is executive chairman and group CEO of Bharti Enterprises. He is a member of the prime minister's Council on Trade and Industry and is also a founder, past president, and member of various telecom industry associations. Mittal is the honorary consul general of the Republic of Seychelles in India. He graduated from Punjab University and completed the Owner/President Management Program from Harvard Business School in 1999.

Nachiket Mor is president of the ICICI Foundation for Inclusive Growth. Formerly, he was deputy managing director of ICICI Bank Ltd. He started his career as an officer in the Corporate Planning and Policy Cell of ICICI in 1987. Mor holds a postgraduate diploma in finance management from the Indian Institute of Management, Ahmedabad, and a doctorate of philosophy in financial economics from the University of Pennsylvania.

P. K. Mukherjee is managing director of Sesa Goa Ltd., a company that produces and distributes iron ore, pig iron, and metallurgical coke. He was appointed as director of Sesa Goa in 2000 and

managing director in 2006. He has twenty-seven years' experience
in finance, accounting, costing, taxation, and legal. He also serves
on the board of the Sesa Community Development Foundation.
Mukherjee has a BCom (honors) FCA, AICWA.

N. R. Narayana Murthy is the joint chairman and chief mentor of
Infosys Technologies Ltd., a Bangalore-based information technology consulting and software services provider with dual listings on
the NASDAQ and BSE stock exchanges, and operations in more
than fifteen countries. In 2008, he was awarded the Padma Vib-
hushan, the second-highest civilian award by India, and the Légion
d'Honneur, the highest civilian award by France.

B. Muthuraman is managing director of Tata Steel Ltd. (Tata
Group). Muthuraman joined Tata Steel as a graduate trainee in
1966 and was appointed executive director (special projects) in 2000.
He became managing director of Tata Steel Ltd. in 2001. Muthuraman has a degree in metallurgical engineering from the Indian Institute of Technology (IIT), Madras, and a master's degree in business
administration from Xavier Labour Relations Institute (XLRI),
Jamshedpur.

Rajat M. Nag is managing director general of Asian Development Bank (ADB). Previously, he headed ADB's Southeast Asia department and served as special adviser to the president on regional
economic cooperation and integration. A Canadian national, he
holds engineering degrees from the University of Saskatchewan
(Canada) and the Indian Institute of Technology, Delhi. He also obtained master's degrees in business administration from Canada
and in economics from the London School of Economics.

M. V. Nair is chairman and managing director (CMD) of Union
Bank of India Ltd., a public-sector bank. He started out with Corporation Bank in 1970 and became CMD of Union Bank in 2006. Nair
is chairman of the Indian Banks' Association, board member of Institute of Banking Personnel Selection, and vice president of the
governing council of the Indian Institute of Banking and Finance.

Vivek Nair is vice chairman and managing director of Hotel Leela
Venture Ltd. He is also the honorary secretary of the Federation of

Hotels and Restaurants Association of India, which represents 1,800 hotels and 800 restaurants in the country. After graduating from St. Xavier's Collage, Mumbai, Nair completed the Postgraduate Program in Hotel Management from Cornell University's School of Hotel Administration in Ithaca, New York.

Lakshmi Narayanan is vice chairman of Cognizant Technology Solutions, a U.S.-based Indian firm specializing in IT services like programming and Web design. In addition, Narayanan serves as chairman of the board of NASSCOM and is a member of the board of the U.S.-India Business Council. He has also received many industry accolades, including the *Economic Times*' Entrepreneur of the Year 2005.

V. R. S. Natarajan is executive chairman and managing director of Bharat Earth Movers Ltd. (BEML), a public-sector undertaking (PSU) based in Bangalore, India. BEML manufactures a wide range of heavy construction machinery to meet the needs of the mining, construction, power, cement, and steel sectors. Natarajan started his career in the sugar and textile industries and served in a variety of PSUs prior to his joining BEML.

Anand Nayak is head of human resource development for ITC Ltd., a diversified Indian tobacco, foods, apparel, and hotels firm with a market capitalization in excess of US$10 billion. He is also a director on the board of ITC Infotech India Ltd. Nayak has been with ITC for more than thirty years. A postgraduate in industrial relations from XLRI, Jamshedpur, Nayak has spent his entire career with ITC.

Vineet Nayar is the CEO of the $2.2 billion HCL Technologies Ltd., leading a team of 54,216 professionals in twenty countries to drive growth in the IT services industry. He also serves on the board of the company as a full-time director. Nayar has instituted several radical programs that began a quiet transformation across the organization. His mantra of "Employee First" and a strong belief in value-based leadership has been recognized globally. *Fortune* magazine has articulated his leadership style as "The World's Most Modern Management."

H. V. Neotia is the former managing director of Ambuja Cement Eastern Ltd. and currently serves as the chairman of Ambuja Realty Group. The government of India gave him the Padma Shri award in 1999 for his initiatives in forging public-private partnerships to develop social housing. He has a BCom (honors) degree and completed the Owner/President Management Program (OPM) at Harvard Business School.

T. V. Mohandas Pai is a board member and director of HR, education and research, and administration for Infosys Technologies Ltd. He joined Infosys in 1994 and has served as a director since 2000. He was the chief financial officer until 2006. He has a bachelor's degree in commerce from St. Joseph's College of Commerce, Bangalore, an LLB degree from Bangalore University, and is a Fellow Chartered Accountant.

Deepak Parekh is executive chairman of Housing Development Finance Corporation Ltd. (HDFC), which promotes Indian home ownership. Parekh joined HDFC in a senior management position in 1978, became a director in 1985, and was appointed chairman in 1993. Parekh is the youngest recipient of the *Economic Times'* Lifetime Achievement Award. He is a Fellow of the Institute of Chartered Accountants (England and Wales).

Allen Pereira is the former executive director of Oriental Bank of Commerce Ltd. He is currently chairman and managing director of the Bank of Maharashtra. He started his banking career as personnel officer with Syndicate Bank in 1973 and eventually became an adviser for personnel and industrial relations for the Indian Banks' Association. He was appointed executive director of Oriental Bank of Commerce in 2006. Pereira has a postgraduate degree in social work with a specialization in labor and personnel administration.

Ajay Piramal is executive chairman of Nicholas Piramal India Ltd. (NPIL), India's second-largest pharmaceutical health-care company, as well as Piramal Enterprises Group. He is a member of the World Economic Forum's Governors' Forum on Healthcare. He is also the chairman of the drugs and pharmaceuticals committee of the Confederation of Indian Industries. Recently, the Entrepreneur of the Year award was conferred on him by Prince Andrew, Duke of York.

Satish Pradhan is executive vice president, group human resources, for Tata Sons Limited (Tata Group). Prior to joining the group in 2001, he worked for various public- and private-sector companies, including SAIL, CMC Ltd., ICI India Ltd., Brook Bond Lipton India Ltd., and ICI Plc. He served on the CII national committee on human resource development and women's empowerment. Pradhan has a master's in history from Delhi University.

G. V. Prasad is vice chairman and chief executive officer of Dr. Reddy's Laboratories Ltd., a major Indian pharmaceutical company with global reach. Previously, he was managing director of Cheminor Drugs Ltd., which merged with Dr. Reddy's. Prasad earned his bachelor's degree in chemical engineering from the Illinois Institute of Technology in Chicago in 1982 and his master's in industrial administration from Purdue University in 1983.

Azim Premji is chairman and managing director of Wipro Ltd., a $5 billion revenue information technology, business process outsourcing, and R&D services organization with a presence in over fifty countries. *BusinessWeek* listed him among the top thirty entrepreneurs in world history (July 2007). He is a nonexecutive director on the board of the Reserve Bank of India. Premji is a graduate in electrical engineering from Stanford University.

Aditya Puri has been managing director of HDFC Bank Ltd. since 1994. He has over twenty-seven years of banking experience in India and abroad. Prior to joining the bank, Puri was the chief executive officer of Citibank, Malaysia, from 1992 to 1994. Puri holds a bachelor's degree in commerce from Punjab University and is an associate member of the Institute of Chartered Accountants of India.

Madhabi Puri-Buch served as executive director of ICICI Bank from June 2007 to January 2009. She has been chief executive officer and managing director of ICICI Securities since February 1, 2009. She is also acting as the head of operations and group corporate brand officer at the bank. She is a graduate in mathematical economics and has a postgraduate degree in management from the Indian Institute of Management, Ahmedabad.

Subir Raha is the former chairman and managing director of Oil and Natural Gas Corporation Ltd. (ONGC), India's number one company in the *Forbes* Global 2000 ranking. He was also chairman of the wholly owned subsidiary, ONGC Videsh Ltd. (OVL), Mangalore Refinery and Petrochem Ltd., and other group companies. Raha was recognized as the Global Petroleum Executive of the Year 2005 by the *Petroleum Economist,* London.

B. Ramalinga Raju is the former executive chairman of Satyam Computer Services Ltd. Raju founded Satyam Computer Services in 1987 and had been instrumental in developing Satyam into one of India's top IT services companies. He resigned in 2009 due to accounting irregularities. Raju received an MBA degree from Ohio University and attended Harvard Business School's Advanced Management Program.

Arun Bharat Ram is executive chairman of SRF Ltd., a producer of chemicals and technical textiles, especially nylon cords for tires. He is the past president of the Association of Synthetic Fibre Industry and has served on many government-industry committees. He was also president of CII (2000–2001) and is currently the chairman of CII International. Ram graduated from the University of Michigan with a degree in industrial engineering.

K. Ramachandran is the former vice chairman, managing director, and CEO-India for Philips Electronics India Ltd. He worked in Tata Administrative Service, Voltas Ltd., before moving to Philips India in 1993. He was appointed vice chairman, managing director, and CEO-India in 1998. Ramachandran has a BE in electrical engineering from BITS, Pilani, and a postgraduate degree in business management from IIM, Calcutta.

S. Ramadorai is the CEO and managing director of Tata Consultancy Services Ltd. (Tata Group). He is a member of the corporate advisory board, Marshall School of Business (USC), a fellow of the

IEEE and the Indian National Academy of Engineers, and a past chairman of the National Association of Software Companies (NASSCOM). In 2006, the government of India honored Ramadorai with the Padma Bhushan award.

K. Ramakrishnan is the former chairman and managing director of Andhra Bank. Prior to joining Andhra Bank in 2005, he was executive director of the Bank of Baroda. From 2005 to 2006, he was a member of the legal and banking operational committee of the Indian Banks' Association. Ramakrishnan has an MBA and was awarded an honorary doctorate of letters from Acharya Nagarjuna University for his contribution to Indian banking.

C. K. Ranganathan is chairman and managing director of CavinKare Pvt. Ltd., which manufactures and markets brands relating to personal care, home care, and food products. The *Economic Times* named him Entrepreneur of the Year in 2004, and in 2008 he served as vice chairman of the Confederation of Indian Industry, Tamil Nadu. He is one of the founder-members of the Ability Foundation, an NGO that rehabilitates the disabled.

G. M. Rao is founder, chairman, and managing director of the GMR Group of companies, which has a strong presence in power, infrastructure, and manufacturing. He is also chairman of the philanthropic GMR Varalakshmi Foundation. Rao is a graduate in mechanical engineering from Andhra University and was awarded a doctorate in philosophy degree by Jawaharlal Nehru Technological University, Hyderabad, in 2005 in recognition of his service to industry.

M. B. N. Rao served as chairman and managing director of Canara Bank from 2005 to 2008. Under Rao's guidance, Canara Bank received the National Award for Excellence in Lending to Micro and Small Enterprises for the Year 2006–2007 from Prime Minister Manmohan Singh. Rao is a member of the Indian Institute of Bankers and the Singapore Institute of Management. He holds a diploma in computer studies from the University of Cambridge and National Computing Centre, London, and a certificate in industrial finance.

Prathap C. Reddy is founder and executive chairman of Apollo Hospitals Enterprise Ltd. Dr. Reddy received the Padma Bhushan award in 1991 for transforming Indian health care; he also received a Citizen of the Year award from Mother Teresa in 1994. Dr. Reddy, a cardiologist, received a bachelor's degree in medicine and surgery (MBBS) from Stanley Medical College, Madras, and is a fellow of the Royal College of Surgeons.

P. V. Ramaprasad Reddy is the chairman of Aurobindo Pharma Ltd., a Hyderabad-based firm that manufactures and exports generic pharmaceuticals and active pharmaceutical ingredients to over one hundred countries. Aurobindo has operations in India, Thailand, the United States, Hong Kong, Brazil, and China, and has annual sales in excess of US$350 million. Reddy, who has a postgraduate degree in commerce, helped cofound the company in 1986.

Mukesh Rohatgi is executive chairman and managing director of Engineers India Ltd. (EIL), which provides engineering and related technical services for petroleum refineries and other large-scale infrastructure projects. Rohatgi has a background in the petroleum industry, having joined Bharat Petroleum Corporation Ltd. (BPCL) in 1982 and becoming its director (refineries) in 2002. *Construction World* named EIL among the "Most Admired Companies" in 2007.

S. K. Roongta is chairman of Steel Authority of India Ltd. (SAIL), the largest steel-producing company in the country. An engineering graduate from BITS, Pilani, and a postgraduate in international trade from the Indian Institute of Foreign Trade (IIFT), New Delhi, Roongta started his career at SAIL in 1972. He became SAIL chairman in 2006 and serves on the board of the International Iron and Steel Institute (IISI) in Brussels.

Raman Roy, widely considered a pioneer in the Indian business process outsourcing (BPO) industry, is chairman and managing director of Quatrro BPO Solutions Pvt. Ltd. Prior to his work with Quatrro, he was chairman and managing director of Wipro Spectramind. Roy was awarded the Dataquest Pathbreaker Award in

2002 for directly creating 35,000-plus jobs in India and indirectly
enabling the employment of 350,000 people by creating the BPO
industry.

Raaj Sah is a professor in the Harris School of Public Policy
Studies and the College, and an associated faculty member in the
Department of Economics, University of Chicago. He has previ-
ously taught at the Massachusetts Institute of Technology, Yale
University, Princeton University, and the University of Pennsylva-
nia. He received a PhD in economics from the University of Penn-
sylvania and an MBA from the Indian Institute of Management,
Ahmedabad.

B. Sambamurthy is executive chairman and managing director
of Corporation Bank. A chartered accountant by training, he joined
Syndicate Bank in 1978, was appointed executive director of Indian
Bank in 2004, and became executive chairman of Corporation Bank
in 2006. Sambamurthy was a member of the Export Advisory Committee and Standing Committee on Forex Clearing for the Reserve
Bank of India. He was also the additional vice chairman of the Foreign Exchange Dealer's Association of India (FEDAI).

T. Sankaralingam served as chairman and managing director
of NTPC Ltd., an energy company, from 2006 to 2008. Previously,
Sankaralingam worked twenty-seven years for NTPC in various
capacities. He also served with Bharat Heavy Electricals Ltd. and
the Tamil Nadu Electricity Board. In recognition of his expertise,
Sankaralingam was elected as vice chairman of CIGRE, India, and
given the Eminent Engineer Award by the Institution of Engineers
(India).

B. Santhanam is chairman and managing director of Saint-
Gobain Glass India Ltd., a manufacturer of automotive glass and
other float-glass products. Santhanam is also promoter-director for
Saint-Gobain Sekurit India Ltd., as well as chairman of the CII,
southern region, Task Force on Skills, Employability, and Affirmative Action. Santhanam has a BTech degree from IIT, Madras, and a
PG Diploma-Management from IIM, Ahmedabad.

R. Santhanam is managing director and executive director of Hindustan Motors Ltd. (Birla Group). He began his career with Telco and served with Eicher Tractors, TVS Suzuki, Hindustan Motors, Mahindra & Mahindra, and Mahindra Holidays Resorts India Ltd. as managing director and CEO. Santhanam is a mechanical engineer from IIT, Madras; has an MBA from IIM, Calcutta; and is a fellow of the Advanced Management Program, Harvard Business School.

Sanjeev Sanyal is a leading Asian economist whose work is widely quoted in the international financial media. From 1997 to 2008, he was an economist at Deutsche Bank in charge of analyzing both Asian and global markets. Sanyal is also the founder of the Sustainable Planet Institute. Sanyal has a BA (honors) from Delhi University and two master's degrees from Oxford University, where he was a Rhodes scholar.

Partha Sarkar is a board member for Capital Factors and Recoveries Ltd., Escorts Automotive Ltd., and Escorts Consumer Credit Ltd. Previously, Sarkar worked for Hindustan Unilever, Tata Finance, RPG Itochu Finance, and Tata Administrative Services. He became CEO of Escorts Finance in 2000 and served as managing director from 2001 to 2006. Sarkar has a BTech from IIT, Delhi, and a PGDBA from IIM, Ahmedabad.

Anil Sharma is vice president, human resources, at ITC's Hotels Division. He began his career in the public sector, followed by stints at Ranbaxy and Modi Cement. He joined ITC in 1985, and working primarily in human resources at the company, he spent six years in the Hotels Division in general management assignments and several years as the general manager, operations, Fortune Hotels. He has also served as an executive assistant to the chairman.

Kamal K. Sharma is managing director of Lupin Ltd., a pharmaceutical manufacturer. In a career spanning more than three decades, Sharma has held a range of senior management positions in the pharmaceuticals and chemicals industries. Sharma is a chemical engineer from IIT, Kanpur, with a postgraduate diploma in industrial management from Jamnalal Bajaj Institute of Management Studies, Mumbai, and a PhD in economics from IIT, Mumbai.

Percy Siganporia is managing director of Tata Tea Ltd. (Tata Group). He first joined the Tata Group of companies in 1974 as a Tata administrative services officer. In 1975 he moved into marketing for Tata Tea and then became executive director in 2000 and managing director in 2004. Siganporia is a graduate in science, and has a postgraduate degree in business management (XLRI).

Analjit Singh is the founder and chairman of Max India Ltd., chairman of Max New York Life Insurance Company Ltd., and chairman and managing director of Max Healthcare Institute Ltd. As the company's first managing director, Singh led the company into the bulk pharma business and its subsequent diversification into telecom, specialty products, electronic components, and chemicals. Singh has an MBA from the Graduate School of Management, Boston University.

Malvinder Mohan Singh is the chairman and CEO of Ranbaxy Laboratories, a prominent Indian pharmaceutical manufacturing firm, which Japan's Daiichi Sankyo acquired in 2008. Singh is a member of the Board of Trade, Ministry of Commerce and Industry, government of India. He is also a member of the national council of the Confederation of Indian Industry. Singh received his MBA from Duke University's Fuqua School of Business.

Ashok Sinha is the chairman and managing director of Bharat Petroleum Corporation Ltd. (BPCL). Prior to his appointment as CMD, he was director (finance) of BPCL. In 2001, the Economic Intelligence Unit (EIU) India and American Express gave him the India CFO Award for information and knowledge management. Sinha is a graduate in electric engineering from IIT, Kanpur, and has an MBA from the Indian Institute of Management, Bangalore.

P. M. Sinha is the former chairman of PepsiCo India Holdings Pvt. Ltd., and the former president of PepsiCo International South Asia and Pepsi Foods Ltd. He currently serves on the boards of BATA India, ICICI Bank, Indian Oil Corporation, and Wipro Ltd.

In addition to his business duties, he has been chair of several FICCI committees. Sinha was educated at the MIT Sloan School of Management.

R. S. P. Sinha is chairman and managing director of Mahanagar Telephone Nigam Ltd. (MTNL), a telecommunications firm majority-owned by the Indian government. Previously, he was director (finance) for MTNL and also director (finance) on the board of Hindustan Organic Chemicals Ltd. (HOCL) and Videsh Sanchar Nigam Ltd. (VSNL). Sinha's educational accomplishments include BS (electrical engineering), master of business management (finance), CAIIB, LLB, and ICWA.

Ashok Soni is the managing director of Voltas Ltd., a refrigeration and heating equipment manufacturer that is part of the Tata Group. Prior to joining Voltas, Soni had worked with the ICI Group for fourteen years as works accountant and corporate taxation manager. He was also associated with Wimco Ltd. for five years, where he held the positions of chief accountant, financial controller, and general manager (finance).

Ashok Soota is chairman and managing director of MindTree Consulting Ltd. Soota was president of the Confederation of Indian Industry during 2002–2003, and served on the Indian prime minister's task force for development of the IT industry. Soota holds a Bachelor of Science degree in electrical engineering from the University of Roorkee (IIT, Roorkee) and an MBA degree from the Asian Institute of Management in the Philippines.

Mallika Srinivasan is a director of Tractors and Farm Equipment (TAFE), a privately held Chennai-based firm that is the second-largest manufacturer of tractors in India. In addition to having chief executive responsibilities at TAFE, she is also on the executive board of the Indian School of Business. In 2007, *Business Today* named her as one of the twenty-five most powerful women in Indian business. She received her MBA from the Wharton School of the University of Pennsylvania.

Ravi Uppal was named managing director and CEO of L&T Power in January of 2009. Prior to that position, he was the head of global markets and member of the group executive committee of ABB Ltd., Switzerland. He is a 2005 graduate of Wharton's Advanced Management Program and serves on the board of governors of the Indian Institute of Management in Bangalore, India.

Questions for the Primary Interviews

We used twelve main questions with the primary interview group, with follow-up questions added as appropriate, and we recorded and transcribed the interviews:

A. Leadership

1. What are the top two leadership capacities that have been most critical for the exercise of your leadership during the past five years?

2. In your experience, how are Indian business leaders different from those from other countries, especially the U.S.?

3. How have you built competitive advantage in your businesses? In what ways do resources beyond the division, such as corporatewide resources or business group resources, contribute to this advantage?

4. Considering your various roles as a CEO, how has your time allocation for each of the following tasks changed over the past three years? Are you spending more time, about the same amount of time, or less time on each task?

    1. Regulatory/compliance issues

    2. Reporting to the board

    3. Shareholder relations

4. Setting strategy

5. Media relations

6. Day-to-day management

7. Fostering workplace diversity

8. Customer relations

B. Governance

1. What are the two most distinctive aspects of corporate governance practices in India compared to the U.S.?

2. Will your governance practices eventually converge with those of the U.S., or will they remain distinct?

3. When it comes to acquisitions, divestitures, and strategic alliances, what value have nonexecutive directors brought to the decisions?

4. What are the two most important criteria you have used in selecting nonexecutive directors?

C. Human Resource Management

1. Please rank the following seven roles for you as a CEO:

   1. A guide or teacher for employees

   2. Chief input for business strategy

   3. Keeper of organizational culture

   4. Representative of owner and investor interests

   5. Representative of other stakeholders (e.g., employees and the community)

    6. Civic leadership within the business community

    7. Civic leadership outside the business community

2. What are the two most important pieces of advice you will give your successor?

3. What are the top two priorities for human resources in the company?

4. Projecting yourself five years into the future, what will be your single most significant "legacy" as leader of the company?

The Survey of Indian Human Resource Executives

To better understand the India Way and to make comparisons with it and U.S. practices more explicit, we identified previous surveys of large American firms on topics of relevance to our work and then replicated those surveys with the Indian companies. The top human resource executives in the Indian companies—virtually all of whom hold titles equivalent to executive vice-president level in U.S. firms—submitted the data for their organization. Of the firms where we interviewed the top executive, 70 percent completed our survey. The Indian firms that responded are identified in table B-4.

We also asked the human resources executives to assess their top executive using a standard assessment of the capabilities of leaders, the Multifactor Leadership Questionnaire. We then compared the results with those from reasonably equivalent surveys in the United States to give us a comparable assessment of American business leaders. The downside of this approach is that we have no control over the sampling frames used in the U.S. surveys. While most of the American surveys we used are based on large companies, they are not drawn from the 150 largest companies in the United States, which would be the Indian equivalent. The sampling frames differ across the various U.S. surveys that we obtained, and their response rates were not always reported, although all those that are reported are lower than for our Indian survey. We should thus be less confident about the U.S. figures than about the Indian results. Because of these limitations, it is appropriate to limit the analyses that compare Indian and American responses to simple descriptive statistics. The comparisons on which we focus are only those where the differences between Indian and American responses are large enough to give us confidence that those differences are real. We recognize the limitations of the U.S. data in particular and therefore the comparisons drawn from them. The survey can be found at http://whartonsurveys.org/hr, and it follows here:

Wharton National HRD Network Survey

The following survey is being conducted by Wharton School faculty for the National Human Resources Development Network (NHRDN) as part of our study of Indian business leadership.

We are surveying the heads of human resources in those companies whose CEOs we have already interviewed—thanks for your help in arranging those interviews. Our goal is to supplement those interviews with some additional information about the management of your companies and also to collect some data on human resource practices that will be of interest to you and your colleagues in NHRDN.

For most of these questions, we also have responses from U.S. employers, so we will be able to report not only about Indian practices but also how they compare to those in the U.S.

The survey is anonymous; while we will combine your responses with those of your CEO for the purposes of analyzing the aggregate results, we will not use or reveal individual responses to this survey.

1. What company do you work for?

2. These questions ask about HR's role in the overall objectives of your company. To what extent is each of the following statements true in your organization. (Please check next to an answer)

HR works closely with senior management in implementing organizational strategies.
__ To no extent
__ To some extent
__ To a large extent

HR works closely with senior management in creating organizational strategies.
__ To no extent
__ To some extent
__ To a large extent

HR has achieved a level of respect that is comparable with other departments in the organization.
__ To no extent
__ To some extent
__ To a large extent

Senior management realizes that investments in HR make financial sense.
__ To no extent
__ To some extent
__ To a large extent

HR implements strategies and processes to drive business results.
__ To no extent
__ To some extent
__ To a large extent

HR is involved in the communication of the business goals.
__ To no extent
__ To some extent
__ To a large extent

HR is involved in the alignment of the business goals.
__ To no extent
__ To some extent
__ To a large extent

The role of HR is increasingly more focused on strategic interests.
__ To no extent
__ To some extent
__ To a large extent

HR involvement is essential in all major business activities and decisions.
__ To no extent
__ To some extent
__ To a large extent

HR is involved in the development of the business goals.
__ To no extent
__ To some extent
__ To a large extent

HR is involved in monitoring the achievement of business goals.
__ To no extent
__ To some extent
__ To a large extent

HR creates strategies and processes to drive business results.
__ To no extent
__ To some extent
__ To a large extent

3. These questions ask about the competencies you believe are important for HR executives and managers.

Level 1: Early Career Level HR Executives and Managers

What are the **five** most important competency domains for early career level HR executives and managers? Please circle five (5) from the following:

Accounting

Business Ethics

Business Law

Change Management

Compensation

Employee Benefits

Employment Law

Financial Management

General Negotiation Skills (Not labor contracts)

Global Business

HR Impact on Mergers and Acquisitions

HR Measurement and Metrics

Information Systems / Information Technology

Interpersonal Communication Skills

Leadership

Management of Diversity

Management of Employees

Marketing

Organizational Development

Performance Management

Presentation Skills

Safety and Security

Staffing and Selection Techniques

Statistics

Strategic Business Management and Planning

Strategic Human Resource Management

Written Communication Skills

Level 2: Mid-Career Level HR Executives
and Managers

What are the **five** most important competency domains for mid-career level HR executives and managers? Please circle five (5) from the following:

Accounting

Business Ethics

Business Law

Change Management

Compensation

Employee Benefits

Employment Law

Financial Management

General Negotiation Skills
(Not labor contracts)

Global Business

HR Impact on Mergers and
Acquisitions

HR Measurement and Metrics

Information Systems / Information
Technology

Interpersonal Communication
Skills

Leadership

Management of Diversity

Management of Employees

Marketing

Organizational Development

Performance Management

Presentation Skills

Safety and Security

Staffing and Selection Techniques

Statistics

Strategic Business Management
and Planning

Strategic Human Resource
Management

Written Communication Skills

Level 3: Senior Career Level HR Executives and Managers

What are the **five** most important competency domains for late career level HR executives and managers? Please circle five (5) from the following:

Accounting

Business Ethics

Business Law

Change Management

Compensation

Employee Benefits

Employment Law

Financial Management

General Negotiation Skills
(Not labor contracts)

Global Business

HR Impact on Mergers and
Acquisitions

HR Measurement and Metrics

Information Systems / Information
Technology

Interpersonal Communication
Skills

Leadership

Management of Diversity

Management of Employees

Marketing

Organizational Development

Performance Management

Presentation Skills

Safety and Security

Staffing and Selection Techniques

Statistics

Strategic Business Management
and Planning

Strategic Human Resource
Management

Written Communication Skills

Not Critical at Any Level

Which competency domains are not critical at any level? Please circle five (5) from the following:

Accounting

Business Ethics

Business Law

Change Management

Compensation

Employee Benefits

Employment Law

Financial Management

General Negotiation Skills
(Not labor contracts)

Global Business

HR Impact on Mergers and
Acquisitions

HR Measurement and Metrics

Information Systems / Information
Technology

Interpersonal Communication
Skills

Leadership

Management of Diversity

Management of Employees

Marketing

Organizational Development

Performance Management

Presentation Skills

Safety and Security

Staffing and Selection Techniques

Statistics

Strategic Business Management
and Planning

Strategic Human Resource
Management

Written Communication Skills

4. These questions ask about the task of learning, training, and development. Please choose the three most important factors from the list below. For each question, chose from the following factors:

Strategic Implementation	Globalization
Transformation	Business Unit Enablement
Leadership Development	Performance Improvement
Capability Building	Innovation
Talent Management	

In what area does learning, training, and development have the largest effect?

_____

In what area does learning, training, and development have the second largest effect?

_____

In what area does learning, training, and development have the third largest effect?

_____

5. The questions below ask about the changes that have taken place in your company over the past two years. Please circle every change that you planned or implemented during the 24 months prior to taking this survey.

New/revised performance management and review process.

Facilities change (e.g., new security procedures, relocation or organization's operations, facility closures).

Organizational culture changes (e.g., executive leadership turnover, organization values changes).

New/revised HR information systems (e.g., time tracking software).

New/revised IT systems (e.g., operating systems, other software).

Organizational repositioning or re-alignment (including centralization or decentralization, international expansion, market expansion or refocusing or organization mission change).

New/revised financial/accounting systems.

Major staffing changes (e.g., downsizing, layoffs).

Diversity and/or cross-cultural communication initiatives.

Operational changes in response to new legislation, changing economic conditions or national/international events.

Product rebranding.

Acquisition.

Offshoring or outsourcing.

Merger.

Initial public offering or corporate ownership change.

6. In your opinion, what are the most important roles for business leaders to play in Indian companies. Please rank the following seven roles *in order of importance*. Please use each number only once.

A guide or teacher for employees	1 2 3 4 5 6 7
Chief input for business strategy	1 2 3 4 5 6 7
Keeper of organizational culture	1 2 3 4 5 6 7
Representative of owner and investor interests	1 2 3 4 5 6 7
Representative of other stakeholders (e.g., employees and the community)	1 2 3 4 5 6 7
Civic leadership within the business community	1 2 3 4 5 6 7
Civic leadership outside the business community	1 2 3 4 5 6 7

7. These questions ask about the leadership style of your organization's chief officer as you perceive it. Please try to answer all of the items. If an item is irrelevant, or if you are unsure or do not know the answer, leave the answer blank.

Please use the following scale when you answer the questions:

1	2	3	4	5
Not at all.	Once in a while.	Sometimes.	Fairly often.	Frequently, if not always.

Provides me with assistance in exchange for my efforts	1 2 3 4 5
Re-examines critical assumptions to question whether they are appropriate	1 2 3 4 5
Fails to interfere until problems become serious	1 2 3 4 5
Focuses attention on irregularities, mistakes, exceptions, and deviations from standards	1 2 3 4 5
Avoids getting involved when important issues arise	1 2 3 4 5
Talks about his/her most important values and beliefs	1 2 3 4 5

Is absent when needed	1	2	3	4	5
Seeks differing perspectives when solving problems	1	2	3	4	5
Talks optimistically about the future	1	2	3	4	5
Instills pride in me for being associated with him/her	1	2	3	4	5
Discusses in specific terms who is responsible for achieving performance targets	1	2	3	4	5
Waits for things to go wrong before taking action	1	2	3	4	5
Talks enthusiastically about what needs to be accomplished	1	2	3	4	5
Specifies the importance of having a strong sense of purpose	1	2	3	4	5
Spends time teaching and coaching	1	2	3	4	5
Makes clear what one can expect to receive when performance goals are achieved	1	2	3	4	5
Shows that he/she is a firm believer in "If it ain't broke, don't fix it."	1	2	3	4	5
Goes beyond self-interest for the good of the group	1	2	3	4	5
Treats me as an individual rather than just as a member of a group	1	2	3	4	5
Demonstrates that problems must become chronic before taking action	1	2	3	4	5
Acts in ways that build my respect	1	2	3	4	5
Concentrates his/her full attention on dealing with mistakes, complaints, and failures	1	2	3	4	5
Considers the moral and ethical consequences of decisions	1	2	3	4	5
Keeps track of all mistakes	1	2	3	4	5
Displays a sense of power and confidence	1	2	3	4	5
Articulates a compelling vision of the future	1	2	3	4	5
Directs my attention toward failures to meet standards	1	2	3	4	5
Avoids making decisions	1	2	3	4	5

Considers me as having different needs, abilities, and aspirations from others	1	2	3	4	5
Gets me to look at problems from many different angles	1	2	3	4	5
Helps me to develop my strengths	1	2	3	4	5
Suggests new ways of looking at how to complete assignments	1	2	3	4	5
Delays responding to urgent questions	1	2	3	4	5
Emphasizes the importance of having a collective sense of mission	1	2	3	4	5
Expresses satisfaction when I meet expectations	1	2	3	4	5
Expresses confidence that goals will be achieved	1	2	3	4	5
Is effective in meeting my job-related needs	1	2	3	4	5
Uses methods of leadership that are satisfying	1	2	3	4	5
Gets me to do more than I expected to do	1	2	3	4	5
Is effective in representing me to higher authority	1	2	3	4	5
Works with me in a satisfactory way	1	2	3	4	5
Heightens my desire to succeed	1	2	3	4	5
Is effective in meeting organizational requirements	1	2	3	4	5
Increases my willingness to try harder	1	2	3	4	5
Leads a group that is effective	1	2	3	4	5

8. How much do you agree with each of the ways the following statement can be answered: Your company faces an environment that is well described as . . .

Very dynamic, changing rapidly in technical, economic, and cultural dimensions.	1	2	3	4	5
Very risky, one false step can mean the firm's undoing.	1	2	3	4	5
Very rapidly expanding through the expansion of old markets and the emergence of new ones.	1	2	3	4	5
Very stressful, exacting, hostile, hard to keep afloat.	1	2	3	4	5

9. How much do you agree that the relationships between
the chief executive of your company and the people in the
positions listed below are strategic partnerships that help
set strategic directions and imperatives for the firm.

Chief financial officer.	1 2 3 4 5
Chief human resources officer.	1 2 3 4 5
Business-unit directors or heads.	1 2 3 4 5
Non-executive independent directors.	1 2 3 4 5

10. Please select the answer that best completes each
sentence.

Compared to other companies, your company's competitive position is presently

1 = Underperforming industry peers.

2

3 = At par with industry peers.

4

5 = Outperforming industry peers.

Compared to other companies, your company's competitive position is presently

1 = in a low growth, mature market

2

3

4

5 = in a high growth, expanding market

Compared to other companies, your company's competitive position is presently

    1 = in a static, largely established environment

    2

    3

    4

    5 = dynamic, rapidly changing environment

11. What percentage of your company's *sales revenue* comes from outside of India?

_____

12. What percentage of your company's *net income* comes from outside of India?

_____

13. What percentage of your company's *employees* come from outside of India?

_____

14. What percentage of your company's *shareholders* come from outside of India?

_____

15. What percentage of your company's shares are held by members of the founding family or families?

_____

16. What is your average annual growth rate in *sales revenue* over the past five years?

_____

17. What is your average annual growth rate in *net income* over the past five years?

_____

18. What is your average annual growth rate in *number of employees* over the past five years?

_____

The remainder of the survey asks factual questions about human resource practices. Although they do not take long to complete, if someone on your staff has such information in hand, it would be fine to ask them to complete the remainder of the questionnaire.

19. These questions ask about basic measures of human resource performance:

What is the overall rate of voluntary turnover in your company?

_____

Think about the job in the company that has the most vacancies to fill every year. How many applicants are there for each vacancy?

_____

How long does it take the company to fill each vacancy?

_____

What percentage of vacancies in the company are filled from within, that is, from internal candidates?

_____

What is your total training budget per year?

_____

For new hires who you expect to be in the management ranks, what kind of initial training do they receive?

_____

What percentage of your employees work in teams of some kind?

_____

What percentage work in self-directed teams, that is, with no direct supervisor directing their day-to-day tasks?

_____

20. These questions ask about the outsourcing of practices to vendors or companies outside your own.

How much of the following activities do you currently out-source? Please circle the answer that best corresponds to the question:

Employee administration/ compliance

None

Small Portion

Large Portion

All

Recruiting

None

Small Portion

Large Portion

All

Payroll

None

Small Portion

Large Portion

All

Health/welfare benefits

None

Small Portion

Large Portion

All

Performance evaluation

None

Small Portion

Large Portion

All

Employee relations

None

Small Portion

Large Portion

All

Pension/retirement

None

Small Portion

Large Portion

All

21. This set of questions asks about the level and structure of pay for your organization's top five executives and your organization's directors.

What was the total compensation of your CEO last year (a rough estimate is fine)?

_____

What percentage of that total was in the form of a base salary?

_____

What percentage of that total was in the form of bonuses?

_____

What percentage of that total was in the form of stock or stock-related instruments?

_____

Please describe the payment structure for members of your board of directors.

_____

What was their total compensation for board service last year?

_____

What percentage, if any, of that compensation was tied to the performance of the company?

_____

22. Please select the practices that your company currently uses to train executives and managers. Please place a check next to all responses that apply:

___ Training other than leadership training

___ Cross-functional training

___ Leadership training

___ Development planning

___ Apprenticeships/internships (to assess potential future hires)

___ Formal coaching

___ Matching employees with 'stretch' assignments/ opportunities

___ High-visibility assignments/ opportunities to work with executives (e.g., executive task forces)

___ Leadership forums (i.e., opportunities for individuals to meet with senior executives in organized events or semiformal settings)

___ Formal identification of high-potential employees

___ Formal succession planning processes

___ Job rotation

___ Formal career mentoring (internal program)

___ Job sharing

___ Formal career mentoring (external program)

23. This question asks about how performance within human resources is assessed.

How often are metrics or analytics used with the following organizational functions? (Please circle your answer)

Recruitment and selection.

Rarely

Sometimes

Frequently

Performance management.

Rarely

Sometimes

Frequently

Compensation management/ reward programs.

Rarely

Sometimes

Frequently

Benefits management.

Rarely

Sometimes

Frequently

Employee relations.

Rarely

Sometimes

Frequently

Health, safety and security programs.

Rarely

Sometimes

Frequently

Budgeting.

Rarely

Sometimes

Frequently

Retention programs.

Rarely

Sometimes

Frequently

Employee communication programs.

    Rarely

    Sometimes

    Frequently

Diversity practices.

    Rarely

    Sometimes

    Frequently

Employee engagement initiatives.

    Rarely

    Sometimes

    Frequently

Analysis of trends and forecasting.

    Rarely

    Sometimes

    Frequently

Leadership development.

    Rarely

    Sometimes

    Frequently

Human capital measurements.

    Rarely

    Sometimes

    Frequently

Retirement planning.

    Rarely

    Sometimes

    Frequently

Talent management initiatives.

    Rarely

    Sometimes

    Frequently

Skills development initiatives.

    Rarely

    Sometimes

    Frequently

Work/life programs.

    Rarely

    Sometimes

    Frequently

Succession planning.

    Rarely

    Sometimes

    Frequently

Employment brand strategy/ employment branding.

    Rarely

    Sometimes

    Frequently

Corporate social responsibility programs.

   Rarely

   Sometimes

   Frequently

Interviews of India Business Leaders Conducted by *Knowledge@Wharton*

Knowledge@Wharton, the online publication of the Wharton School, has interviewed or profiled a number of Indian business leaders—a valuable resource from which we have also drawn. The interviews are all available online:

Vikram Akula, founder and CEO of SKS Microfinance

http://knowledge.wharton.upenn.edu/india/article.cfm?articleid=4284

Mukesh and Anil Ambani, promoters, Reliance Group (now split in two)

   http://knowledge.wharton.upenn.edu/india/article.cfm?articleid=4043

Subroto Bagchi, chief operating officer, MindTree Consulting

http://knowledge.wharton.upenn.edu/india/article.cfm?articleid=4184
http://knowledge.wharton.upenn.edu/india/article.cfm?articleid=4188

Rahul Bajaj, chairman, Bajaj Group

http://knowledge.wharton.upenn.edu/india/article.cfm?articleid=4117

Sumit Banerjee, CEO, ACC (formerly Associated Cement Companies)

http://knowledge.wharton.upenn.edu/india/article.cfm?articleid=4313

Sabeer Bhatia, cofounder, Hotmail Corporation

http://knowledge.wharton.upenn.edu/india/article.cfm?articleid=4385

Kishore Biyani, managing director and promoter-director, Pantaloon Retail (India)

http://knowledge.wharton.upenn.edu/india/article.cfm?articleid=4235

Dilip Chhabria, boutique car designer, DC Design

http://knowledge.wharton.upenn.edu/india/article.cfm?articleid=4260

T. P. Chopra, CEO, GE India

http://knowledge.wharton.upenn.edu/india/article.cfm?articleid=4293
http://knowledge.wharton.upenn.edu/india/article.cfm?articleid=4215

Ajai Chowdhry, CEO, HCL Infosystems

http://knowledge.wharton.upenn.edu/india/article.cfm?articleid=4240

Bharat Desai, CEO and cofounder, Syntel (Michigan-based IT company)

http://knowledge.wharton.upenn.edu/india/article.cfm?articleid=4128

Vinod Dham, "Father of the Pentium" at Intel; cofounder and managing director of NewPath Ventures and NEA-IndoUS Ventures

http://knowledge.wharton.upenn.edu/india/article.cfm?articleid=4270

Dr. Raj Dharampuriya, cofounder and chief medical officer, eClinicalWorks

http://knowledge.wharton.upenn.edu/india/article.cfm?articleid=4404

Rono Dutta, former CEO, Air Sahara (now JetLite)

http://knowledge.wharton.upenn.edu/india/article.cfm?articleid=4111

Ramesh Emani, president, Wipro Technologies' Product Engineering Services business unit

http://knowledge.wharton.upenn.edu/india/article.cfm?articleid=4046

Sunil Gavaskar, former cricket captain for Team India

http://knowledge.wharton.upenn.edu/india/article.cfm?articleid=4371

Adi Godrej, chairman, Godrej Group

http://knowledge.wharton.upenn.edu/india/article.cfm?articleid=4135

S. Gopalakrishnan, CEO of Infosys

http://knowledge.wharton.upenn.edu/india/article.cfm?articleid=4332

G. R. Gopinath, founder and managing director of Air Deccan (now Kingfisher Red).

http://knowledge.wharton.upenn.edu/india/article.cfm?articleid=4154

Rajiv Gulati, director of India-China strategy and corporate strategic planning, Eli Lilly

http://knowledge.wharton.upenn.edu/india/article.cfm?articleid=4325

Ajay Gupta, founder and CEO, ruralnaukri.com

http://knowledge.wharton.upenn.edu/india/article.cfm?articleid=4362

Rajat Gupta, former worldwide managing director, McKinsey & Company

http://knowledge.wharton.upenn.edu/india/article.cfm?articleid=4125

Yusuf Hamied, chairman and managing director of Cipla Pharmaceuticals

http://knowledge.wharton.upenn.edu/india/article.cfm?articleid=4374

Shushil Handa, founder and CEO, Claris Lifesciences

http://knowledge.wharton.upenn.edu/india/article.cfm?articleid=4360

Remi Hinduja, chairman of HTMT Global Solutions, and **Sashi Reddi,** CEO of AppLabs Technologies

http://knowledge.wharton.upenn.edu/india/article.cfm?articleid=4199

Suresh Hiranandani, founder and managing director, Hiranandani Group

http://knowledge.wharton.upenn.edu/india/article.cfm?articleid=4120

Rajesh Hukku, executive director and managing director, i-Flex
Solutions

http://knowledge.wharton.upenn.edu/india/article.cfm?articleid=4176
http://knowledge.wharton.upenn.edu/india/article.cfm?articleid=4180

Raj Jain, president, Wal-Mart India

http://knowledge.wharton.upenn.edu/india/article.cfm?articleid=4305

Rajat Jain, managing director, Walt Disney India

http://knowledge.wharton.upenn.edu/india/article.cfm?articleid=4171

Rajesh Jain, CEO, Netcore

http://knowledge.wharton.upenn.edu/india/article.cfm?articleid=4069

Hasit Joshipura, vice president–South Asia, and managing
director, GlaxoSmithKline

http://knowledge.wharton.upenn.edu/india/article.cfm?articleid=4373

K. V. Kamath, managing director and CEO, ICICI Bank

http://knowledge.wharton.upenn.edu/article.cfm?articleid=1529
http://knowledge.wharton.upenn.edu/india/article.cfm?articleid=4356

Shobana Kamineni, executive director of new initiatives, Apollo
Hospitals

http://knowledge.wharton.upenn.edu/india/article.cfm?articleid=4363

Rana Kapoor, managing director and CEO, Yes Bank

http://knowledge.wharton.upenn.edu/india/article.cfm?articleid=4153

Rajeev Karwal, founder and CEO, Milagrow Business and
Knowledge Solutions

http://knowledge.wharton.upenn.edu/india/article.cfm?articleid=4323

Farrokh Kavarana, director of Tata Sons

http://knowledge.wharton.upenn.edu/india/article.cfm?articleid=4368

Chanda Kochhar, joint managing director and CFO, ICICI Bank

http://knowledge.wharton.upenn.edu/india/article.cfm?articleid=4257
http://knowledge.wharton.upenn.edu/india/article.cfm?articleid=4357

Kiran Mazumdar-Shaw, executive chairman and managing director, Biocon

http://knowledge.wharton.upenn.edu/india/article.cfm?articleid=4144

Hital R. Meswani, executive director, Reliance Industries

http://knowledge.wharton.upenn.edu/india/article.cfm?articleid=4042

Aditya Mittal, CFO and member the group membership board, Mittal Steel (now ArcelorMittal)

http://knowledge.wharton.upenn.edu/india/article.cfm?articleid=4054

Sunil Bharti Mittal, chairman, Bharti Enterprises

http://knowledge.wharton.upenn.edu/india/article.cfm?articleid=4306

N. R. Narayana Murthy, chairman and chief mentor of Infosys

http://knowledge.wharton.upenn.edu/india/article.cfm?articleid=4001
http://knowledge.wharton.upenn.edu/india/article.cfm?articleid=4004

Shiv Nadar, chairman and CEO, HCL Technologies

http://knowledge.wharton.upenn.edu/article.cfm?articleid=1558
http://knowledge.wharton.upenn.edu/article.cfm?articleid=1563

Shantanu Narayen, president and chief operating officer, Adobe Systems

http://knowledge.wharton.upenn.edu/india/article.cfm?articleid=4191

Vineet Nayar, CEO, HCL Technologies

http://knowledge.wharton.upenn.edu/india/article.cfm?articleid=4334

Nandan Nilekani, former CEO of Infosys

http://knowledge.wharton.upenn.edu/article.cfm?articleid=2290

Girish Paranjape and Suresh Vaswani, co-CEOs of Wipro

http://knowledge.wharton.upenn.edu/india/article.cfm?articleid=4298

Vivek Paul, partner, Texas Pacific Group

http://knowledge.wharton.upenn.edu/india/article.cfm?articleid=4049

Rajendra S. Pawar, chairman and cofounder, NIIT

http://knowledge.wharton.upenn.edu/india/article.cfm?articleid=4123

Ravilochan Pola, CEO of U.S. operations, Kotak Mahindra

http://knowledge.wharton.upenn.edu/india/article.cfm?articleid=4311

Azim Premji, chairman, Wipro

http://knowledge.wharton.upenn.edu/india/article.cfm?articleid=4297
http://knowledge.wharton.upenn.edu/india/article.cfm?articleid=4059
http://knowledge.wharton.upenn.edu/india/article.cfm?articleid=4060

V. Raghunathan, managing director of GMR Group

http://knowledge.wharton.upenn.edu/india/article.cfm?articleid=4222

Sri Rajan, partner and head of Bain & Company's private equity practice in India

http://knowledge.wharton.upenn.edu/india/article.cfm?articleid=4291

Sudhakar Ram, CEO, Mastek

http://knowledge.wharton.upenn.edu/india/article.cfm?articleid=4342

Suneeta Reddy, executive director of finance, Apollo Hospitals

http://knowledge.wharton.upenn.edu/india/article.cfm?articleid=4301

Raman Roy, founder of Spectramind; current chairman of Quatrro BPO Solutions

http://knowledge.wharton.upenn.edu/india/article.cfm?articleid=4018
http://knowledge.wharton.upenn.edu/india/article.cfm?articleid=4019

Manish Sabharwal, chairman, TeamLease

http://knowledge.wharton.upenn.edu/india/article.cfm?articleid=4186
http://knowledge.wharton.upenn.edu/india/article.cfm?articleid=4026

Ronnie Screwvala, managing director and founder-CEO, UTV
Software Communications

http://knowledge.wharton.upenn.edu/india/article.cfm?articleid=4299

Ranjit Shahani, country president, Novartis Group (India)

http://knowledge.wharton.upenn.edu/india/article.cfm?articleid=4286

Gaurav Sharma, strategist, Providence Equity Partners

http://knowledge.wharton.upenn.edu/india/article.cfm?articleid=4388

Manmohan Shetty, chairman, Adlabs

http://knowledge.wharton.upenn.edu/india/article.cfm?articleid=4177

V. G. Siddhartha, chairman, Café Coffee Day

http://knowledge.wharton.upenn.edu/india/article.cfm?articleid=4300

Malvinder Mohan Singh, CEO and managing director, Ranbaxy
Laboratories (now part of Daiichi Sankyo in Japan)

http://knowledge.wharton.upenn.edu/india/article.cfm?articleid=4296

Dean Pramath Sinha, founding dean of Hyderabad-based Indian
School of Business (ISB)

http://knowledge.wharton.upenn.edu/india/article.cfm?articleid=4399#

Rohan Sippy, film producer-director

http://knowledge.wharton.upenn.edu/india/article.cfm?articleid=4377

V. Srinivasan, CEO of IT Services, 3i Infotech, Edison, NJ

http://knowledge.wharton.upenn.edu/india/article.cfm?articleid=4231

Mak Teje, CEO of AppLabs

http://knowledge.wharton.upenn.edu/india/article.cfm?articleid=4314

T. N. Thakur, chairman and managing director, Power Trading Corporation

http://knowledge.wharton.upenn.edu/india/article.cfm?articleid=4393

Gautam Thapar, chairman, Avantha Group

http://knowledge.wharton.upenn.edu/india/article.cfm?articleid=4351

Y. V. Verma, director of human resources and management support, LG India

http://knowledge.wharton.upenn.edu/india/article.cfm?articleid=4285

Dilip Vellodi, CEO, Sutherland Global Services

http://knowledge.wharton.upenn.edu/india/article.cfm?articleid=4345

Vivek Wadhwa, executive-in-residence, Duke University School of Engineering

http://knowledge.wharton.upenn.edu/india/article.cfm?articleid=4307

Cultural Roots of the India Way

THE PRACTICES THAT CONSTITUTE the India Way clearly reflect the country's culture and history, yet the India Way is not a simple application of that culture. Indian business leaders learned a great deal from Anglo-American practices, but they assimilated those lessons in a unique way. The new, competitive environment following the economy's liberalization of the early 1990s played a special role in the creation of the India Way as did the rise of exemplary business firms, especially in the wide-open information technology sector, that built world-class capabilities and offered breakthrough innovations in products and management practices. What arose from this mix is not a mere echo with Indian accents; it is something remarkably fresh.

Ignoring the Legacy Model

Indian business leaders and researchers have been keen students of the U.S. literature on business practices. In functional areas, they know the latest financial and marketing techniques, and U.S. management books are routinely best sellers in India. American business schools have also long had an honored presence on the subcontinent. The Indian Institute of Management, Calcutta, began in 1961 with the help of the MIT Sloan School of Management, and the Indian Institute of Management, Ahmedabad, began in the same year in collaboration with the Harvard Business School.

There is little evidence, though, that the India Way was simply borrowed from American models or imported from American scholars. Historian Ramachandra Guha has argued that the most important models for India after independence in 1947 were actually the Soviet Union and Japan, in both cases emphasizing the role of a central government directing economic activity and development.[1] Relations between America and India were strained in the 1960s at a time when U.S. multinationals were expanding in other countries. British enterprises had a far bigger presence on the subcontinent. Among those corporations, Hindustan Unilever stood head and shoulders above all others in terms of influence, perhaps especially in terms of transferring lessons about hiring and development practices.

But while international corporations like Hindustan Unilever clearly had an influence on Indian business, their presence was dwarfed by the sheer scale of the country and by the dominant driver and determinant of economic decisions, which was then the government. Privately owned businesses were heavily regulated in their product market practices and especially in the area of labor, where strong unions combined with extensive regulation to restrict severely the ability of employers to shape their own organizations.[2] The most basic underpinnings of the multinational companies had a hard time being absorbed in a country where the traditional Indian business ethos placed great emphasis on family ownership and treating the company as a large clan. Kinship-controlled firms still dominated the landscape, even though many were publicly listed. While Indian businesses clearly learned lessons from abroad, their response—like that of Indian culture to foreign influences throughout its long history—was to assimilate rather than mimic or reject, producing a novel recombination in the process.

The management practices of indigenous Indian businesses are equally difficult to reconcile with the contemporary American model. With respect to day-to-day management, Indian practices were deeply hierarchical. An Indian colleague of ours remembered how it was at a local factory when his immediate supervisor would visit from headquarters: the employees of the facility would line the pathway to the building and sprinkle flower petals on it as he approached. Similarly, former Procter & Gamble executive and commentator Gurcharan Das reported great resistance from established management cadres to the idea of giving his lower-level employees any amount of influence or autonomy over how they did their work.[3]

To the extent that there was a legacy model for managing employees in this era, it was not a helpful one: limited scope for leaders to act, a narrowly restricted sense of purpose that was driven mainly by national politics, strongly hierarchical supervision, and a fixation on seniority as the criterion for workplace decisions. The contemporary model of Indian business leadership thus does not represent a legacy of historical modes of operating.

Moreover, the new generation of leaders who created the India Way for the most part did not come from the executive ranks of the legacy companies. Rather, they were by and large entrepreneurs who started from scratch or, in the case of existing companies like Bank of Baroda, with a mandate to reshape the drawing board. The India Way model they created responded to the remarkably different environment for business offered up by the 1991 reforms and the economic context those reforms then created. The new model was further shaped by the fact that the leading companies in India were in industries that did not even exist before the 1991 reforms. Information technology companies like Wipro, HCL, and Infosys, and service

companies like Tata Consultancy Services, did not have to break free
of a traditional industry pattern, because none existed.

Cultural Influences, Not Cultural Hegemony

While the India Way fits into the national culture in important and
intriguing ways, the full picture, we found, was far more compli-
cated than that. It is easy, for instance, to see the Hindu stress on
service to others reflected in the social mission of Indian business,
but other aspects of the India Way are not so easy to square with
the country's culture.

Researchers Suresh Gopalan and Joan Rivera have summarized
the accepted views about Indian national culture as they relate to
business as follows: that the Hindu religion's belief in predestina-
tion reduced personal ambition and persistence; that the country's
deep historical orientation led to conformity with the past and resistance to change; and that a long tradition of hierarchical social
relations made individual leaders more important than the goals
they pursue.[4] Others have made similar arguments—for example,
that Indian salespersons performed better under more hierarchical
authority arrangements than did U.S. counterparts, and that the
greater power imbalance between superiors and subordinates in Indian society required leadership styles that are much more task oriented, leaving little room for individual autonomy.[5] These views of
Indian culture, however, are hard to reconcile with the fast-moving,
innovative Indian business scene, empowered employees, and ambitious leaders who populate the India Way.

We have found bits and pieces of the India Way in many other
contexts—the sophistication of selection and talent development
looked like U.S. companies in the 1950s, for example, and the concern
with employee engagement was similar to Japanese practices, while
the focus on credentials and skill development reminded one of
German companies. And aspects of the portrait that emerged are little different from the American way or the Japanese way or the

Chinese way. Wherever they operate and in whatever field, virtually all business managers favor an enduring set of qualities. A cross-national study of some 16,000 middle managers of 825 companies in 64 countries, ranging from Albania to Zimbabwe, found, for instance, that the most valued attributes of company leadership, regardless of country, are dynamism, decisiveness, and honesty; a capacity to motivate and negotiate with others; and a focus on performance. The company managers also universally agreed on several unfavorable traits: autocratic, egocentric, and irritable.[6] And in specific ways, India proved little different from the United States: compared with other regions, managers in both countries displayed relatively favorable attitudes toward charismatic and individualistic leaders.[7]

But the complete package of the India Way could be found nowhere else. And parts of the system, especially the focus on a broader social mission, were uniquely Indian and deeply formative. The priority and value placed on service to others and the widely held belief that one's goal in life should extend beyond oneself, especially beyond one's material needs, has been crucial to the India Way. The third of the four stages of Hindu life, with its focus on the search for meaning, helping others, and a gradual withdrawal from the competitive business world, also neatly coincides with the typical age (over fifty) of senior business leaders. In the same research noted above, the Indian region scored the highest of any area in desiring leaders who were humane, compassionate, and generous.[8] That preference fit nicely with the aspect of national culture manifesting service to others as a source of motivation.

Notes

Chapter One

1. Eric Bellman, "All in the Family: $100 Billion," *Wall Street Journal,* November 24, 2007.

2. Thomas S. Robertson, e-mail message to "the Wharton Community," November 28, 2008; *Times of India,* "Day After, Mumbai Limping to Normalcy," November 30, 2008; and Joe Nocera, "Mumbai Finds Its Resiliency," *New York Times,* January 4, 2009.

3. Mark Landler, "Seeking Business Allies, Clinton Connects with India's Billionaires," *New York Times,* July 18, 2009.

4. Vikas Bajaj, "India Undertakes Ambitious ID Card Plan," *New York Times,* June 25, 2009.

5. Anusha Chari, Wenjie Chen, and Kathryn M. E. Dominguez, "Foreign Ownership and Firm Performance: Emerging Market Acquisitions in the United States," working paper, NBER, 2009.

6. China has become a useful source of new management principles as well, as seen in Tarun Khanna, *Billions of Entrepreneurs: How China and India Are Reshaping Their Futures—and Yours* (Boston: Harvard Business School Press, 2007); Robyn Meredith, *The Elephant and the Dragon: The Rise of India and China and What It Means for All of Us* (New York: W. W. Norton & Company, 2007); and Pete Engardio, *Chindia: How China and India Are Revolutionizing Global Business* (New York: McGraw-Hill, 2007).

7. James P. Womack, Daniel T. Jones, and Daniel Roos, *The Machine That Changed the World: Based on the Massachusetts Institute of Technology 5-Million Dollar 5-Year Study on the Future of the Automobile* (New York: Rawson Associates, 1990); James P. Womack and Daniel T. Jones, *Lean Thinking: Banish Waste and Create Wealth in Your Corporation* (New York: Free Press, 2003); James P. Womack and Daniel T. Jones, *Lean Solutions: How Companies and Customers Can Create Value and Wealth Together* (New York: Free Press, 2005); and Ceci Connolly, "Toyota Assembly Line Inspires Improvements at Hospital," *Washington Post,* June 3, 2005.

8. Unless otherwise indicated, quotations from these business leaders are drawn from the authors' interviews with them from 2007 to 2009.

9. Nick Kurczewski, "And Now, for Some Serious Belt-Tightening," *New York Times,* June 28, 2009.

10. T. Surender and J. Bose, "I'm in a Lonely Phase of My Life: Ratan Tata," *Times of India,* January 11, 2008.

11. Heather Timmons, "A Tiny Car Is the Stuff of 4-Wheel Dreams for Millions of Drivers in India," *New York Times,* March 23, 2009.

12. Peter Cappelli, *Talent on Demand: Managing Talent in an Age of Uncertainty* (Boston: Harvard Business Press, 2008); P. Christopher Earley and Harbir Singh, eds., *Innovations in International and Cross-Cultural Management* (Thousand Oaks, CA: Sage Publications, 2000); Ravi Rama-murti and Jitendra V. Singh, eds., *Emerging Multinationals in Emerging Markets* (Cambridge: Cambridge University Press, 2009); and Michael Useem, *Investor Capitalism: How Money Managers Are Changing the Face of Corporate America* (New York: HarperCollins/Basic Books, 1996).

13. A host of books on business leadership, some by the business leaders themselves, have informed our commentary, including Gita Piramal, *Business Maharajas* (New Delhi: Viking, 1996); Geoff Hiscock, *India's Global Wealth Club: The Stunning Rise of Its Billionaires and Their Secrets of Success* (Somerset, NJ: Wiley, 2007); Gurcharan Das, *India Unbound: The Social and Economic Revolution from Independence to the Global Information Age* (New York: Random House, 2000); Steve Hamm, *Bangalore Tiger: How Indian Tech Startup Wipro Is Rewriting the Rules of Global Competition* (New York: McGraw-Hill, 2007); Kishore Biyani, *It Happened in India: The Story of Pantaloons, Big Bazaar, Central and the Great Indian Consumer* (New Delhi: Rupa & Company, 2007); and Nandan Nilekani, *Imagining India: The Idea of a Nation Renewed* (New York: Penguin Press, 2009).

Chapter Two

1. Daniel Yergin and Joseph Stanislaw, *The Commanding Heights: The Battle for the World Economy* (New York: Free Press, 2002).

2. Gurcharan Das, *India Unbound: The Social and Economic Revolution from Independance to the Global Information Age* (New York: Random House, 2000).

3. India in Business, "India's Economic Reforms," Economy page, http://www.indiainbusiness.nic.in/economy/economic_reforms.htm.

4. Ibid.

5. Arvind Panagariya, "India in the 1980s and 1990s: A Triumph of Reforms," working paper WP/04/43, IMF, March 2004, http://www.imf.org/external/pubs/ft/wp/2004/wp0443.pdf.

6. Joe Nocera, "Mumbai Finds Its Resiliency," *New York Times,* January 4, 2009; and Heather Timmons, "India Maintains Sense of Optimism and Growth," *New York Times,* March 1, 2009.

7. KPMG, *India Fraud Survey Report 2008* (New Delhi: KPMG, 2009), http://www.in.kpmg.com/TL_Files/Pictures/FraudSurveyReport_08.pdf.

8. The 1991 reforms and their aftermath are assessed in Montek S. Ahluwalia, "Economic Reforms in India Since 1991: Has Gradualism Worked?" *Journal of Economic Perspectives* 16 (2002): 67–88; Stephen P. Cohen, *India: Emerging Power* (Washington, DC: Brookings Institution Press, 2002); Gurcharan Das, *The Elephant Paradigm: India Wrestles with Change* (New Delhi: Penguin Books, 2002); Gurcharan Das, "The India Model," *Foreign Affairs* 85 (2006): 2–16; Edward Luce, *In Spite of the Gods: The Rise of Modern India* (New York: Random House, 2007); Kishore Mahbubani, *The New Asian Hemisphere: The Irresistible Shift of Global Power to the East* (New York: Public Affairs, 2008); Robyn Meredith, *The Elephant and the Dragon: The Rise of India and China and What It Means for All of Us* (New York: W. W. Norton & Company, 2007); Organization for Economic Co-operation and Development, *Economic Survey of India, 2007, OECD Policy Brief* (Paris, France: Organization for Economic Co-operation and Development, 2007); Arvind Panagariya, "India's Economic Reforms: What Has Been Accomplished? What Remains to Be Done?" ERD Policy Brief Series, Economics and Research Department, Asian Development Bank, 2002; Panagariya, "India in the 1980s and 1990s"; Ravi Ramamurti and Jitendra V. Singh, eds., *Emerging Multinationals in Emerging Markets* (Cambridge: Cambridge University Press, 2009); Jeffrey D. Sachs, Ashutosh Varshney, and Nirupam Bajpai, eds., *India in the Era of Economic Reforms* (New York: Oxford University Press, 2000); and Fareed Zakaria, *The Post-American World* (New York: W. W. Norton & Company, 2008).

9. Rajesh Chakrabarti, William Megginson, and Pradeep K. Yadav, "Corporate Governance in India," *Journal of Applied Corporate Finance* 20, no. 1 (2008): 59–72; Reserve Bank of India, *Report on Foreign Exchange Reserves,* 2008, http://rbidocs.rbi.org.in/rdocs/AnnualReport/DOCs/86606.xls; and Jina Saha and Tarumoy Chaudhuri, "Rising Foreign Exchange Reserves: A Potential Source for Infrastructural Development in India?" February 10, 2008, http://ssrn.com/abstract=1266716.

10. *BusinessWeek,* "The Trouble with India: Crumbling Roads, Jammed Airports, and Power Blackouts Could Hobble Growth," March 19, 2007; and *Economist,* "Battling the Babu Raj," March 8, 2008.

11. Atul Gawande, *Better: A Surgeon's Notes on Performance* (New York: Picador, 2008).

12. Martin J. Wiener, *English Culture and the Decline of the Industrial Spirit, 1850–1980,* 2nd ed. (Cambridge: Cambridge University Press, 2004).

13. See the Reserve Bank of India sources at http://rbidocs.rbi.org.in/rdocs/Bulletin/PDFs/89876.pdf.

14. India Brand Equity Foundation, "Foreign Direct Investments," September 8, 2008, http://www.ibef.org/economy/fdi.aspx; Lauren A. E. Schuker, "Spielberg, India's Reliance to Form Studio," *Wall Street Journal,*

September 20, 2008; and Abhishek Bhattacharya and Vidhika Sehgal, "Money Magic: Market Cap Races Past GDP," *Economic Times,* October 17, 2006, http:// economictimes.indiatimes.com/articleshow/2181063.cms.

15. See the Reserve Bank of India sources at http://rbidocs.rbi.org.in/ rdocs/Bulletin/PDFs/89874.pdf.

16. Somnath   Temple,   http://en.wikipedia.org/wiki/somnath,   and "Somnath—The Symbol of National Pride," http://agmkonleave.sulekha.com/ blog/post/2007/04/the-symbol-of-national-pride.htm.

Chapter Three

1. David Kirkpatrick, "The World's Most Modern Management—In India," *Fortune,* April 14, 2006.

2. Vineet's Blog, Leading a Transformational Journey, "Destroying the Office of the CEO," March 11, 2008, http://vineet.hclblogs.com/?p=51.

3. For a useful overview of the "employee first" model, see Kamalini Ramdas and Ravindra Gajulapalli, "HCL Technologies: Employee First, Customer Second," Case UV1085-PDF-ENG (Boston: Harvard Business School, 2008).

4. Vijaya Murthy and Indra Abeysekera, "Human capital value creation practices of software and service exporter firms in India," *Journal of Human Resource Costing & Accounting* 11, no. 2 (2007): 84.

5. This is the case for the most recent 2007 annual reports for the five biggest IT employers in the United States: IBM, Hewlett-Packard, Microsoft, Oracle, and Cisco. The closest statement to the India model is a reasonably generic sentence in Cisco's shareholder letter, which says, "While we're proud of the financial results we delivered," we "are also very proud of our people, our culture, and the way Cisco operates as a company."

6. David Hoyt and Hayagreeva Rao, "Infosys: Building a Talent Engine to Sustain Growth," working paper, Stanford Graduate School of Business, Palo Alto, CA, 2007.

7. In addition to our own interviews and visits with Infosys, a description of company policies and those of other IT companies can be found in Jo Johnson, "How India Raises an Army; Runaway Growth in the Country's IT Outsourcing Industry Has Pushed Human Resources to New Extremes," *Financial Times,* May 22, 2007.

8. Dr. Reddy's Laboratories, http://www.drreddys.com/careers/working_ performance.html.

9. For further details on Yes Bank's employment philosophy, see "Employee Value Proposition," http://www.yesbank.in/evp.htm.

10. See Table 5 in U.S. Bureau of Labor Statistics, Economic New Release, http://www.bls.gov/news.release/sept.t05.htm. This data is from 1995, for employees in establishments with more than fifty employees. Large employers, like the Indian companies referred to earlier, no doubt do much more training in the United States.

11. Brian Caplen, "Technology: India's Outsourcing Reinvention," *Banker*, March 2008, 1.

12. William H. Whyte, *The Organization Man* (New York: Simon and Schuster, 1956).

13. Gurcharan Das, *India Unbound: The Social and Economic Revolution from Independence to the Global Information Age* (New York: Random House, 2000), 143.

14. Ibid., 266.

15. MindTree, About Us, "People Focused Innovation," http://www.mindtree.com/aboutus/people_focused_innovation.html.

16. MindTree, About Us, "Integrity Policy," http://www.mindtree.com/aboutus/integrity_policy.html.

17. For a description of the company and its practices, see "Single Status for All," Express Computer, July 23, 2007. http://www.expresscomputeronline.com/20070723/technologylife04.shtml.

18. The Indian figure is from our survey; the U.S. figure is from Society for Human Resource Management, *Strategic HR Management Survey Report* (McLean, VA: Society for Human Resource Management, 2006).

Chapter Four

1. Max Weber, *The Protestant Ethic and the Sprit of Capitalism,* trans. Talcott Parsons (New York: Scribner, 1958; originally published in German in 1905); Reinhard Bendix, *Work and Authority in Industry: Ideologies of Management in the Course of Industrialization* (Berkeley: University of California Press, 1974); and Mauro F. Guillén, *Models of Management: Work, Authority, and Organization in a Comparative Perspective* (Chicago: University of Chicago Press, 1994).

2. Thomas J. Peters and Robert H. Waterman, *In Search of Excellence: Lessons from America's Best-Run Companies* (New York: Harper & Row, 1982); James C. Collins and Jerry I. Porras, *Built to Last: Successful Habits of Visionary Companies* (New York: HarperBusiness, 1994); and James C. Collins, *Good to Great: Why Some Companies Make the Leap—and Others Don't* (New York: HarperBusiness, 2001).

3. C. K. Prahalad, *The Fortune at the Bottom of the Pyramid: Eradicating Poverty Through Profits* (Upper Saddle River, NJ: Wharton School Publishing, 2006).

4. *Business Standard,* "The Top 10 Business Bestsellers," April 8, 2008, http://www.business-standard.com/india/storypage.php?autono=319288; and *Wall Street Journal Online,* "Wall Street Journal Book Index," August 8, 2008, http://online.wsj.com/public/resources/documents/retro-BOOKLIST.html.

5. Graduate Program, Wharton School, August 8, 2008. The data include those who graduated from both the regular MBA program and the executive MBA program.

6. Graduate Management Admission Council, *Asian Geographic Trend Report for Examinees Taking the Graduate Management Admission Test, 2002-2006* (McLean, VA: Graduate Management Admission Council, 2007); and Graduate Management Admission Council, *Asian Geographic Trend Report for GMAT Examinees, 2003-07* (McLean, VA: Graduate Management Admission Council, 2008).

7. Robert J. House et al., *Culture, Leadership, and Organizations: The Globe Study of 62 Societies* (Thousand Oaks, CA: Sage Publications, 2004).

8. ISI Emerging Markets, "Western Business Model Cannot Be Replicated in India: Kamath," Press Trust of India Ltd., May 23, 2008.

9. New York Stock Exchange, *CEO Report 2007: Planning for Growth, Valuing People* (Princeton, NJ: Opinion Research Corporation, 2006).

10. Lauren Baranowska, *Growing Globally in an Age of Disruptions— How India's Top Companies Are Meeting the Challenge* (New York: The Conference Board, July 2007), File A-0241-07-EA.pdf.

11. Telecomm Regulatory Authority of India, "10.81 Million Wireless Subscribers Added in December 2008; Broadband Subscribers Reaches 5.45 Million Mark; Tele-density Reaches 33.23% Mark," news release, January 21, 2009, http://www.trai.gov.in/WriteReadData/trai/upload/PressReleases/644/pr21jan09no11.pdf.

12. Robyn Meredith, *The Elephant and the Dragon: The Rise of India and China and What It Means for All of Us* (New York: W. W. Norton & Company, 2007), 44; Edward Luce, *In Spite of the Gods: The Rise of Modern India* (New York: Random House, 2007), 78–79; and Diana Farrell, Noshir Kaka, and Sascha Strüze, "Ensuring India's Offshoring Future," *McKinsey Quarterly* (Special Edition, 2005).

13. Edward Luce, "India to Dip into Forex Reserves to Build Roads," *Financial Times,* October 16, 2004.

14. Bernard M. Bass and Ronald E. Riggio, *Transformational Leadership* (Mahwah, NJ: Lawrence Erlbaum Associates, 2005).

15. The MLQ survey is a proprietary instrument whose individual components cannot be reproduced here. For a description, see B. M. Bass and B. J. Avolio, *Multifactor Leadership Questionnaire* (Palo Alto, CA: Consulting Psychologists Press, 1993). The survey can be acquired from Mind Garden Inc., http://www.mindgarden.com.

16. The U.S. studies only use part of the MLQ. The data from the first study comes from David A. Waldman et al., "Does Leadership Matter? CEO Leadership Attributes and Profitability Under Conditions of Perceived Environmental Uncertainty," *Academy of Management Journal* 44, no. 1 (2001): 134–143; and from the second study from H. L. Tosi et al., "CEO Charisma, Compensation, and Firm Performance," *Leadership Quarterly* 15, no. 3 (2004): 405–420. Thanks to professor Vilmos Misangyi from Pennsylvania State University for making the latter data available to us.

17. Information on ICICI's operation is available from many useful sources, including Datamonitor, "ICICI Bank Limited: Company Profile," April 17, 2008, http://www.datamonitor.com.

18. *Financial Express,* "ICICI Aims to Be Among World's Top 10," January 14, 2008, http://www.financialexpress.com/news/icici-aims-to-be-among-worlds-top-10/261339.

19. Indrajit Gupta, T. Surendar, and Neelima Mahajan-Bansal, "How ICICI Bank Discovered Its New Leader," *Network 18 Business Magazine,* December 24, 2008, http://ibnlive.in.com/news/how-icici-bank-discovered-its-new-leader/81257-7.html.

20. James P. Womack, Daniel T. Jones, and Daniel Roos, *The Machine That Changed the World: Based on the Massachusetts Institute of Technology 5-Million Dollar 5-Year Study on the Future of the Automobile* (New York: Rawson Associates, 1990).

21. John F. Krafcik, "Triumph of the Lean Production System," *Sloan Management Review* 30, no. 1 (1988); and F. K. Pil and J. P. MacDuffie, "What Makes Transplants Thrive: Managing the Transfer of 'Best Practice' at Japanese Auto Plants in North America," *Journal of World Business* 34, no. 4 (1999): 372–391.

22. Luisa Kroll, "Special Report: The World's Billionaires," *Forbes,* March 5, 2008.

Chapter Five

1. Wharton Graduate Program Office, December 22, 2008.

2. Alfred Dupont Chandler, *Strategy and Structure: Chapters in the History of the Industrial Enterprise* (Cambridge, MA: MIT Press, 1962).

3. Rebecca Buckman, "Outsourcing with a Twist: Indian Phone Giant Bharti Sends Jobs to Western Firms in a Multinational Role Switch," *Wall Street Journal,* January 18, 2005.

4. Clay Chandler, "Wireless Wonder: India's Sunil Mittal," *Fortune,* January 17, 2007.

5. Ibid.

6. Steve Hamm, "Why Does Cognizant Grow So Fast? Part II," *Business-Week Online,* August 14, 2007, http://www.businessweek.com/ globalbiz/blog/globespotting/archives/2007/08/how_does_cogniz.html.

7. Niko Canner, "The Issue: For Cognizant, Two's Company," *BusinessWeek Online,* January 17, 2008, http://www.businessweek.com/globalbiz/blog/globespotting/archives/2007/08/how_does_cogniz.html.

8. Ibid.

9. United Nations Development Program, *Human Development Report 2007/2008* (New York: United Nations Development Program, 2007–2008).

10. C. K. Prahalad, *The Fortune at the Bottom of the Pyramid: Eradicating Poverty Through Profits* (Upper Saddle River, NJ: Wharton School Publishing, 2006).

Chapter Six

1. Business Roundtable, *Principles of Corporate Governance* (New York: Business Roundtable, 2005), 5.

2. Robert A. G. Monks and Nell Minow, *Corporate Governance,* 4th ed. (Hoboken, NJ: Wiley-Blackwell, 2008), chap. 3.

3. For an account of the scandals through the mid-2000s, see Jerry W. Markham, *A Financial History of Modern U.S. Corporate Scandals: From Enron to Reform* (Armonk, NY: M. E. Sharpe, 2006).

4. Spencer Stuart, *Spencer Stuart Board Index* (Spencer Stuart, 2008). http://content.spencerstuart.com/sswebsite/pdf/lib/SSBI_08.pdf.

5. Organization for Economic Co-operation and Development, "OECD Principles of Corporate Governance 2004," http://www.oecd.org/dataoecd/32/18/31557724.pdf.; and World Bank Group, "Reports on the Observance of Standards and Codes (ROSC)" Program, http://www.worldbank.org/ifa/rosc_cg.html.

6. Niraj Sheth, Jackie Range, and Geeta Anand, "Corporate Scandal Shakes India," *Wall Street Journal,* January 9, 2009; Heather Timmons, "India's Enron Moment," *New York Times,* January 8, 2009; and Joe Nocera, "In India, Crisis Pairs with Fraud," *New York Times,* January 10, 2009.

7. B. Ramalinga Raju, "Memo to the Board of Directors, Satyam Computer Services Ltd.," January 7, 2009, http://www.bseindia.com/xml-data/corpfiling/announcement/Satyam_Computer_Services_Ltd_070109.pdf.

8. Rajesh Chakrabarti, "Corporate Governance in India—Evolution and Challenges," January 17, 2005, http://ssrn.com/abstract=649857; and Moody's-ICRA, "Corporate Governance and Related Credit Issues for Indian Family-Controlled Companies," October 2007, http://v3.moodys.com/sites/products/AboutMoodysRatingsAttachments/2007000000448489.pdf.

9. Tarun Khanna and Jan W. Rivkin, "Estimating the Performance Effects of Business Groups in Emerging Markets," *Strategic Management Journal* 22, no. 1 (2001): 45–74; and Robert Lensink, Remco Van der Molen, and Shubashis Gangopadhyay, "Business Groups, Financing Constraints and Investment: The Case of India," *Journal of Development Studies* 40, no. 2 (2003): 93–119.

10. Michael Useem, *Investor Capitalism: How Money Managers Are Changing the Face of Corporate America* (New York: HarperCollins/Basic Books, 1996); and Michael Useem, "Corporate Leadership in a Globalizing Equity Market," *Academy of Management Executive* 12, no. 4 (1998): 43–59.

11. G. Epstein, ed., *Financialization and the World Economy* (Aldershot, England: Edward Elgar, 2005); and Vidhi Chhaochharia and Luc Laeven, "Corporate Governance Norms and Practices," International Monetary Fund, CEPR, and ECGI, February 20, 2008, http://ssrn.com/paper=965733.

12. Darryl Reed and Sanjoy Mukherjee, *Corporate Governance, Economic Reforms, and Development: The Indian Experience* (New Delhi: Oxford University Press, 2004); and Randall K. Morck and Lloyd Steier, "The Global

History of Corporate Governance—An Introduction," working paper 11062, National Bureau of Economic Research, Cambridge, MA, January 2005, http://www.nber.org/papers/w11062.

13. Confederation of Indian Industry, "Desirable Corporate Governance: A Code," April 1998, http://www.acga-asia.org/public/files/CII_Code_1998.pdf.

14. In the 2003 SEBI report on corporate governance, Narayana Murthy observed, "Corporate governance is beyond the realm of law. It stems from the culture and mindset of management, and cannot be regulated by legislation alone." N. R. Narayana Murthy, "Report of the SEBI Committee on Corporate Governance," February 8, 2003, http://www.acga-asia.org/public/files/India_MurthyCtee_Feb03.pdf., section 1.1.3.

15. Tom Perkins, "The Compliance Board," *Wall Street Journal,* March 2, 2007.

16. Rahul Bajaj, "Avoid Pessimism and Face the Recession," *Economic Times,* December 26, 2008, http://economictimes.indiatimes.com/Features/Corporate_Dossier/Avoid_pessimism_and_face_the_recession_Rahul_Bajaj/rssarticleshow/3893077.cms.

17. Tata Council for Community Initiates, March 2003, http://www.tata.com/ourcommitment/articles/inside.aspx?artid=ZeYh3v7WOxB=.

18. Securities and Exchange Board of India, "Original Clause 49 Memo," SMDRP/POLICY/CIR-10/2000, February 21, 2000, Asian Corporate Governance Association, http://www.acga-asia.org/public/files/IndiaClause49.doc. For an assessment of India's corporate governance system in recent years, see Asian Corporate Governance Association (ACGA), "Country Snapshots—India," http://www.acga-asia.org/content.cfm?SITE_CONTENT_TYPE_ID=11&COUNTRY_ID=264.

19. For a summary of Clause 49, see N. Balasubramanian, Bernard S. Black, and Vikramaditya Khanna, "Firm-Level Corporate Governance in Emerging Markets: A Case Study of India," 2008, http://ssrn.com/abstract=992529.

20. Klaus Gugler, Dennis C. Mueller, and B. Burcin Yurtoglu, "The Impact of Corporate Governance on Investment Returns in Developed and Developing Countries," *Economic Journal* 113 (2003): F511–539; and Rajesh Chakrabarti, William Megginson, and Pradeep K. Yadav, "Corporate Governance in India," *Journal of Applied Corporate Finance* 20, no. 1 (2008): 59–72.

21. Y. R. K. Reddy, "When Non-Compliance Is Self-Defeating," *Financial Express,* January 6, 2007; Balasubramanian, Black, and Khanna, "Firm-Level Corporate Governance in Emerging Markets"; and Arinam Gupta and Anupam Parua, "An Enquiry into Compliance of Corporate Governance Codes by the Private Sector Indian Companies" (paper presented at the Indian Institute of Capital Markets Conference, December 18, 2006). See also Rajesh Chakrabarti, "Foreign Exchange Markets in India," January 17, 2005, http://ssrn.com/abstract=649858.

22. Derek Higgs, "Review of the Role and Effectiveness of Non-Executive Directors," U.K. Department of Trade and Industry, January 2003,

http://www.berr.gov.uk/files/file23012.pdf; and The Conference Board, "Corporate Governance Handbook 2007: Legal Standards and Board Practices," Research Report R-1405-07-RR, http://www.conference-board.org.

23. Mauro F. Guillen, "Convergence in Global Governance?" *Corporate Board* 21, no. 121 (2000): 17; and Tarun Khanna, Joe Kogan, and Krishna Palepu, "Globalization and Similarities in Corporate Governance: A Cross-Country Analysis," *Review of Economics and Statistics* 88, no. 1 (2006): 69–90.

24. Jeffrey A. Sonnenfeld, "What Makes Great Boards Great," *Harvard Business Review,* September 2002, 106–113; and U.S. Senate, Permanent Subcommittee on Investigations of the Committee on Governmental Affairs, *The Role of the Board of Directors in Enron's Collapse,* Report 107-70, July 8, 2002, http://fl1.findlaw.com/news.findlaw.com/hdocs/docs/enron/senpsi70802rpt.pdf.

25. Enron, "Code of Ethics," July 2000, http://bobsutton.typepad.com/files/enron-ethics.pdf; John C. Coffee Jr., "Understanding Enron: It's About the Gatekeepers, Stupid," working paper 207, Columbia Law and Economics, New York, July 30, 2002, http://ssrn.com/abstract=325240, or DOI: 10.2139/ssrn.325240; and Stuart L. Gillan and John D. Martin, "Corporate Governance Post-Enron: Effective Reforms, or Closing the Stable Door?" *Journal of Corporate Finance* 13, no. 5 (2007): 929–958.

26. Infosys Technologies Ltd., Annual Report 2007–2008. This annual report and others are available at http://www.infosys.com/investors/reports-filings/annual-report/default.asp.

27. Ibid.

28. See Infosys, Awards, "Financial Reporting," http://www.infosys.com/about/awards/about-awards-financial.asp.

29. The third author served as an independent director of Infosys from 2000 to 2003.

30. Justin Doebele, "CEO Pay: The Softest Pillow," *Forbes.com,* September 2, 2002, http://www.forbes.com/global/2002/0902/036.html; and Tarun Khanna and Krishna Palepu, "Globalization and Convergence in Corporate Governance: Evidence from Infosys and the Indian Software Industry," *Journal of International Business Studies* 35, no. 6 (2004): 484–507.

31. Pitabas Mohanty, "Institutional Investors and Corporate Governance in India," Research Initiative Paper 15, National Stock Exchange of India, May 12, 2003, http://ssrn.com/abstract=353820, or DOI: 10.2139/ssrn.353820.

Chapter Seven

1. There is a long literature on the attributes of the U.S. model as well as a separate literature, more developed outside the United States, on the spread of U.S. practices abroad. One of the seminal works in this area is M. Djelic, *Exporting the American Model: The Postwar Transformation of European Business* (Oxford: Oxford University Press, 1993).

2. Whether there was real convergence toward the U.S. model continues to be the subject of debate. For the convergence view, see Moses Abramovitz, "Catch-up and Convergence in the Postwar Growth Boom and After," in *Convergence of Productivity: Cross-National Studies and Historical Evidence,* eds. William J. Baumol, Richard R. Nelson, and Edward N. Wolff (Oxford: Oxford University Press, 1994). For the view that the process was more about learning and adapting, see J. Zeitlin and G. Herrigel, eds., *Americanization and Its Limits: Reworking U.S. Technology and Management in Postwar Europe and Japan* (Oxford: Oxford University Press, 2000).

3. Alexis de Tocqueville, "How the Americans Combat Individualism by the Principle of Self-Interest Rightly Understood," in *Democracy in America* (New York: Alfred A. Knopf, 1976; originally published in 1835).

4. George Soros, "The Capitalist Threat," *Atlantic Monthly,* February 1997.

5. See, for instance, J. Williamson, "Democracy and the Washington Consensus," *World Development* 21 (1993): 1329–1336.

6. A. Greenspan, "Statement to Congress, May 21 (Asian Financial Crisis)," *Federal Reserve Bulletin,* July 1998, 536–537, http://www. federalreserve .gov/boarddocs/testimony/1998/19980521.htm.

7. E. Potter and J. Youngman, *Keeping America Competitive: Employment Policy for the 21st Century* (Lakeland, CO: Glenbridge Publishers, 1994).

8. A. L. Saxenian, *Regional Advantage: Culture and Competition in Silicon Valley and Route 128* (Cambridge, MA: Harvard University Press, 1994).

9. G. Epstein, ed., *Financialization and the World Economy* (Aldershot, England: Edward Elgar, 2005).

10. R. Dore, "Financialization of the Global Economy," *Industrial and Corporate Change* 17 (2006): 1097–1112.

11. Brian J. Hall and Kevin J. Murphy, "The Trouble with Stock Options," *Journal of Economic Perspectives* 17 (Summer 2003): 49–70.

12. Klaus Gugler, Dennis C. Mueller, and B. Burcin Yurtoglu, "The Impact of Corporate Governance on Investment Returns in Developed and Developing Countries," *Economic Journal* 113 (2003): F511–539.

13. General Accounting Office, *Financial Statement Restatements: Trends, Market Impacts, Regulatory Responses, and Remaining Challenges,* GAO-03-138 (Washington, DC: General Accounting Office, 2002).

14. John C. Coffee Jr., "A Theory of Corporate Scandals: Why the USA and Europe Differ," *Oxford Review of Economic Policy* 21 (2005): 198–211.

15. The National Bureau of Economic Research determines recessions based on trends in a complex set of economic variables. Interestingly, unemployment is not one of those variables, although it is the measure most frequently associated with recessions. U.S. unemployment in 1982 peaked at 10.8 percent and stands in December 2009 at 10.0 percent. See Bureau of Labor Statistics, "Labor Force Statistics from the Current Population Survey," http://www.bls.gov/cps/.

16. C. Dougherty and K. Bennhold, "Russia and China Blame Capitalists," *New York Times,* January 28, 2009.

17. *Economist,* "American International Group: Cranking Up the Outrage-O-Meter," March 21, 2009, 77–78.

18. Government Printing Office, National Intelligence Council, *Global Trends 2025: A Transformed World,* GPO Stock #041-015-00261-9 (Washington, DC: U.S. Government Printing Office, 2008).

19. For a thorough history and critique of the financialization approach and its effects on business and society, see Gerald F. Davis, *Managed by the Markets: How Finance Re-Shaped America* (New York: Oxford University Press, 2009). Justin Fox describes the intellectual history behind this approach and how ignoring caveats in the original ideas behind modern financial models led to this extreme version; see Justin Fox, *The Myth of the Rational Market: A History of Risk, Reward, and Delusion on Wall Street* (New York: HarperBusiness, 2009).

20. Jonathan Doh et al., "How to Retain Talent in Fast-Moving Labor Markets: Some Findings from India," excerpted in *MIT Sloan Management Review* 50 (Fall 2008).

21. Michael E. Porter and Klaus Schwab, *The Global Competitiveness Report 2008–2009* (Geneva, Switzerland: World Economic Forum, 2008), and prior World Economic Forum annual reports going back to 1999, available at http://www.weforum.org.

22. *Time,* "Engine Charlie," October 6, 1961, http://www.time.com/time/magazine/article/0,9171,827790,00.html.

23. *Hindustan Times,* "21st Century Will Be India's: Mukesh Ambani," March 8, 2009.

24. Jean Strouse, *Morgan: American Financier* (New York: Harper, 2000); and Jean Strouse, "When the Economy Really Did 'Fall Off a Cliff,'" *New York Times,* March 23, 2009.

25. Sebastian Raisch et al., "Organization Ambidexterity: Balancing Exploitation and Exploration for Sustained Performance," *Organization Science* 20 (2009): 685–695.

Appendix A

1. The Economist Intelligence Unit had forecast GDP growth in India in 2008–2009 of 5.6 percent, and in 2009–2010 of 5.2 percent. For assessments and prognostications pointing toward continued rapid growth, see Martin Wolf, "What India Must Do If It Is to Be an Affluent Country," *Financial Times,* July 7, 2009; Centennial Group for the Emerging Markets Forum, *India 2039: An Affluent Society in One Generation* (Manila, Philippines: Asian Development Bank, 2009); Vikas Bajaj and Keith Bradsher, "Investors in Developing Markets See Optimism," *New York Times,* June 4, 2009; Heather Timmons, "India Feels Less Vulnerable as Outsourcing Presses On,"

New York Times, June 3, 2009; Jackie Range and Neelabh Chaturvedi, "India's Economy Grows 5.8%," *Wall Street Journal,* June 1, 2009; and Peter Wonacott, "India Defies Slump, Powered by Growth in Poor Rural States," *Wall Street Journal,* April 10, 2009.

Appendix B

1. Anthony J. Mayo, Nitin Nohria, and Laura G. Singleton, *Paths to Power: How Insiders Shaped American Business Leadership* (Boston: Cambridge University Press, 2006).

2. Nine additional companies opted to respond anonymously to the survey.

Appendix C

1. Ramachandra Guha, *India After Gandhi: The History of the World's Largest Democracy* (New York: Ecco, 2007).

2. While the government did talk about developing human resources for the economy, in practice those efforts were limited to basic education. See T. V. Rao, "Human Resource Development as National Policy in India," *Advances in Developing Human Resources* 6 (2004): 288–297.

3. Gurcharan Das, *India Unbound: The Social and Economic Revolution from Independence to the Global Information Age* (New York: Random House, 2000).

4. Suresh Gopalan and Joan B. Rivera, *International Journal of Organizational Analysis* 5, no. 2 (April 1997): 156.

5. S. Agarwal, "Influence of Formalization on Role Stress, Organizational Commitment, and Work Alienation of Salespersons: A Cross-National Comparative Study," *Journal of International Business Studies* 24 (1993): 715–739; J. B. P. Sinha, "Power in Superior-Subordinate Relationships: The Indian Case," *Journal of Social and Economic Studies* 6 (1978): 205–218.

6. Robert J. House et al., *Culture, Leadership, and Organizations: The Globe Study of 62 Societies* (Thousand Oaks, CA: Sage Publications, 2004).

7. M. Javidan, P. W. Dorfman, M. S. de Luque, and R. House, "In the Eye of the Beholder: Cross-Cultural Lessons in Leadership from Project GLOBE," *Academy of Management Perspectives* (February 2006): 67–90.

8. Ibid.

Bibliography

Abramovitz, Moses. "Catch-up and Convergence in the Postwar Growth Boom and After." In *Convergence of Productivity: Cross-National Studies and Historical Evidence*, edited by William J. Baumol, Richard R. Nelson, and Edward N. Wolff. Oxford: Oxford University Press, 1994.

Agarwal, S. "Influence of Formalization on Role Stress, Organizational Commitment, and Work Alienation of Salespersons: A Cross-National Comparative Study." *Journal of International Business Studies* 24 (1993): 715–739.

Ahluwalia, Montek S. "Economic Reforms in India Since 1991: Has Gradualism Worked?" *Journal of Economic Perspectives* 16 (2002): 67–88.

Ahmed, Zubair. "India Attracts Western Tech Talent." *BBC News,* September 5, 2006. http://news.bbc.co.uk/go/pr/fr/-/2/hi/south_asia/5272672.stm.

American Society for Training & Development. *C-Level Perceptions of the Strategic Value of Learning*. Alexandria, VA: American Society for Training & Development, 2006.

Asian Corporate Governance Association (ACGA). "Country Snapshots—India." http://www.acga-asia.org/content.cfm?SITE_CONTENT_TYPE_ID=11&COUNTRY_ID=264.

Bajaj, Rahul. "Avoid Pessimism and Face the Recession." *Economic Times,* December 26, 2008. http://economictimes.indiatimes.com/Features/Corporate_Dossier/Avoid_pessimism_and_face_the_recession_Rahul_Bajaj/ rssarticleshow/3893077.cms.

Bajaj, Vikas. "India Undertakes Ambitious ID Card Plan." *New York Times*, June 25, 2009.

Bajaj, Vikas, and Keith Bradsher. "Investors in Developing Markets See Optimism." *New York Times,* June 4, 2009.

Balasubramanian, N., Bernard S. Black, and Vikramaditya Khanna. "Firm-Level Corporate Governance in Emerging Markets: A Case Study of India." 2008. http://ssrn.com/abstract=992529.

Baranowska, Lauren. *Growing Globally in an Age of Disruptions—How India's Top Companies Are Meeting the Challenge*. New York: The Conference Board, July 2007. File A-0241-07-EA.pdf.

Bass, B. M., and B. J. Avolio. *Multifactor Leadership Questionnaire*. Palo Alto, CA: Consulting Psychologists Press, 1993.

Bass, Bernard M., and Ronald E. Riggio. *Transformational Leadership*. Mahwah, NJ: Lawrence Erlbaum Associates, 2005.

Basu, Kaushik, and Annemie Maertens. "The Pattern and Causes of Economic Growth in India." *Oxford Review of Economic Policy* 23 (2007): 143–167.

Baum, J. Robert, and Stefan Wally. "Strategic Decision Speed and Firm Performance." *Strategic Management Journal* 24 (2003): 1107–1129.

Bellman, Eric. "All in the Family: $100 Billion." *Wall Street Journal,* November 24, 2007.

Bendix, Reinhard. *Work and Authority in Industry: Ideologies of Management in the Course of Industrialization*. Berkeley: University of California Press, 1974.

Bhattacharya, Abhishek, and Vidhika Sehgal. "Money Magic: Market Cap Races Past GDP." *Economic Times*, October 17, 2006. http://economictimes. indiatimes.com/articleshow/2181063.cms.

Biyani, Kishore, and Dipayan Baishya. *It Happened in India: The Story of Pantaloons, Big Bazaar, Central and the Great Indian Consumer*. New Delhi: Rupa & Company, 2007.

British Broadcasting Corporation. "World's Cheapest Car Goes on Show." January 10, 2008. http://news.bbc.co.uk/2/hi/business/7180396.stm.

Buckman, Rebecca. "Outsourcing with a Twist: Indian Phone Giant Bharti Sends Jobs to Western Firms in a Multinational Role Switch." *Wall Street Journal*, January 18, 2005.

Business Roundtable. *Principles of Corporate Governance*. New York: Business Roundtable, 2005.

Business Standard. "The Top 10 Business Bestsellers." April 8, 2008. http:// www.business-standard.com/india/storypage.php?autono=319288.

BusinessWeek. "The Trouble with India: Crumbling Roads, Jammed Airports, and Power Blackouts Could Hobble Growth." March 19, 2007.

Canner, Niko. "The Issue: For Cognizant, Two's Company." *BusinessWeek Online,* January 17, 2008. http://www.businessweek.com/managing/content/ jan2008/ca20080117_999307_page_2.htm.

Cappelli, Peter. *Talent on Demand: Managing Talent in an Age of Uncertainty*. Boston: Harvard Business Press, 2008.

Centennial Group for the Emerging Markets Forum. *India 2039: An Affluent Society in One Generation*. Manila, Philippines: Asian Development Bank, 2009.

Central Statistical Organization, Government of India, 2009, http://mospi .nic.in/mospi_cso_rept_pubn.htm.

Chakrabarti, Rajesh. "Corporate Governance in India—Evolution and Challenges." January 17, 2005. http://ssrn.com/abstract=649857.

———. "Foreign Exchange Markets in India." January 17, 2005. http://ssrn
.com/abstract=649858.

Chakrabarti, Rajesh, William Megginson, and Pradeep K. Yadav. "Corporate Governance in India." *Journal of Applied Corporate Finance* 20, no. 1 (2008): 59–72.

Chandler, Alfred Dupont. *Strategy and Structure: Chapters in the History of the Industrial Enterprise*. Cambridge, MA: MIT Press, 1962.

Chandler, Clay. "Wireless Wonder: India's Sunil Mittal." *Fortune*, January 17, 2007.

Chari, Anusha, Wenjie Chen, and Kathryn M. E. Dominguez. "Foreign Ownership and Firm Performance: Emerging Market Acquisitions in the United States." Working Paper, NBER, 2009.

Chhaochharia, Vidhi, and Luc Laeven. "Corporate Governance Norms and Practices." International Monetary Fund, CEPR, and ECGI. February 20, 2008. http://ssrn.com/paper=965733.

Coffee, John C., Jr. "A Theory of Corporate Scandals: Why the USA and Europe Differ." *Oxford Review of Economic Policy* 21 (2005): 198–211.

———. "Understanding Enron: It's About the Gatekeepers, Stupid." Working paper 207, Columbia Law and Economics, New York, July 30, 2002. http://ssrn.com/abstract=325240, or DOI: 10.2139/ssrn.325240.

Cohen, Stephen P. *India: Emerging Power*. Washington, DC: Brookings Institution Press, 2002.

Collins, James C. *Good to Great: Why Some Companies Make the Leap—and Others Don't*. New York: HarperBusiness, 2001.

Collins, James C., and Jerry I. Porras. *Built to Last: Successful Habits of Visionary Companies*. New York: HarperBusiness, 1994.

Collins, Jim. *How the Mighty Fall: And Why Some Companies Never Give In*. Jim Collins, 2009.

Confederation of Indian Industry. "Desirable Corporate Governance: A Code." April 1998. http://www.acga-asia.org/public/files/CII_Code_1998.pdf.

Conference Board, The. "Corporate Governance Handbook 2007: Legal Standards and Board Practices." Research Report R-1405-07-RR. http://www
.conference-board.org.

Connolly, Ceci, "Toyota Assembly Line Inspires Improvements at Hospital." *Washington Post,* June 3, 2005.

Conyon, M. J., S. Peck, and G. V. Sadler. "Compensation Consultants and Executive Pay: Evidence from the United States and the United Kingdom." *Academy of Management Perspectives* 23 (2009): 43–55.

Das, Gurcharan. *The Elephant Paradigm: India Wrestles with Change*. New Delhi: Penguin Books, 2002.

———. "The India Model." *Foreign Affairs* 85 (2006): 2–16.

———. *India Unbound: The Social and Economic Revolution from Independence to the Global Information Age*. New York: Random House, 2000.

———. "The Next World Order." *New York Times*, January 2, 2009.

Datamonitor. "ICICI Bank Limited: Company Profile." April 17, 2008. http://www.datamonitor.com.

Davis, Gerald F. *Managed by the Markets: How Finance Re-Shaped America*. New York: Oxford University Press, 2009.

Djelic, M. *Exporting the American Model: The Postwar Transformation of European Business*. Oxford: Oxford University Press, 1993.

Doebele, Justin. "CEO Pay: The Softest Pillow." *Forbes.com*, September 2, 2002. http://www.forbes.com/global/2002/0902/036.html.

Doh, Jonathan, Walter Tynon, Stephen A. Strumpf, and Michael Haid. "How to Retain Talent in Fast-Moving Labor Markets: Some Findings from India." Excerpted in *MIT Sloan Management Review* 50 (Fall 2008).

Dore, R. "Financialization of the Global Economy." *Industrial and Corporate Change* 17 (2006): 1097–1112.

Dossani, Rafiq. *India Arriving: How This Economic Powerhouse Is Redefining Global Business*. New York: AMACOM, 2008.

Dougherty, C., and K. Bennhold. "Russia and China Blame Capitalists." *New York Times,* January 28, 2009.

Earley, P. Christopher, and Harbir Singh, eds. *Innovations in International and Cross-Cultural Management*. Thousand Oaks, CA: Sage Publications, 2000.

Economist. "American International Group: Cranking Up the Outrage-O-Meter." March 21, 2009, 77–78.

———. "Battling the Babu Raj." March 8, 2008.

———. "The Madoff Affair: Dumb Money and Dull Diligence." December 20, 2008, 17–18.

Eisenhardt, K. "Agency Theory: An Assessment and Review." *Academy of Management Review* 14, no. 1 (1989): 57–74.

Elliott, John. "Riding the Elephant: Kochhar of ICICI Leads Indian Women Bankers to the Top." *Fortune*, October 22, 2007.

Engardio, Pete, ed. *Chindia: How India and China Are Revolutionizing Global Business*. New York: McGraw-Hill, 2007.

Engardio, Pete, and Jena McGregor. "Karma Capitalism." *BusinessWeek,* October 19, 2006.

Enron. "Code of Ethics." July 2000. http://bobsutton.typepad.com/files/enron-ethics.pdf.

Epstein, G., ed. *Financialization and the World Economy*. Aldershot, England: Edward Elgar, 2005.

EquityMaster.com. "You Will Have 2-3 Strong Players in the Next Few Years with Consolidation Speeding Up." Interview with Madhabi Puri Buch. February, 22, 2002. http://www.equitymaster.com/DETAIL.ASP?story=2&date=2/22/2002.

Euromonitor International. Global Market Information Database. September 2008. http://www.euromonitor.com/.

Farrell, Diana, Noshir Kaka, and Sascha Strüze. "Ensuring India's Off-shoring Future." *McKinsey Quarterly* (Special Edition, 2005).

Financial Express. "ICICI Aims to Be Among World's Top 10." January 14, 2008.

Forbes.com. "Special Report: The World's Biggest Companies." 2009. http://www.forbes.com/2009/04/08/worlds-largest-companies-business-global-09-global_land.html.

Fortune. "The Top Companies for Leaders." October 1, 2007.

———. "World's Largest Corporations." July 21, 2008, 165–174.

Fox, Justin. *The Myth of the Rational Market: A History of Risk, Reward, and Delusion on Wall Street.* New York: HarperBusiness, 2009.

Frank, Robert H. "Can Socially Responsible Firms Survive in a Competitive Environment?" In *Codes of Conduct: Behavioral Research into Business Ethics,* edited by David Messick and Ann Tenbrunsel, 86–103. New York: Russell Sage Foundation, 1996.

Gawande, Atul. *Better: A Surgeon's Notes on Performance.* New York: Picador, 2008.

General Accounting Office. *Financial Statement Restatements: Trends, Market Impacts, Regulatory Responses, and Remaining Challenges*, GAO-03-138. Washington, DC: General Accounting Office, 2002.

Gillan, Stuart L., and John D. Martin. "Corporate Governance Post-Enron: Effective Reforms, or Closing the Stable Door?" *Journal of Corporate Finance* 13, no. 5 (2007): 929–958.

Gopalan, Suresh, and Joan B. Rivera. *International Journal of Organizational Analysis* 5, no. 2 (April 1997): 156.

Government Printing Office. National Intelligence Council. *Global Trends 2025: A Transformed World.* GPO Stock #041-015-00261-9. Washington, DC: U.S. Government Printing Office, 2008.

Graduate Management Admission Council. *Asian Geographic Trend Report for Examinees Taking the Graduate Management Admission Test, 2002-2006.* McLean, VA: Graduate Management Admission Council, 2007.

———. *Asian Geographic Trend Report for GMAT Examinees, 2003-07.* McLean, VA: Graduate Management Admission Council, 2008.

———. *Asian Geographic Trend Report for GMAT Examinees, 2004-08.* McLean, VA: Graduate Management Admission Council, 2009.

Greenspan, A. "Statement to Congress, May 21 (Asian Financial Crisis)." *Federal Reserve Bulletin,* July 1998, 536–537. http://www.federalreserve.gov/boarddocs/testimony/1998/19980521.htm.

Grynbaum, Michael M. "Greenspan Concedes Error on Regulation." *International Herald Tribune,* October 23, 2008.

Gugler, Klaus, Dennis C. Mueller, and B. Burcin Yurtoglu. "The Impact of Corporate Governance on Investment Returns in Developed and Developing Countries." *Economic Journal* 113 (2003): F511–539.

Guha, Ramachandra. *India After Gandhi: The History of the World's Largest Democracy.* New York: Ecco, 2007.

Guillen, Mauro F. "Convergence in Global Governance?" *Corporate Board* 21, no. 121 (2000): 17.

———. *Models of Management: Work, Authority, and Organization in a Comparative Perspective.* Chicago: University of Chicago Press, 1994.

Gupta, Arinam, and Anupam Parua. "An Enquiry into Compliance of Corporate Governance Codes by the Private Sector Indian Companies." Paper presented at the Indian Institute of Capital Markets Conference, December 18, 2006.

Gupta, Indrajit, T. Surendar, and Neelima Mahajan-Bansal. "How ICICI Bank Discovered Its New Leader." *Network 18 Business Magazine,* December 24, 2008. http://ibnlive.in.com/news/how-icici-bank-discovered-its-new-leader/81257-7.html.

Hamm, Steve. *Bangalore Tiger: How Indian Tech Startup Wipro Is Rewriting the Rules of Global Competition.* New York: McGraw-Hill, 2007.

———. "Why Does Cognizant Grow So Fast? Part II." *BusinessWeek Online,* August 14, 2007. http://www.businessweek.com/globalbiz/blog/globespotting/archives/2007/08/how_does_cogniz.html.

Herrod, A. "Labor as an Agent of Globalization and as a Global Agent." In *Spaces of Globalization: Reasserting the Power of the Local,* edited by K. R. Cox. New York: Guilford Press, 1997.

Hewitt Associates. *Global Top Companies for Leaders Announced.* Lincolnshire, IL: Hewitt Associates, September 19, 2007.

Higgs, Derek. "Review of the Role and Effectiveness of Non-Executive Directors." U.K. Department of Trade and Industry, January 2003. http://www.berr.gov.uk/files/file23012.pdf.

Hindustan Times. "21st Century Will Be India's: Mukesh Ambani." March 8, 2009.

Hiscock, Geoff. *India's Global Wealth Club: The Stunning Rise of Its Billionaires and Their Secrets of Success.* Somerset, NJ: Wiley, 2007.

House, Robert J., Paul J. Hanges, Mansour Javidan, Peter Dorfman, and Vipin Gupta. *Culture, Leadership, and Organizations: The Globe Study of 62 Societies.* Thousand Oaks, CA: Sage Publications, 2004.

Hoyt, David, and Hayagareeva Rao, "Infosys: Building a Talent Engine to Sustain Growth." Working paper, Stanford University, Palo Alto, CA, 2007.

Infosys Technologies Ltd. Annual Report 2007–2008. This annual report and others are available at http://www.infosys.com/investors/reports-filings/annual-report/default.asp.

———. Members of the Board, 2009. http://www.infosys.com/about/management-profiles/default.asp.

International Monetary Fund. World Economic Outlook Database. http://www.imf.org/external/datamapper/index.php.

ISI Emerging Markets. "Western Business Model Cannot Be Replicated in India: Kamath." Press Trust of India Ltd., May 23, 2008.

Iwata, Edward. "Infosys Kicks Up Growth Mode." *USA Today*, August 3, 2006.

Jensen, M., and W. Meckling. "Theory of the Firm: Managerial Behavior, Agency Costs and Ownership Structure." *Journal of Financial Economics* 3, no. 4 (1976): 305–360.

Kafka, Franz, and J. A. Underwood. *The Castle*. Penguin Twentieth-Century Classics. London: Penguin, 1997.

Khanna, Tarun. *Billions of Entrepreneurs: How China and India Are Reshaping Their Futures—and Yours*. Boston: Harvard Business School Press, 2007.

Khanna, Tarun, Joe Kogan, and Krishna Palepu. "Globalization and Similarities in Corporate Governance: A Cross-Country Analysis." *Review of Economics and Statistics* 88, no. 1 (2006): 69–90.

Khanna, Tarun, and Krishna Palepu. "Globalization and Convergence in Corporate Governance: Evidence from Infosys and the Indian Software Industry." *Journal of International Business Studies* 35, no. 6 (2004): 484–507.

Khanna, Tarun, and Jan W. Rivkin. "Estimating the Performance Effects of Business Groups in Emerging Markets." *Strategic Management Journal* 22, no. 1 (2001): 45–74.

Khurana, Rakesh, and Andy Zelleke. "You Can Cap the Pay, But the Greed Will Go On." *Washington Post*, February 8, 2009.

Kirkpatrick, David. "The World's Most Modern Management—In India." *Fortune,* April 14, 2006.

KPMG. *India Fraud Survey Report 2008*. New Delhi: KPMG, 2009. http://www.in.kpmg.com/TL_Files/Pictures/FraudSurveyReport_08.pdf.

Krafcik, John F. "Triumph of the Lean Production System." *Sloan Management Review* 30, no. 1 (1988).

Kroll, Luisa. "Billionaire Blowups of 2008." *Forbes,* December 22, 2008. http://www.forbes.com/billionaires/2008/12/22/billionaires-mitttal-ross-biz-billies-cz_lk_1222billieblowups.html.

———. "Special Report: The World's Billionaires." *Forbes,* March 5, 2008.

Kurczewski, Nick. "And Now, for Some Serious Belt-Tightening." *New York Times,* June 28, 2009.

Lacey, Robert. *Ford: The Men and the Machine*. Boston: Little, Brown, 1986.

Landler, Mark. "Seeking Business Allies, Clinton Connects with India's Billionaires." *New York Times*, July 18, 2009.

Lensink, Robert, Remco Van der Molen, and Shubashis Gangopadhyay. "Business Groups, Financing Constraints and Investment: The Case of India." *Journal of Development Studies* 40, no. 2 (2003): 93–119.

Luce, Edward. "India to Dip Into Forex Reserves to Build Roads." *Financial Times*, October 16, 2004.

———. *In Spite of the Gods: The Rise of Modern India.* New York: Random House, 2007.

Mahbubani, Kishore. *The New Asian Hemisphere: The Irresistible Shift of Global Power to the East.* New York: Public Affairs, 2008.

Markham, Jerry W. *A Financial History of Modern U.S. Corporate Scandals: From Enron to Reform.* Armonk, NY: M. E. Sharpe, 2006.

Mayo, Anthony J., Nitin Nohria, and Laura G. Singleton. *Paths to Power: How Insiders Shaped American Business Leadership.* Boston: Cambridge University Press, 2006.

Mazzetti, M. "Global Economy Top Threat to U.S., Spy Chief Says." *New York Times,* February 12, 2008.

Meredith, Robyn. *The Elephant and the Dragon: The Rise of India and China and What It Means for All of Us.* New York: W. W. Norton & Company, 2007.

Mohanty, Pitabas. "Institutional Investors and Corporate Governance in India." Research Initiative Paper 15, National Stock Exchange of India, May 12, 2003. http://ssrn.com/abstract=353820, or DOI: 10.2139/ssrn.353820.

Monks, Robert A. G., and Nell Minow. *Corporate Governance.* 4th ed. Hoboken, NJ: Wiley-Blackwell, 2008.

Moody's-ICRA. "Corporate Governance and Related Credit Issues for Indian Family-Controlled Companies." October 2007. http://v3.moodys.com/sites/products/AboutMoodysRatingsAttachments/2007000000448489.pdf.

Morck, Randall K., and Lloyd Steier. "The Global History of Corporate Governance—An Introduction." Working paper 11062, National Bureau of Economic Research, Cambridge, MA, January 2005. http://www.nber.org/papers/w11062.

Murthy, N. R. Narayana. "Report of the SEBI Committee on Corporate Governance." February 8, 2003. http://www.acga-asia.org/public/files/India_MurthyCtee_Feb03.pdf.

New York Stock Exchange. *CEO Report 2007: Planning for Growth, Valuing People.* Princeton, NJ: Opinion Research Corporation, 2006.

Nilekani, Nandan. *Imagining India: The Idea of a Nation Renewed.* New York: Penguin Press, 2009.

Nocera, Joe. "In India, Crisis Pairs with Fraud." *New York Times*, January 10, 2009.

———. "Mumbai Finds Its Resiliency." *New York Times*, January 4, 2009.

Opinion Research Corporation. "NYSE CEO Report 2007: Planning for Growth, Valuing People." May 2006. http://www.nyse.com/pdfs/2007CEOReport.pdf.

Organization for Economic Co-operation and Development. *Economic Survey of India, 2007, OECD Policy Brief.* Paris, France: Organization for Economic Co-operation and Development, 2007.

———. "OECD Principles of Corporate Governance 2004." http://www.oecd.org/dataoecd/32/18/31557724.pdf.

Palepu, Krishna, and Tarun Khanna. "Product and Labor Market Globalization and Convergence of Corporate Governance: Evidence from Infosys and the Indian Software Industry." Working Paper 02-30, Harvard NOM, Cambridge, MA; Working Paper 02-040, Harvard Business School, Boston, September 2001. http://proxy.library.upenn.edu:3071/abstract=323142 or DOI: 10.2139/ssrn.323142.

Panagariya, Arvind. "India in the 1980s and 1990s: A Triumph of Reforms." Working Paper WP/04/43, IMF, March 2004. http://www.imf.org/external/pubs/ft/wp/2004/wp0443.pdf.

———. "India's Economic Reforms: What Has Been Accomplished? What Remains to Be Done?" ERD Policy Brief Series, Economics and Research Department, Asian Development Bank. 2002.

Perkins, Tom. "The Compliance Board." *Wall Street Journal*, March 2, 2007.

Peters, Thomas J., and Robert H. Waterman. *In Search of Excellence: Lessons from America's Best-Run Companies.* New York: Harper & Row, 1982.

Pil, F. K., and J. P. MacDuffie. "What Makes Transplants Thrive: Managing the Transfer of 'Best Practice' at Japanese Auto Plants in North America." *Journal of World Business* 34, no. 4 (1999): 372–391.

Piramal, Gita. *Business Maharajas.* New Delhi: Viking, 1996.

Piramal, Gita, and Jennifer Netarwala. *Smart Leadership: Insights for CEOs.* New Delhi: Portfolio, published by the Penguin Group, 2005.

Porter, Michael E., and Klaus Schwab. *The Global Competitiveness Report 2008–2009.* Geneva, Switzerland: World Economic Forum, 2008. (These GCR reports are produced annually by the World Economic Forum and are available at http://www.weforum.org.)

Potter, E., and J. Youngman. *Keeping America Competitive: Employment Policy for the 21st Century.* Lakeland, CO: Glenbridge Publishers, 1994.

Prahalad, C. K. *The Fortune at the Bottom of the Pyramid: Eradicating Poverty Through Profits.* Upper Saddle River, NJ: Wharton School Publishing, 2006.

Raisch, Sebastian, Julian Birkinshaw, Gilbert Probst, and Michael L. Tushman, "Organization Ambidexterity: Balancing Exploitation and Exploration for Sustained Performance." *Organization Science* 20 (2009): 685–695.

Rajadhyaksha, Niranjan. *The Rise of India: Its Transformation from Poverty to Prosperity.* Hoboken, NJ: John Wiley & Sons, 2006.

Raju, B. Ramalinga. "Memo to the Board of Directors, Satyam Computer Services Ltd." January 7, 2009. http://www.bseindia.com/xml-data/corpfiling/announcement/Satyam_Computer_Services_Ltd_070109.pdf.

Ramamurti, Ravi, and Jitendra V. Singh, eds. *Emerging Multinationals in Emerging Markets.* Cambridge: Cambridge University Press, 2009.

Range, Jackie, and Neelabh Chaturvedi. "India's Economy Grows 5.8%." *Wall Street Journal*, June 1, 2009.

Rao, T. V. "Human Resource Development as National Policy in India." *Advances in Developing Human Resources* 6 (2004): 288–297.

Reddy, Y. R. K. "When Non-Compliance Is Self-Defeating." *Financial Express,* January 6, 2007.

Reed, Darryl, and Sanjoy Mukherjee. *Corporate Governance, Economic Reforms, and Development: The Indian Experience.* New Delhi: Oxford University Press, 2004.

Reserve Bank of India. *Report on Foreign Exchange Reserves.* 2008. http://rbidocs.rbi.org.in/rdocs/AnnualReport/DOCs/86606.xls.

Robertson, Thomas S. E-mail message to "the Wharton Community," November 28, 2008.

Sachs, Jeffrey D., Ashutosh Varshney, and Nirupam Bajpai, eds. *India in the Era of Economic Reforms.* New York: Oxford University Press, 2000.

Saha, A. "Basic Human Nature in India Tradition and Its Economic Consequences." *International Journal of Sociology and Social Policy* 12, no. 1-2 (1992): 1–50.

Saha, Jina, and Tarumoy Chaudhuri. "Rising Foreign Exchange Reserves: A Potential Source for Infrastructural Development in India?" February 10, 2008. http://ssrn.com/abstract=1266716.

Sana, Arunoday. "The Caste System in India and Its Consequences." *International Journal of Sociology and Social Policy* 13, no. 3-4 (1993): 1–76.

Saxenian, A. L. *Regional Advantage: Culture and Competition in Silicon Valley and Route 128.* Cambridge, MA: Harvard University Press, 1994.

Schuker, Lauren A. E. "Spielberg, India's Reliance to Form Studio." *Wall Street Journal,* September 20, 2008.

Schumpeter, Joseph Alois. *Capitalism, Socialism, and Democracy.* New York: Harper Perennial Modern Classics, 2008. (Originally published in 1942.)

Securities and Exchange Board of India. "Original Clause 49 Memo." SMDRP/POLICY/CIR-10/2000, February 21, 2000. Asian Corporate Governance Association, http://www.acga-asia.org/public/files/India Clause49 .doc.

Sen, Amartya. *The Argumentative Indian: Writings on Indian History, Culture and Identity.* New York: Penguin, 2005.

Sheth, Niraj, Jackie Range, and Geeta Anand. "Corporate Scandal Shakes India." *Wall Street Journal,* January 9, 2009.

Simmons, B. A., F. Dobbin, and G. Garrett. "Introduction: The International Diffusion of Liberalism." *International Organization* 60 (2006): 781–810.

Sinha, J. B. P. "Power in Superior-Subordinate Relationships: The Indian Case." *Journal of Social and Economic Studies* 6 (1978): 205–218.

Society for Human Resource Management. *HR Outsourcing Survey Report.* McLean, VA: Society for Human Resource Management, 2004.

———. *SHRM/Catalyst Employee Development Survey Report.* McLean, VA: Society for Human Resource Management, 2007.

———. *Strategic HR Management Survey Report*. McLean, VA: Society for Human Resource Management, 2006.

Sonnenfeld, Jeffrey A. "What Makes Great Boards Great." *Harvard Business Review,* September 2002, 106–113.

Soros, George. "The Capitalist Threat." *Atlantic Monthly,* February 1997.

Spencer Stuart. *Spencer Stuart Board Index*. Spencer Stuart, 2008. http://content.spencerstuart.com/sswebsite/pdf/lib/SSBI_08.pdf.

Stiglitz, Joseph. "The Economic Crisis: Capitalist Fools." *Vanity Fair,* January 2009. http://www.vanityfair.com/magazine/2009/01/stiglitz200901.

Strouse, Jean. *Morgan: American Financier*. New York: Harper, 2000.

———. "When the Economy Really Did 'Fall Off a Cliff.'" *New York Times,* March 23, 2009.

Subramanian, Arvind. *India's Turn: Understanding the Economic Transformation*. New Delhi: Oxford University Press, 2008.

Surender, T., and J. Bose. "I'm in a Lonely Phase of My Life: Ratan Tata." *Times of India*, January 11, 2008.

Telecom Regulatory Authority of India. "10.81 Million Wireless Subscribers Added in December 2008; Broadband Subscribers Reaches 5.45 Million Mark; Tele-density Reaches 33.23% Mark." News release, January 21, 2009. http://www.trai.gov.in/WriteReadData/trai/upload/PressReleases/644/pr21jan09no11.pdf.

Time. "Engine Charlie." October 6, 1961. http://www.time.com/time/magazine/article/0,9171,827790,00.html.

Times of India. "Day After, Mumbai Limping to Normalcy." November 30, 2008.

Timmons, Heather. "India Feels Less Vulnerable as Outsourcing Presses On." *New York Times,* June 3, 2009.

———. "India Maintains Sense of Optimism and Growth." *New York Times,* March 1, 2009.

———. "India's Enron Moment." *New York Times*, January 8, 2009.

———. "A Tiny Car Is the Stuff of 4-Wheel Dreams for Millions of Drivers in India." *New York Times*, March 23, 2009.

Tocqueville, Alexis de. "How the Americans Combat Individualism by the Principle of Self-Interest Rightly Understood." In *Democracy in America*. New York: Alfred A. Knopf, 1976. (Originally published in 1835.)

Tosi, H. L., V. F. Misangyi, A. Fanelli, D. A. Waldman, and F. J. Yammarino. "CEO Charisma, Compensation, and Firm Performance." *Leadership Quarterly* 15, no. 3, (2004): 405–420.

Transparency International. *2008 Corruption Perceptions Index and Methodological Note*. Berlin: Transparency International, 2008. http://www.transparency.org/policy_research/surveys_indices/cpi.

United Nations Development Program. *Human Development Report 2007/2008*. New York: United Nations Development Program, 2007–2008.

Useem, Michael. "Corporate Leadership in a Globalizing Equity Market." *Academy of Management Executive* 12, no. 4 (1998): 43–59.

―――. *Investor Capitalism: How Money Managers Are Changing the Face of Corporate America*. New York: HarperCollins/Basic Books, 1996.

U.S. Senate. Permanent Subcommittee on Investigations of the Committee on Governmental Affairs. *The Role of the Board of Directors in Enron's Collapse*. Report 107-70, July 8, 2002. http://fl1.findlaw.com/news.findlaw .com/hdocs/docs/enron/senpsi70802rpt.pdf.

Varma, Pavan K. *Being Indian*. New Delhi: Penguin Books, 2006.

Wadhwa, Vivek, Una Kim de Vitton, and Gary Gereffi. "How the Disciple Became the Guru: Is It Time for the U.S. to Learn Workforce Development from Former Disciple India?" School of Engineering, Duke University, 2008.

Waldman, David A., Gabriel G. Ramirez, Robert J. House, and Phanish Puranam. "Does Leadership Matter? CEO Leadership Attributes and Profitability Under Conditions of Perceived Environmental Uncertainty." *Academy of Management Journal* 44, no. 1 (2001): 134–143.

Wall Street Journal Book Index (Business). http://online.wsj.com/public/ resources/documents/retro-BOOKLIST.html.

Weber, Max. *Economy and Society*. Edited by Guenther Roth and Claus Wittich. Berkeley: University of California Press, 1978.

―――. *The Protestant Ethic and the Sprit of Capitalism*. Translated by Talcott Parsons. New York: Scribner, 1958. (Originally published in German in 1905.)

―――. *The Theory of Social and Economic Organization*. Edited by Talcott Parsons. New York: Free Press, 1997. (Originally published in 1947.)

Whitley, R. *Divergent Capitalisms: The Social Structuring and Change of Business Systems*. Oxford: Oxford University Press, 1999.

Wiener, Martin J. *English Culture and the Decline of the Industrial Spirit, 1850–1980*. 2nd ed. Cambridge: Cambridge University Press, 2004.

Williamson, J. "Democracy and the Washington Consensus." *World Development* 21 (1993): 1329–1336.

Wilson, Dominic, and Roopa Purushothaman. "Dreaming with BRICs: The Path to 2050." Global Economic Paper 99, Goldman Sachs, 2003.

Wolf, Martin. "What India Must Do If It Is to Be an Affluent Country." *Financial Times*, July 7, 2009.

Womack, James P., and Daniel T. Jones. *Lean Solutions: How Companies and Customers Can Create Value and Wealth Together*. New York: Free Press, 2005.

―――. *Lean Thinking: Banish Waste and Create Wealth in Your Corporation*. New York: Free Press, 2003.

Womack, James P., Daniel T. Jones, and Daniel Roos. *The Machine That Changed the World: Based on the Massachusetts Institute of Technology 5-Million Dollar 5-Year Study on the Future of the Automobile*. New York: Rawson Associates, 1990.

Wonacott, Peter. "India Defies Slump, Powered by Growth in Poor Rural States." *Wall Street Journal,* April 10, 2009.

World Bank. *Doing Business 2008: India.* Washington, DC: World Bank, 2008. http://www.doingbusiness.org/.

———. *World Development Indicators,* WDI Online. http://www.worldbank .org/.

———. *World Development Indicators 2006.* Washington, DC: World Bank, 2007. http://www.worldbank.org/.

World Bank Group. "Reports on the Observance of Standards and Codes (ROSC)" Program. http://www.worldbank.org/ifa/rosc_cg.html.

Yergin, Daniel, and Joseph Stanislaw. *The Commanding Heights: The Battle for the World Economy.* New York: Free Press, 2002.

Zakaria, Fareed. *The Post-American World.* New York: W. W. Norton & Company, 2008.

Zeitlin, J., and G. Herrigel, eds. *Americanization and Its Limits: Reworking U.S. Technology and Management in Postwar Europe and Japan.* Oxford: Oxford University Press, 2000.

Acknowledgments

We would like to thank Mukesh Ambani of Reliance Industries for financial backing of this study; the National Human Resources Development Network for exceptional support in coordinating our research efforts in India; Anand Nayak of ITC Ltd. for leading NHRDN's initiative and Aruma George Mahoot of ITC (and now RSA Insurance) for managing the initiative; Sok Be of the Wharton Mack Center for Technological Innovation, Sandhya Karpe of Wharton Executive Education, and independent researcher Mark Hanna for their untiring efforts on multiple fronts; and Melinda Merino, executive editor of Harvard Business Press, and independence editor Howard Means for their excellent editorial guidance of the book throughout its preparation. This book would not have been possible without their invaluable support and guidance.

We also want to express our special gratitude to the Wharton School of the University of Pennsylvania and the following individuals and institutions for their backing and assistance during the research and writing of the book.

Bruce J. Avolio, University of Washington
Rob Bell, Archomai Ltd.
Brendan Callahan, Wharton School Graduate Program
Dhruv Chandhok, ICICI Bank
Thomas Colligan, Wharton Executive Education
Jonathan Heckman, Wharton School
Chris Higgins, Wharton School

David Huang, Wharton School
Indian School of Business
Anjani Jain, Wharton School
Devesh Kapur, Center for Advanced Study of India, University
    of Pennsylvania
Jeff Klein, Wharton School
Nandani Lynton, China Europe International Business School
Nathan Means, independent editor
Jason Mercer, Wharton School
Vilmos Misangyi, Pennsylvania State University
Sandeep Mukherjee, McKinsey
Mukul Pandya, editor, *Knowledge@Wharton*, Wharton School
Vivek Paranjpe, Reliance Industries Ltd.
Satish Pradhan, Tata Sons
Ramkumar Ranganathan, Wharton School
Hema Ravichandar, independent consultant
Roberta Shell, editor, *Knowledge@Wharton*, Wharton School
Sarah Simons, Wharton School
Naomi Tschoegl, Wharton School
Jerry Useem, independent writer

Index

About the Authors

Peter Cappelli is George W. Taylor Professor of Management and director of the Center for Human Resources at the Wharton School, University of Pennsylvania. He holds a doctorate from the University of Oxford, and he conducts research in human resources practices, talent and performance management, and public policy related to employment. He was the editor of *Academy of Management Perspectives*, and is the author of *The New Deal at Work: Managing the Market-Driven Workforce* and *Talent on Demand: Managing Talent in an Age of Uncertainty*.

Harbir Singh is William and Phyllis Mack Professor of Management and codirector of the Mack Center for Technological Innovation at the Wharton School. He has been Chair of the Business Policy and Strategy Division of the Academy of Management, and was Chair of Wharton's Management Department. He holds a bachelor's degree in technology from the Indian Institute of Technology, an MBA from the Indian Institute of Management, Ahmedabad, and a PhD from the University of Michigan. He is widely published in the areas of strategy, governance, acquisitions, joint ventures, and restructuring, and is the coeditor of *Innovations in International and Cross-Cultural Management*.

Jitendra Singh is Saul P. Steinberg Professor of Management at the Wharton School, where he previously served as Vice Dean for International Academic Affairs. From 2007 to 2009, he was Dean and

Shaw Foundation Chair Professor of Strategy, Management and Organization at the Nanyang Business School of Nanyang Technological University in Singapore. He holds an MBA degree from the Indian Institute of Management, Ahmedabad, and a PhD from Stanford University. His earlier research has focused on evolutionary approaches to strategy and organization, organizational change, business process outsourcing, and the Indian software services sector. He has coauthored several books, including *Emerging Multinationals in Emerging Markets*, and he has served on the boards of several companies, from established firms to start-ups, including Infosys Technologies and Emcure Pharmaceuticals in India and, more recently, SPRING Singapore, and has been on the board of governors of SAFTI Military Institute in Singapore.

Michael Useem is William and Jacalyn Egan Professor of Management and director of the Center for Leadership and Change Management at the Wharton School. He holds a PhD from Harvard University, and his research has focused on leadership, decision making, governance, and corporate change. He has presented leadership development programs in India, China, and elsewhere, and with Harbir Singh and Jitendra Singh has offered an annual program on corporate governance in Mumbai. He is the author of several books on leadership, including *The Inner Circle*, *Investor Capitalism*, and *The Leadership Moment*.

DATE DUE